50 Hikes in Wisconsin

50 *Hikes*

In Wisconsin

Walks, Hikes, and Backpacks in the Badger State

First Edition

JOHN AND ELLEN MORGAN

Backcountry Guides

Woodstock, Vermont

AN INVITATION TO THE READER

Over time trails can be rerouted and signs and landmarks altered. If you find that changes have occurred on the routes described in this book, please let us know so that corrections may be made in future editions. The author and publisher also welcome other comments and suggestions. Address all correspondence to:

Editor, 50 Hikes™ Series
Backcountry Guides
P.O. Box 748
Woodstock, VT 05091

Library of Congress Cataloging-in-Publication Data has been applied for.

ISBN 0-88150-624-9

Cover and interior design by Glenn Suokko
Composition by Doug Porter, Desktop Services
and Publishing
Cover photo © Tom Bean
Interior photographs by the authors unless otherwise specified
Maps by Mapping Specialists, Ltd.,
Madison, WI, © The Countryman
Press

Published by The Countryman Press
P.O. Box 748
Woodstock, Vermont 05091
www.countrymanpress.com

Distributed by W. W. Norton & Company, Inc.
500 Fifth Avenue
New York, NY 10110

Printed in the United States of America

10 9 8 7 6 5 4 3 2 1

DEDICATION

To our parents for getting us out on the trails in the first place.

50 Hikes in Wisconsin at a Glance

HIKE	REGION
1. Stockton Island	NW, Bayfield
2. Mount Valhalla	NW, Washburn
3. Pattison State Park	NW, Superior
4. Copper Falls State Park	NW, Mellen
5. Rock Lake Trail	NW, Cable
6. Willow River State Park	NW, Hudson
7. Kinnickinnic State Park	NW, Prescott
8. Hoffman Hills State Recreation Area	NW, Menomonie
9. Chippewa Moraine Ice Age Reserve	NW, Bloomer
10. Brunet Island State Park	NW, Cornell
11. Rib Mountain State Park	NW, Wausau
12. Fallison Lake Nature Trail	NE, Woodruff
13. Lost Lake	NE, Florence
14. Ed's Lake	NE, Crandon
15. Barkhausen Waterfowl Preserve	NE, Green Bay
16. UW Green Bay	NE, Green Bay
17. Potawatomi State Park	NE, Sturgeon Bay
18. Whitefish Dunes State Park	NE, Jacksonport
19. The Ridges Sanctuary	NE, Baileys Harbor
20. Peninsula State Park	NE, Fish Creek
21. Newport State Park	NE, Ellison Bay
22. Rock Island State Park	NE, Washington Island
23. Perrot State Park	SW, Trempealeau
24. Black River State Forest	SW, Black River Falls
25. Roche-A-Cri State Park	SW, Friendship

DISTANCE (miles)	DIFFICULTY	GOOD FOR KIDS	FEATURES	CAMPING	NORDIC SKIING	SNOWSHOEING	NOTES
4.2	3.5		H, W, F, S, G	★			
3.3	2.5	★	H, W, F	★	★		
4.7	3.5		H, G, W, F, WF, V	★	★	★	
2.5	4.0		H, G, F, V, WF	★	★		
4.0	3.5		H, G, W, F	★	★	★	
3.0	2.5	★	H, S, W, F, V, WF, G	★	★	★	
2.8	2.0	★	W, S, F, V		★	★	
2.7	3.0		W, F, V	★	★	★	Group camping only
4.5	3.5		H, G, W, F, V	★	★	★	Backcountry camping only
3.0	2.0		G, W, F, S	★	★	★	
3.1	4.5		H, G, F, V, W	★	★	★	
2.0	2.5	★	H, W, F		★	★	No pets allowed
4.5	3.5		W, F, V	★	★	★	
3.5	2.5		W, F	★	★		
3.5	2.0	★	W, F, V		★		
4.1	2.5	★	W, F, V		★		
3.5	2.5		G, V, F	★	★	★	
2.8	2.5	★	H, G, W, F, V, S		★	★	
2.6	2.0	★	H, G, W, F, V, S			★	No pets allowed
4.0	4.0		V, H, G, F, S, W	★	★	★	
5.0	2.5		W, V, S, F	★	★	★	Backpack camping only
3.5	3.0		H, F, V, S	★			
1.5	5.0		H, G, V, F, W	★	★	★	
4.0	3.5		F, V, W	★	★		Backcountry camping only
4.5	2.0	★	H, G, W, V, F	★	★	★	

DIFFICULTY
1 = easiest
5 = most difficult

FEATURES
H history
G geology
W wildlife
F flora
V scenic views
S swimming
WF waterfalls

50 Hikes in Wisconsin at a Glance

HIKE	REGION
26. Jersey Valley County Park	SW, Westby
27. Wildcat Mountain State Park	SW, Ontario
28. Wyalusing State Park	SW, Prairie du Chien
29. Mirror Lake State Park	SW, Wisconsin Dells
30. Devil's Lake State Park	SW, Baraboo
31. Governor Dodge State Park	SW, Dodgeville
32. Yellowstone Lake State Park	SW, Blanchardville
33. Indian Lake County Park	SW, Cross Plains
34. UW Madison Arboretum	SW, Madison
35. UW Madison Picnic Point	SW, Madison
36. Cherokee Marsh	SW, Madison
37. Magnolia Bluff County Park	SW, Evansville
38. Ice Age Trail, Waupaca/Portage	SE, Waupaca
39. High Cliff State Park	SE, Kaukauna
40. Point Beach State Forest	SE, Two Rivers
41. Kettle Moraine State Forest, Parnell Observation Tower	SE, Plymouth
42. Horicon National Wildlife Refuge	SE, Waupun
43. Lake Kegonsa State Park	SE, Stoughton
44. Kettle Moraine State Forest, Pike Lake	SE, Hartford
45. Nashotah Park	SE, Oconomowoc
46. Kettle Moraine State Forest, Lapham Peak	SE, Hartland
47. Kettle Moraine State Forest, Scuppernong	SE, Eagle
48. Schlitz Audubon Nature Center	SE, Bayside
49. Wehr Nature Center	SE, Hales Corners
50. Richard Bong State Recreation Area	SE, Union Grove

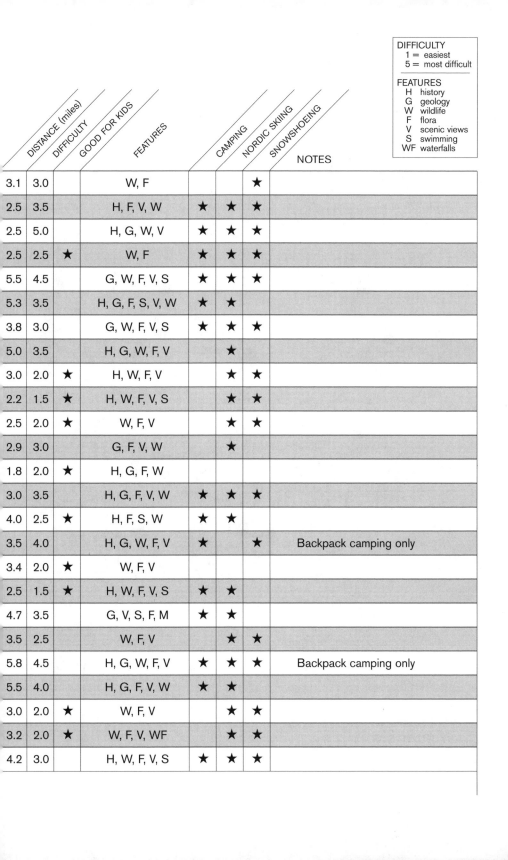

DISTANCE (miles)	DIFFICULTY	GOOD FOR KIDS	FEATURES	CAMPING	NORDIC SKIING	SNOWSHOEING	NOTES
3.1	3.0		W, F			★	
2.5	3.5		H, F, V, W	★	★	★	
2.5	5.0		H, G, W, V	★	★	★	
2.5	2.5	★	W, F	★	★	★	
5.5	4.5		G, W, F, V, S	★	★	★	
5.3	3.5		H, G, F, S, V, W	★	★		
3.8	3.0		G, W, F, V, S	★	★	★	
5.0	3.5		H, G, W, F, V		★		
3.0	2.0	★	H, W, F, V		★	★	
2.2	1.5	★	H, W, F, V, S		★	★	
2.5	2.0	★	W, F, V		★	★	
2.9	3.0		G, F, V, W		★		
1.8	2.0	★	H, G, F, W				
3.0	3.5		H, G, F, V, W	★	★	★	
4.0	2.5	★	H, F, S, W	★	★		
3.5	4.0		H, G, W, F, V	★		★	Backpack camping only
3.4	2.0	★	W, F, V				
2.5	1.5	★	H, W, F, V, S	★	★		
4.7	3.5		G, V, S, F, M	★	★		
3.5	2.5		W, F, V		★	★	
5.8	4.5		H, G, W, F, V	★	★	★	Backpack camping only
5.5	4.0		H, G, F, V, W	★	★		
3.0	2.0	★	W, F, V		★	★	
3.2	2.0	★	W, F, V, WF		★	★	
4.2	3.0		H, W, F, V, S	★	★	★	

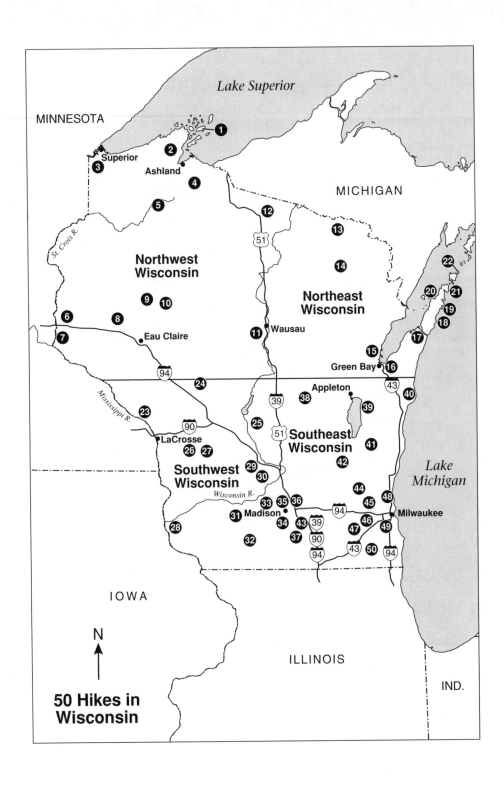

Lake Superior

MINNESOTA

Superior

Ashland

MICHIGAN

St. Croix R.

**Northwest
Wisconsin**

51

**Northeast
Wisconsin**

Eau Claire

Wausau

94

Green Bay

43

Mississippi R.

LaCrosse

Appleton

**Southeast
Wisconsin**

90

39

51

**Southwest
Wisconsin**

Wisconsin R.

Madison

90

94

*Lake
Michigan*

Milwaukee

IOWA

N

ILLINOIS

IND.

**50 Hikes in
Wisconsin**

CONTENTS

IV. Southeast Wisconsin

Acknowledgments

Books, like trails, are a cumulative product of the efforts of many. This book is no exception.

First, *50 Hikes in Wisconsin* wouldn't have our names on it were it not for the thoughtfulness and foresight of a true trekker, Mary Makarushka. Thanks again. Thanks to Jeannie Hanson, an exceptional agent who, along with Kermit Hummel at Countryman Press, gave us the opportunity to write this book. And a special thanks to a terrific editor, Bill Bowers, for assisting in putting the finishing touches on this book.

Because we love our dog but hate to hike with her, we have to thank our respective parents for doubling as dog-sitters and surrogate parents, often for days on end, and often to the point that lines of loyalty began to blur...in the dog's eyes.

To all the friends and family who found time to hike with us, house us, and/or feed us on our tour of the state, including seasoned hikers Mary and Al, young hikers Chloe and Isabella, cool moms like Patty, and our Oregon Duck friends, Jen and Greg. Your support and friendship are invaluable.

A sincere thanks and nod to the dedicated staff of all the Wisconsin state parks and forests, the Chequamegon-Nicolet National Forest, the Apostle Islands National Lakeshore, Vernon County Parks, Dane County Parks, the University of Green Bay Cofrin Arboretum, the Barkhausen Waterfowl Preserve, Schlitz Audubon Nature Center, The Ridges Sanctuary, University of Wisconsin Arboretum, and Wehr Nature Center. These people represent a dedicated cadre of professionals whose lives and work are truly invaluable to the preservation and conservation of Wisconsin's natural environment.

Also, this book is full of observations and sketches of the natural world from a trail's-eye view. John thanks Beloit College for giving him the tools to tell a story about a state through the lens of a hiking book—the kind of thing you don't learn just anywhere. And thanks to the School of Journalism at UW Madison for honing and sharpening those tools needed to tell the story well.

Finally, to the great State of Wisconsin and all of those who have cared for it to this point, including the Native Americans who first called this place home. And to Aldo Leopold, John Muir, August Derleth, Steve Hopkins, Ben Logan, George Vukelich, and other great conservationists, who trod lightly before us. We'll try to do the same.

Thanks.

Introduction

Wisconsin is an outdoorsperson's paradise, with rivers, lakes, forests, prairies, and beaches around every corner. Equally beneficial is the fact that as a culture, Wisconsinites expect their state government to provide them with trails on which to tread and parks in which to play. As a demonstration of their devotion to the outdoors, it's not unusual to see the windshields of residents' cars riddled with several years' worth of state park stickers.

In essence, we sought to write the Wisconsin hiking book that we wish we had in our glove compartment. We wanted a book that represented trails all across the state, a book whose hikes would get us huffing and puffing and sweaty, a book with trails that would be worth visiting more than once, a book that offered some information about the natural features we were hiking past, and, most important, a book with trails that were only loop hikes. These 50 trails fit all these criteria.

Due to the many geological alterations to the state, the hiking trails found here are tours of Wisconsin's past as much as they are paths through the present. Just under 30,000 years ago, Wisconsin played host to a catastrophic geological event: a glacier. For nearly 20,000 years, this ice sheet, almost a mile thick, advanced and blanketed the state, driving away wildlife and leaving very little, if any, plant life. The line of the farthest advance of the glacier starts just north of Hudson and goes east to about 30 miles northeast of Wausau before diving south to Janesville and finally heading northeast toward Green Bay. This line is commemorated by a trail-in-progress, the thousand-mile Ice Age Trail, several sections of which are included in this book.

Just about everything north of this line is the direct result of the glacier: the thousands of lakes; the lush northern forests filled with hemlock, pine, and spruce; the rolling hills; the bogs, prairies, and rivers; and of course, two Great Lakes, Superior and Michigan. Everything south of this line falls in what is appropriately called the Driftless Area. Here you won't find much in the way of lakes, but you will find deep coulees and high ridges—a hilly topography spared from the glacier's plow—covered in prairies and hardwood forests and forming a landscape that looks almost European. The trails in this book will take you into, around, atop, and over these valleys and ridges and acquaint you with Wisconsin from a trail's-eye view.

ABOUT THE TRAILS

In this book you will find a range of trails with a range of difficulty. Hikers with varying degrees of ability can attempt almost all these trails. Only a few trails are recommended solely for advanced hikers. Yet, seasoned hikers looking for some great trails should find most of these hikes relatively challenging.

The trails themselves are found in 33 different counties. We have included hikes in state parks, forests, and recreation areas; county parks; city parks, nonprofit conservancies and sanctuaries; university arboreta; national forests; and areas administered by the National Park Service, including a national lakeshore and parts of the Ice Age and North Country Trails. Two of the trails are found on remote islands unpopulated during the colder months and accessible only by boat or passenger ferry during the warmer months. These are a day's drive from the state's major metropolitan areas. Yet, the majority of the trails are within striking distance of cities and major highways. We estimate that no matter where you are in Wisconsin, one or more of these trails will be within an hour's drive.

In order to organize these hikes, we have divided the state into quadrants (Northwest, Northeast, Southwest, and Southeast). The center axis is Stevens Point, with US 51 forming the dividing line between east and west. A dividing line between north and south is formed by drawing an imaginary line westward from Green Bay, through Stevens Point, and straight to the western edge of the state. Our system corresponds roughly with the state park and forest map, which is divided into similar quadrants. The map also lists camping facilities on state lands, and is available from the Wisconsin Department of Natural Resources by calling 608-266-2181 or TTY: 608-267-2752.

HOW TO USE THIS BOOK

Each chapter includes basic information on the hike itself, including location, distance, approximate time to hike the trail, a difficulty rating ranging from 1 to 5 (1 being very easy, 3 being moderately difficult, and 5 being very difficult), vertical rise, and the title of the United States Geological Survey (USGS) map(s) depicting the hike. (See additional notes on maps below.) Following this are directions to the trail, including page numbers and coordinates that correspond with the DeLorme *Wisconsin Atlas and Gazetteer,* a very helpful atlas for anyone planning to travel the state extensively; an overview of the trail, including natural history and historical information about the area; and a step-by-step walk-through of the trail itself that gives information on footing, terrain, and scenery.

The maps used in this book were generated from the USGS 7½-minute topographic maps of Wisconsin. These maps depict elevation change and significant geological details. They are available from many map stores and camping equipment outfitters, or from the USGS directly at 1-888-275-8747 or www.usgs.gov.

Distances are provided based on the trail maps available from the trail administrators, or roughly calculated by the authors. Due to possible inaccuracies in calculating lengths or to subsequent changes in trail routes, actual distances may differ from those provided at the time of publication. Vertical rise was calculated using the corresponding USGS map. For all hikes where the vertical rise is less than 100 feet, this is noted as "minimal." Information on where to obtain the most recent maps is provided in each chapter, as well as a contact phone number.

Difficulty ratings are derived from a combination of terrain, distance, hiking time, and footing. Thus, a short hike that takes a long time—such as the Perrot Ridge Trail at Perrot State Park—has a relatively high difficulty rating due to the fact that it takes over an hour to cover little more than a mile. (Perrot Ridge receives a rating of 5.0.) Conversely, a relatively flat hike of a few miles that can be hiked in an hour or so probably receives a rating of 2.0 or 2.5, between very easy and moderately difficult. All this is very subjective, of course, whereas the trail descriptions in each chapter should provide you with a more detailed, objective idea of what the hike will entail in terms of footing, terrain, and overall difficulty.

Hiking times are based upon our own hiking pace, which we consider to be a bit faster than average but not blistering. You will undoubtedly need to hike two or three of these trails to calibrate your own hiking time with ours. Our basic means of providing a time range was to take the time that it took us to hike the trail and add an additional 15 to 30 minutes. For example, if it took us 1 hour, 45 minutes to hike the Brown Loop at Kettle Moraine State Forest, Pike Lake Unit, then we provide a hiking time of 1 hour, 45 minutes to 2 hours, 15 minutes.

UNDERSTANDING WISCONSIN ROADS

If you are unfamiliar with Wisconsin roads, you will need some tips regarding the directions given. Basically, Wisconsin's roads are part of a hierarchy. Starting at the top, there are federally sponsored roadways such as I-94 or US 51. Then there are the state highways, such as WI 70. Next are the roads that fall under the counties. These are named using single and double letters (or sometimes even triple letters), such as County Route T (CR T) or County Route TT (CR TT). There is often no rhyme or reason to the order of these roads, geographically speaking; thus a CR A might be near a CR Z.

The only other road type of note is the forest roads (FR) that weave through the national forests. Almost all are dirt and/or gravel and are designed chiefly for logging and maintenance purposes. You will often encounter deep ruts and potholes in these roads. And, due to the loose gravel atop hard-packed dirt, they are very slippery, especially when wet. The best way to drive these is to go slowly and stay away from the edges, which are often unsupported and can leave your axle stuck in sand, or worse.

VEHICLE STICKERS AND CAMPING INFORMATION

When entering a Wisconsin state park, forest, or recreation area, you will be required to obtain either a daily or annual vehicle permit. In 2003, the rates for these stickers were $20 per year or $5 daily for Wisconsin residents, and $30 per year or $10 daily for nonresidents. (Note: A second sticker can be obtained for a reduced rate for another vehicle registered at the same address.) For more information, call 608-266-2181 or TTY: 608-267-2752. Stickers are available at every state park office as well.

Anyone parking at trailhead parking lots in the Chequamegon-Nicolet National Forest also must have an annual parking sticker or pay a daily use fee. In 2003, the annual rate was $10, and the daily fee was $3. Contact the Chequamegon-Nicolet National Forest supervisor's office in Park Falls at 715-762-2461 or TTY: 715-762-5701 for information on obtaining a sticker. There are several district offices and local merchants who also sell them. And, while you may be in the middle of nowhere, don't expect to finish many five-mile hikes without returning to a parking ticket! Besides, you're paying for the maintenance of those great trails that you hike and ski.

Camping is available at the majority of the trail locations covered in this book. For camping in the state parks and forests, all reservations—as of 2003—are handled through Reserve America at 1-888-947-2757 or

TTY: 1-800-274-7275 or on the web at www.wiparks.net. Camping information for the Chequamegon-Nicolet can be obtained by contacting the Park Falls forest supervisor's office at 715-762-2461 or TTY: 715-762-5701. Remote camping on the islands of the Apostle Islands National Lakeshore is also available. Contact the National Park Service, Apostle Islands National Lakeshore at 715-779-3397 or on the web at www.nps.gov/apis for more information.

AUTUMN IN WISCONSIN MEANS HUNTING IN WISCONSIN

In case you are new to Wisconsin, or new to exploring its parks and trails, you will note that there are several hunting seasons that begin in the fall months. It is important to know that many state parks and forests, national forests, county parks, and recreation lands allow hunting in the same areas as trails or in adjoining areas at some point during the fall. The first hunting seasons begin in mid-September, and the best bet is to inquire at the park office about any hunting in or near the park you are visiting, to ensure a safe hike. Contact phone numbers are provided for each hike in this book.

HIKING HAZARDS: PROTECTING YOURSELF

There are several potential hazards to think about before heading off into the wilds of Wisconsin. These are particularly important to consider when hiking, especially since the "trail" may require some bushwhacking and may not be a ten-foot-wide swath of gravel that sweeps through the forest out of the reach of any hazard. From microorganisms to bears to dehydration, there are some simple tactics to reduce the risk of exposure to most problems, yet you will never totally eliminate them.

Ticks, Mosquitoes, and Flies

First, in addition to thousands of species of wildlife, Wisconsin is home to a few rather pesky insects. These include deer (or bear) ticks, wood ticks, mosquitoes, and a whole assortment of flies. The infamous deer tick is the carrier of Lyme disease, a troublesome disorder that can cause lifelong neurological and joint maladies. There are several ways to prevent the bite, and embedding, of a deer tick. First and foremost, wear tall socks and long pants. The deer tick isn't much of a jumper; instead you need to brush against some vegetation where ticks are waiting to grab hold of you and climb toward skin. Thus, long pants that are tucked into socks or draped over your boots make for a good defense. Light-colored material is helpful, too, in order to see the little pinhead-sized ticks and remove them. Once suited up, spray your bootlaces, the area where your socks meet your skin, your socks, and then your pants (the entire circumference) with a spray that repels deer ticks. There are many options for sprays, including new "natural" repellents made from ingredients like eucalyptus and oil of citronella.

The same holds true for above the knees. Tuck in your shirt and spray all the way around your waist. Long sleeves are better than short, but just make sure to spray. Then, spray your neck areas and spray your wide-brimmed hat (great for holding bugs at bay and even better for shade from hot sun) before you put it on. There are also several creams that work well for your arms, neck, and face. We use a combination of spray and cream to cover most of our bodies. Also, this tends to ward off flies and mosquitoes, too. But you're not done yet! There are two ways to prevent deer ticks from wreaking havoc. Once home, take off your hiking clothes, dump them in the washer, and do a tick check on your body. Then, take a hot and extra-soapy shower. Ticks tend to dislike lots of hot, soapy water and may flush off. But, if you find a tick, be very careful in removing it. You must remove the head using a tweezers. When in doubt, see a doctor.

Unfortunately, even after all this, you still may develop the telltale bull's-eye rash of the tick. If you do, you may or may not develop Lyme disease. Initial symptoms include headache, fever, achiness, and more. See a doctor right away if you suspect that a deer tick has bitten you; the sooner you start to fight Lyme disease, the better.

Wood ticks, much larger than deer ticks, are about the circumference of a pencil eraser and are dark brown to black in color. They, too, will seek to embed in your skin and benefit from your blood. While these ticks do not carry Lyme disease, to the best of our knowledge, they can and do carry other diseases. Thus, it is just as important to prevent them from accessing your skin and to check for them after hiking as well. Again, removal of the tick's entire head and mouthparts with a tweezers is essential.

As for mosquitoes and flies, the same preventive treatment works for them as well, the only caveat being that Wisconsin-bred mosquitoes don't back down from much! While you may be able to ward off an onslaught of bites, you're going to get bitten by mosquitoes eventually if you're hiking in Wisconsin. Again, the more clothes, the better. And consider packing a lightweight head net in your hip pack to pull out in those situations where you feel like you actually might lose your mind from the attack of hundreds of the little menaces. As for West Nile virus or the several forms of encephalitis, the transmission and behavior of these diseases aren't necessarily well understood. A simple solution is to ward off mosquito bites as best you can. But if you feel feverish or unwell after a weekend or week in the wild, go to the doctor immediately and express your concerns. Better to be safe than sorry.

All in all, when going into the wilds of Wisconsin, you're entering an ecosystem that couldn't be any happier to welcome fresh, untapped blood. You are like a large, walking piece of red meat to bloodthirsty mosquitoes and ticks. The best defense is to cover up as much as possible, to protect yourself with sprays, and to tick-check and soap up afterwards. None of this will guarantee that you won't be bitten, but you'll be a lot better off than if you wore sport sandals, shorts, and a T-shirt.

While this advice is far from a guarantee, being careful before you start hiking will undoubtedly help at least a little. For more information about Lyme disease, West Nile virus, and encephalitis, the United States Centers for Disease Control (www.cdc.gov) maintains several web sites devoted to the explanation of and treatment for these diseases. There are also nonprofit groups, such as the Lyme Disease Network (www.lymnet.org), that offer good tips, precautions, and information about the disease.

Dangerous Plants
The two main herbaceous hazards along the trails of Wisconsin are poison ivy and wild parsnip. Poison ivy is a relatively short plant and is distinguishable by its characteristic three spade-shaped green leaves, which tend to be a bit glossy and often have a slight notch near the base. Poison ivy can be a standalone plant or part of a

vine. The biggest problem with poison ivy is that it tends to reside in great patches, and you often won't know that you've stumbled into it until it's too late. Again, with the clothing barriers recommended above, you will have a much better defense than if you were in shorts.

As for wild parsnip, this tall, rough-stalked plant grows primarily out in the open and likes to hang out with prairie plants. It has small yellow flowers that grow in bunches—almost like broccoli—and it resembles yarrow in its structure. The problem with parsnip is that it contains a phototoxin—that is, if you get the toxin on your skin it will cause you to blister very badly when your skin is exposed to light. By not touching parsnip, and especially not breaking the stem, you should be fine after being in its presence. Because it's tall, you can see it coming and avoid it. Also, it tends not to creep onto trails. But there are some hikes in this book that require bushwhacking and take you right through parsnip country. Again, pants and long-sleeved shirts are the key.

If pants and long-sleeved shirts don't seem like fun on a hot summer day, do what we do. We tend to resign ourselves to being hotter and sweatier than we'd like on the trail in exchange for being protected from these plant and insect hazards. Then, back at the car, we change into shorts and sandals.

Wild parsnip

Poison ivy

Hunger and Hydration

It's important, when planning a day hike, to drink at least two or three glasses of water before you head out and to have a good meal, too. Granola, yogurt, and fruit make for great ways to start a morning of hiking, and sub sandwiches, fruit, and a granola bar make for a great lunch. You need to load up before heading out on long hikes. Once on the trail, you'll need more water, sometimes lots of it. We each carry 32 ounces of water and make two to four stops while hiking, so we've finished off the entire bottle by the end of the hike. Also, while you won't feel too hungry when you start hiking, you will by the time you've climbed your first set of hills or found yourself two miles and almost an hour away from the parking lot. We bring complex carbohydrate snacks, like whole-grain granola bars, as well as some fruit or carrots and some protein, such as string cheese. You may even want to bring along a lunch and stop halfway to enjoy a view and dine in the wild. Whatever you do, never go onto the trail without food and water.

Black Bears

Many experienced hikers would argue that bears aren't really a hiking hazard at all. But, in a state with a burgeoning black bear population, the issue should be addressed; unfortunately, there's no hard-and-fast way to do so. Some people say that in the event of an encounter with an unhappy bear, you should play dead. Others will say you ought to act big, while still others will advise you to run like heck. Some hikers carry bear mace.

Yet, the best way to avoid bears is probably to understand them better. Bears tend to be pretty reclusive, and want nothing more than to never see you up close in the first place. This being true, one way to help them avoid you is to make some noise as you hike. Talking helps, and some people will put a bell on their dog or even on their backpack. And, by the time you've applied the various sprays and creams recommended above, you shouldn't have any trouble announcing your presence to a bear, whose olfactory abilities are thousands of times better than ours.

Even so, people do have encounters with bears, particularly on the Apostle Islands, where bears are very unused to people and consequently pretty unafraid and curious. Thus, it's hard to give a solid recommendation other than to recognize, again, that if you're hiking in northern Wisconsin you're going into an ecosystem that includes black bears and now includes you, too. For many hikers, it's this wilderness that they came for in the first place.

HIKING PREPARATIONS

Supplies—What to Bring?

There are a few simple things that we carry with us when we're hiking. We both carry a hip pack, which holds our water bottles and snacks. In addition to those, we've found that having a wildflower and tree identification book is essential. We also carry a multi-tool that includes a scissors, knife, tweezers, and other handy gadgets, a compass of course, and a small first aid kit. The kit includes a roll of under-wrap (thin foam wrap to use under tape), a roll of medical tape, a few gauze pads, a few Band-Aids of various sizes, and some Q-tips. This is in addition to the comprehensive medical pack that we carry in our car with everything from small bottles of rubbing alcohol and hydrogen peroxide to more tape and larger gauze wraps.

We also carry two things in our packs that most hikers probably don't: Neoprene ankle and knee braces—the kind that athletes use. We figure that if one of us sprains a knee or ankle, having those braces will be well worth carrying the extra half pound. Other than some bug spray and lip balm, that's it. It all fits around our waists and, while they start out a bit heavy, the packs lighten up after slugging down some water on the trail.

Hiking Boots and Socks— Never Compromise

We've talked about clothing and hats, but the single most important piece of hiking gear is a great pair of boots over a great pair of socks. No matter what looks cool or what is on sale, you have to wear what is comfortable and sturdy. Go to a good outdoor clothing store and plan on staying there for an hour or two. Put on a liner sock and then a high-quality wool-blend hiking sock. Then, have the salesperson bring you everything she or he has in your size that is marketed as a good to great hiking boot.

Never buy anything that doesn't cover your ankles or anything that feels flimsy. Unfortunately, boots need to be a bit stiff at first. It will take about a month of hiking, but you'll develop a relationship with your boots after that. We can't say enough for waterproof boots. They're more expensive, but they tend to last longer, and you'll be a very happy hiker on that cool spring day when you're sloshing through icy cold snowmelt with warm, dry feet. And as for cost, a boot that costs $150 will probably last at least three to four seasons for us—at least. That's probably well over a thousand miles. And that's a conservative estimate. Not a bad return for never getting blisters and being able to blaze through shallow streams while others try their best to hopscotch across slippery logs and rocks. Once you find the boots that are right for you, wear them to work and on walks in the neighborhood for a week or two, and then start hitting the trails.

Hiking Fitness—Hitting the Trails in Shape

While trail hiking can be a weekend athlete's dream activity, it probably shouldn't be. We "train" for our weekend sports by working out in a gym twice weekly and combining cardiovascular training with light weight training. This fitness schedule makes hopping along a trail on the weekends a lot easier. It also keeps your immune system up to par and lessens the number of injuries you might otherwise get. There are some really tough hikes in this book that assume a certain level of fitness going into them. So make sure you're

prepared for trail hiking before simply hitting the trail. If you are new to hiking or are seeking to start a workout plan, check with your doctor first. It's a good idea to have a physician advise you before undertaking any new fitness activities.

ADDITIONAL READING AND RESOURCES

Just as it is critical to have a good map once in the woods, it's equally important to have a trusty road atlas to get you there. The DeLorme Mapping Company makes what may be the best road atlases one can find. Our own DeLorme *Wisconsin Atlas and Gazetteer,* now shored up with duct tape, is the first thing we pick up on the way out the door.

There are a lot of field guides to choose from, but we have found Stan Tekiela's small, pocket-sized identification guides very good companions. These books are specific to the state and include color photographs. We carry the *Trees of Wisconsin, Birds of Wisconsin,* and *Wildflowers of Wisconsin* guides, all published by Adventure Publications of Cambridge, Minnesota.

A great guide to have along while traveling Wisconsin is Jeanette and Chet Bell's *County Parks of Wisconsin,* published by Wisconsin Trails of Black Earth, Wisconsin. This guide is incredibly comprehensive and is a great resource if you are looking to really explore Wisconsin one county at a time.

Another helpful guide, if you're focused more on the southern part of the state, is *Walking Trails of Southern Wisconsin* by Bob Crawford (University of Wisconsin Press, Madison). This book covers trails, hikes, and paths in fifteen southern Wisconsin counties.

No one book sums up the birth of the study of ecology from its roots in Wisconsin as does *A Sand County Almanac* by Aldo Leopold (Oxford University Press). While many of us simply throw our hiking boots in our cars and speed off to the nearest trailhead to thoroughly enjoy the outdoors in the company of fellow creatures, we may not have thought about why we value this recreation. Reading Leopold's book helps to put our current actions in a historical perspective.

HELPFUL CONTACT INFORMATION

For information on Wisconsin state parks, forests, recreation areas, and trails, contact the Wisconsin Department of Natural Resources at 608-266-2181 or TTY: 608-267-2752, on the web at www.wiparks.com, or by e-mail at wiparks@ dnr.state.wi.us. The mailing address is: Wisconsin Department of Natural Resources, Bureau of Parks and Recreation, P.O. Box 7921, Madison, WI 53707-7921.

Contact the Chequamegon-Nicolet National Forest, forest supervisor's office at 715-762-2461 or TTY: 715-762-5701.

The mailing address is: 1170 4th Avenue South, Park Falls, Wisconsin 54552.

The Wisconsin Department of Tourism can be reached at 1-800-432-8747 or on the web at www.travelwisconsin.com.

The Apostle Islands National Lakeshore (administered by the National Park Service) can be reached directly at 715-779-3397 or on the web at www.nps.gov/apis/home.htm. Their address in Bayfield is: Route 1, Box 4, Bayfield, Wisconsin 54814.

AUTHORS' NOTE

While we have tried our best to provide reliable directions for and descriptions of the following trails, we stress that hiking is an unpredictable endeavor, as is any outdoor activity. Also, we do not guarantee that following the advice offered in this book—or taking for granted any absence of information—will assure safety or prevent bodily harm of any degree. Hike these trails at your own risk.

I

Northwest Hikes

1

Stockton Island

Total distance: 4.2 miles

Hiking time: 1 hour, 45 minutes to 2 hours, 15 minutes

Difficulty: 3.5

Vertical rise: Minimal

Maps: USGS 7½' Stockton Island, Wisconsin; DeLorme Wisconsin Atlas & Gazetteer, p. 103 (A-8)

It's October 1905 and you're on the crew of the schooner-barge Noquebay, steaming out of Bayfield en route to Michigan with an immense cargo of 600,000 board feet of hemlock bound for lumber yards in New York. After setting your course, you and your shipmates sit down for lunch before the long journey across the bitterly cold and highly unpredictable autumn seas of Lake Superior. Before you know it, a fire engulfs the ship and sends you and your mates into the water just offshore of Stockton Island. No one dies, but yet another vessel finds the bottom of this unforgiving lake.

If you have not captured the idea of the force of glaciers, wait until you chug across the icy waters of Lake Superior and explore the Apostle Islands archipelago. This massive lake is the most visible remnant of the most recent Ice Age. The largest freshwater lake in the world—with an average depth of 500 feet and plunging to 1,300 feet at its deepest—it is basically what's left over when a mile-thick and miles-wide block of ice melts. Should you decide to venture out away from a protected bay for some swimming, you'll find yourself in waters that never get much above 40 degrees Fahrenheit—cold enough to cause hypothermia within minutes and death in half an hour. Typical summer weather around the islands ranges anywhere from 48 to 78 degrees F, and sees extremes of 22 and 104 degrees. The "Old Lady," as Superior is called, is teeming with shipwrecks, entombed inside her icy coffin. In fact, as you stride along the exceptionally beautiful and tranquil beach at Julian Bay, you'd never guess that the wreck

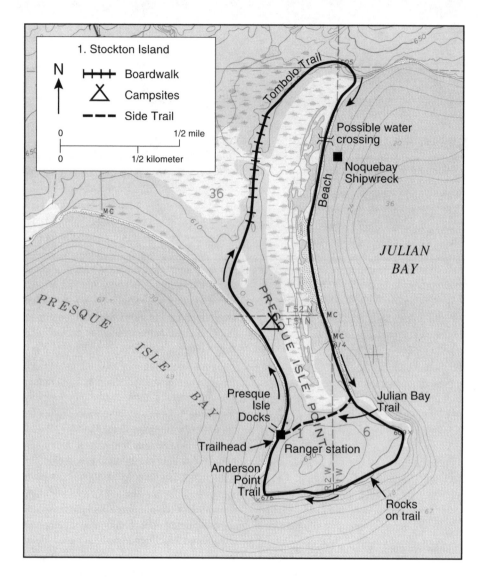

1. Stockton Island

|↔| Boardwalk
|△| Campsites
|- - -| Side Trail

N

0   1/2 mile
0   1/2 kilometer

Tombolo Trail

Possible water crossing

Noquebay Shipwreck

Beach

JULIAN BAY

PRESQUE ISLE BAY

PRESQUE ISLE POINT

T 52 N
T 51 N

Presque Isle Docks

Julian Bay Trail

Trailhead

Ranger station

Anderson Point Trail

Rocks on trail

resulting from the fiery demise of the Noquebay is lying just offshore in 10 feet of water.

No longer crowded with schooners, the waters around the Apostle Islands are blanketed with sailboats and ferries now. Stockton Island, the largest island included in the National Lakeshore, is over ten thousand acres of wilderness. There are no

cars, roads, phones, restaurants, or lighted sidewalks here. Instead, you'll find a rich diversity of hundreds of species of plants and animals ranging from tiny trailside flowers to towering hemlocks, and from little toads to rather large bears.

The Tombolo Trail loop hike seeks to show you the many beauties of the island in the short two-and-a-half-hour layover that

The "trail" along the beach at Stockton Island

you have as a day hiker. If you are camping, this hike can be done in a much more leisurely way, but even on a day trip you should have plenty of time. It is also possible to cut off the Anderson Point part of the trail and head directly back to the ferry dock, if you are running out of time. Be aware that if you miss the ferry, you're spending the night on Stockton, and not returning until late afternoon the next day.

A bit of advice: If you attempt this trip, you are crossing a large body of water and docking at a wilderness island. This hike is somewhere next to magical, but you should really be a serious hiker to attempt it as a day hike. We wouldn't recommend dragging the kids along, unless you have an up-and-coming trekker on your hands who's serious about hiking. Keep in mind that a twisted ankle on the middle of Stockton Island is pretty serious business. Just know your limits before heading over for this immensely beautiful hike.

How to Get There

Unless you have your own boat, the only way to Stockton Island is via the Manitou/Stockton Shuttle aboard the Eagle Island passenger ferry out of Bayfield. Be aware that this ferry often fills up on weekends, so reservations are recommended. As of summer 2003, the boat left at noon and returned at 5:15 pm, spending about two and a half hours on Stockton, after first stopping for a half-hour interpretive program at a historic fishing camp on Manitou Island.

For more information, contact the Apostle Islands National Lakeshore at 715-779-3397 or at www.nps.gov/apis. For ferry information, contact the Apostle Islands Cruise Service at 715-779-3925 or 1-800-323-7619 or at www.apostleisland.com.

The Trail

This clockwise loop is a combination of the Tombolo and Anderson Point Trails. After hopping off the ferry, visitors will be corralled

Boardwalk at Stockton Island

by a ranger for a short orientation. If you know that you are going to do this hike, you should mention it to the ranger right away. Head up the boardwalk off the dock and up to the map kiosk outside the visitors center and restrooms. A boardwalk heading northeast out of this kiosk area will take you up to the trailhead.

Turn left and head northwest along the Quarry Bay/Tombolo Trail toward the campground on the shore of Presque Isle Bay. You will travel behind these campsites, among tall pines and on a soft pine-needle bed, for about 0.5 mile before coming to the turnoff for the Tombolo Trail. Take this to the right (north) and head deeper into the woods of the island. The trail will meander back and forth and up and down small rises and valleys among beds of ferns and under the shelter of pines and birch. The trail is narrow, but the footing is pretty good. You will even pass over a few boardwalks, making the footing exceptionally good.

Eventually, you will emerge from the woods and approach a long boardwalk taking you across a marshy area that is just west of Julian Bay. In fact, from the boardwalk you can see the beach and the bay to your right. This makes for a great place to have a water break and a snack before working your way to the beach itself.

Head back into the woods and follow the path through a pretty boggy, yet wooded area. There is also a boardwalk through a sometimes wet area back here, and the footing stays quite good. Eventually, you will turn to the right (south) and head up toward a small dune, taking you over to the beach. The trail is the beach, in fact. For the best hiking, head down to just where the soft sand meets the more wave-compacted sand. Though slanted, this makes for pretty good footing. You can always kick off the boots, too, because if you look all the way to the end of the beach, that's where you're headed—where the sand meets the woods about a mile to the south. Soon after starting along the beach, you'll be in the exact place where the Noquebay perished and its crew came ashore. While you won't be plunging into the lake, you may need to make a short water crossing. When we visited, a small inlet forced us to cross about 10 feet of knee-deep water, and the ranger mentioned that until recently it had been passable without wading.

Eventually, you will meet back up with the woods and begin a very different hike. As you duck into the woods, you will pass the Julian Bay Trail to the right (west). Take it if you think you're running out of time. The Anderson Point Trail will head left (southeast) and take you along the shore. The trail skirts along the edge of the shore, just inside the woods. It is a remarkable setting as you hike amidst towering old-growth hemlock and amble over huge sheets of the brown-red sandstone, or brownstone, emblematic of the region. Eventually, this quiet, wooded path will take you back to the Julian Bay Trail. Take it left (west) a few steps back to the visitors center area and down toward the dock.

Hiking in a leisurely fashion, but not making too many stops, we finished the hike in 1:45, leaving plenty of time before the ferry left. This phenomenal hike, in one of the most pristine and protected wilderness areas of the state, is well worth the visit for an experienced hiker. Just don't forget to call ahead, or the only hiking you'll be doing will be in and out of the shops of downtown Bayfield—a fun activity in its own right, but not quite the same.

2

Mount Valhalla

Total distance: 3.3 miles

Hiking time: 1 hour to 1 hour, 15 minutes

Difficulty: 2.5

Vertical rise: 100 feet

Maps: USGS 7½' Mt. Valhalla, Wisconsin; DeLorme Wisconsin Atlas & Gazetteer, p. 102 (C-4)

From the time of European settlement in Wisconsin to the time of the Great Depression, millions of acres of land in the state were denuded of their trees. Whether logged for boom-and-bust timber companies or farmland clearing, this vast wasteland of stumps and sandy soil became known as the "cutover region." Covering the state were logging camps, sawmills, and frontier towns crowded with lumberjacks. While those historic towns–like Bayfield, Washburn, and Ashland–still exist today, their focus has switched noticeably toward tourism, recreation, and forestry as opposed to deforestation. Sure, trucks still ramble along the gravel forest roads with their cargoes of logs, but now they are removing trees from one of the most successful reforestation efforts in the world, rather than decimating it.

The two most significant chunks of this massive northern forest make up the Chequamegon and Nicolet National Forests (merged into the Chequamegon-Nicolet National Forest in 1998). With its boundaries stretching into 11 counties, this great forest includes over a million and a half acres and stretches all the way from Bayfield County in the west to Florence County in the east. Included in this natural masterpiece are tens of thousands of non-motorized and designated wilderness areas.

There are also trails, 1,183 miles of them at last count. And, thanks to the large expanse of forest, these are long, uninterrupted trails that take hikers, mountain

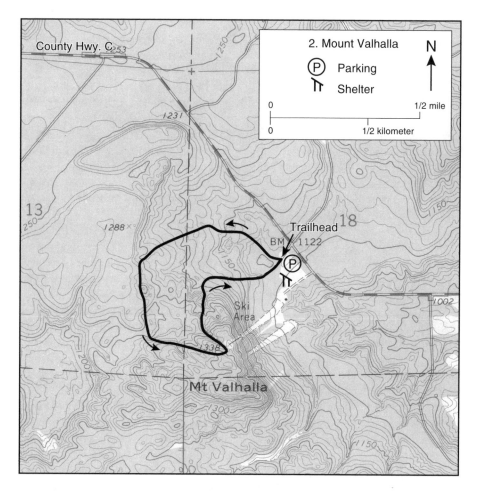

bikers, skiers, horseback riders, snowmobilers, and ATV riders deep into the woods. In a farsighted move, the planners of this immense recreational area thought enough to give each group not only their own trails, but often their own areas. Thus, while the Chequamegon-Nicolet is packed full of ATVs in the warmer months, you'll seldom see them. In the winter, this also means miles and miles of Nordic ski trails, for gliding and skating on only, and separated from the equally impressive snowmobile trails.

In fact, the trails at Mount Valhalla are so attractive that they were once used as a training ground for the United States Olympic Nordic Ski Team. As you meander along this wide trail (obviously a groomed ski trail) and roll up and down the hilly side of Mount Valhalla, you'll understand quickly why an Olympic team would value the terrain. This trail is perfect for hiking, too, and is actually one of several found in the Mount Valhalla area. From the trailhead parking area, you will head counterclockwise up into the still young maple and birch forest, dancing with bright green leaves in the summer, along an uphill stretch before looping back around and down through a steep descent.

Though not overly challenging, it does give you some hill work. Don't be too discouraged about your ability to ski this trail. There are several other, easier loops available for easy to moderate difficulty skiing, if you choose to come back in the winter.

How to Get There

From the southeast and east, take County Route C west out of Washburn and travel about 8.5 miles to the trailhead, which is marked with a large national forest sign for the Teuton and Valkyrie trail system, on the left. There are actually two parking lots here and two entrances; park in the second, more westerly one.

From the north, take CR C south, east out of Cornucopia about 11.5 miles to the trailhead on the right. The parking area will be marked.

From the southwest, take US 2 to the junction with WI 13 outside of Ashland. Turn left (north) on WI 13 and take it 6.7 miles to CR C in Washburn. From there, follow the direction from the southeast/east above.

Note: All the parking areas in the Chequamegon-Nicolet require either a day or seasonal parking pass. In 2003, this cost $3 per day or $10 for a seasonal sticker. Day use fees are payable at any parking lot, while seasonal passes are sold in all the district Chequamegon-Nicolet offices and at many local businesses throughout northern Wisconsin. Remember, these nominal extra fees help to maintain these great trails and the access roads to get you there.

For more information, contact the Chequamegon National Forest, Washburn Ranger District at 715-373-2667.

The Trail

The Teuton Ski Trail is a counterclockwise trail that leaves the trailhead parking area and follows Loop B (approximately 3.3 miles or 5.3 kilometers) of the Teuton Trail System, which meanders along the side of Mount Valhalla. Perfect for skiing, this wide trail begins by taking you into the young maple and birch forest, alive in the summer with bright green leaves and pale bark emerging from a fern-covered forest floor. Soon after starting, you will come to the intersection with another trail, Loop A, but you will follow the trail to the left, which is marked with a sign for the Benchmark and is Loop B.

From here, you will curve to the southwest, and the trail will head up a steep slope for its first and only really challenging section. Again, you will converge with the return intersection of Loop A, but head straight and continue slightly uphill along Loop B. Eventually, the trail will turn southward as you begin to descend just slightly. The trail gets a bit grassier here, but there is usually a good path running through the middle of the grass.

Again, you will pass a trail intersection, this time with Loop C heading off to the right. Stay straight and begin the more prominent downhill section. The trail, obviously a ski trail, will begin to zigzag its way downhill, now among some larger trees. This is a perfect place to round a bend and come upon a deer munching on grass in the open, so keep your eyes peeled. The edge habitat is also good for spotting wildflowers and birds.

The trail will make its final turn eastward and down a steep decline through the only really significant stand of red pine on the trail. You will meet back up with Loop C before heading left (north) back to the trailhead and parking area.

This great little hike along a ski trail is perfect for scouting out your winter ski destinations, stretching your legs while passing through the area, or taking younger hikers out for a short trek. While it's not a narrow path meandering through old-growth woods, it is a great hike in a forest that will be full of towering maples by the time those youngsters are adults.

3

Pattison State Park

Total distance: 4.7 miles

Hiking time: 1 hour 45 minutes to 2 hours, 15 minutes

Difficulty: 3.5

Vertical rise: 100 feet

Maps: USGS 7½' Sunnyside, Wisconsin; DeLorme Wisconsin Atlas & Gazetteer, p. 100 (D-4)

Hiking through the woods of Pattison State Park is like thumbing through the pages of a natural-history book. A billion years ago this entire area flowed with lava, leaving the dark brown rock, called basalt, that is the foundation of the park and the waterfalls today. On top of much of this basalt is sandstone left by the bed of glacial Lake Superior at the close of the last Ice Age about 10,000 years ago. To top this off, a third geological phenomenon—the Douglas Fault—also runs through this area. The uncommon thrust of rock upwards, on a line from Ashland to the Twin Cities, caused the older basalt, curiously, to end up on top of the younger sandstone—one of those marvels that demonstrate the awesome forces of the earth.

All these historical occurrences led to the formation of the principal scenic feature of Pattison, Big Manitou Falls. At 165 feet tall and the fourth highest falls east of the Rockies, Big Manitou serves as quite an attraction—sort of Wisconsin's Niagara Falls. Indeed, this has always been the case. After the retreat of the most recent glacier, nomadic people moved here. Several Native American cultures, including the Archaic and Old Copper cultures, inhabited the region. Later, the area supported a trading post and was a hotbed for copper mining. Eventually, a logging camp was built along the banks of the Black River by Martin Pattison (1841–1918), who went on to become very wealthy thanks to logging and iron mining.

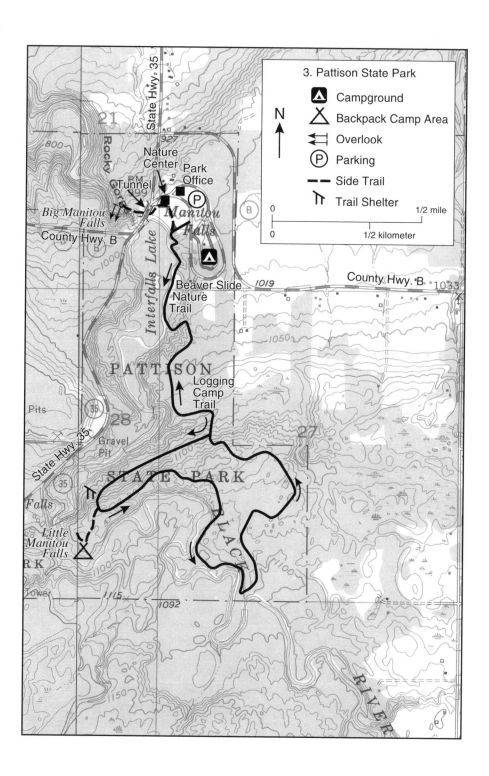

3. Pattison State Park

- Campground
- Backpack Camp Area
- Overlook
- P Parking
- Side Trail
- Trail Shelter

N

0 ___ 1/2 mile
0 ___ 1/2 kilometer

State Hwy. 35

927

Nature Center
Park Office
RM 899
Tunnel
Big Manitou Falls
County Hwy. B
Manitou Falls

800

Rocky

1000

Interfalls Lake

Beaver Slide Nature Trail

1019
County Hwy. B
1033

B

1050

PATTISON

Logging Camp Trail

Pits
35
28
Gravel Pit

State Hwy. 35

35

Falls

STATE PARK

1100

27

Little Manitou Falls

PLACE

1100

RK

Tower

1115
1092

1150

RIVER

Pattison's wealth allowed him to stealthily buy up all the land needed to thwart a proposed damming of the river, which would have eliminated the falls. Today this 1,400-acre park, way up in Wisconsin's northwest corner, is home to more than 200 species of birds and mammals, including timber wolves, moose, black bears, eagles, ospreys, and a variety of reptiles. Hiking through history at Pattison is definitely more fun than reading about it!

Unless you're from Superior, Wisconsin or Duluth, Minnesota—both within sight of the park on a clear day—you have probably traveled off the beaten path to arrive at Pattison. For this reason, a good, long hike is in order. Thus, the following hike takes you around most of the park, through the backpacking campsite area, and to a great view of the Little Manitou Falls (although "little" doesn't do them justice). The loop is about 4.7 miles and will take about two hours with little stopping. Be ready for two things if it is wet: Sloshing around in ankle-deep water and bloodthirsty mosquitoes. On a recent early summer hike, with long pants and shirts, waterproof boots, and some bug juice, these drawbacks were overcome by the beauty and solitude of the hike. This certainly isn't a shorts, T-shirt, and tennis shoes hike, however, and it isn't for kids or those who aren't in shape; what it lacks in vertical rise it makes up for in distance.

How to Get There

From the north or northwest, take WI 35 south from Superior; the park is about 12 miles outside the city. From the east, south and southeast, take County Route B from US 53. Follow CR B for approximately 17 miles to WI 35. Turn left on WI 35 and head south; the park is about 0.25 mile on the left.

For more information, contact Pattison State Park at 715-399-3111.

The Trail

While it is excruciatingly tempting to go there first, try saving Big Manitou Falls until after you finish the hike. This gives you something to look forward to and it makes the little falls seem pretty respectable when you get there.

After passing the park office, follow the road past the several rows of parking spots; take one near the end row to be closer to your vehicle when you finish the hike. The Logging Camp Trail starts near the lake, and there are signs at the southwest corner of the parking lot marking its beginning. The Logging Camp Trail shares a route with the Beaver Slide Nature Trail for a while as they pass Interfalls Lake. The trail follows the lake for about 0.25 mile and is a good warm-up before splitting with the nature trail. Take a left and head up a steep rise deep into the woods on a well-maintained Nordic ski trail. At the apex of the climb there will be a bench and overlook area with views of the lake and the nature trail bridge below. This serves as a good place for a water break or to adjust boots and backpacks, or apply bug juice.

The trail meanders downhill, amidst a wide variety of woodland plants including bunchberries, wild rose, many types of ferns, and sarsaparilla. The trail is almost all shaded and is seldom exposed to the sun. As you wind down from the overlook area, you will merge with a trail not found on the park's maps. This Nordic trail heads straight north and almost looks like an access road. Don't take it. Instead, head right and down into a low marshy area and back up the other side of the valley. Again, there will be a confusing confluence of trails. To do

Big Manitou Falls, Pattison State Park

the loop counterclockwise, take a right. (Straight ahead is your return trail.) You will skirt along the side of the Black River valley as you climb through a mixed hardwood forest, less dense and more open than at the beginning of the hike. About a mile since the last break, you will come to a trail shelter. Again, this area serves as a great spot to break for water or have a snack. If you're packing a lunch, you may want to wait a few more minutes, however, and have a sandwich on the banks of Little Manitou Falls. But, it is a tricky little backcountry-style trail that gets you to the falls. It is steep and slippery, and can be a dangerous bit of trail.

To get to the falls, if you choose to go there, head out of the shelter area and take the next right. This is a dead-end trail that leads to all three backcountry sites. Take this trail to the White Birch Campsite Trail. Go through the site, and a service trail will exit it toward the falls. The very steep and slippery descent is a short one, and you will emerge on a rock outcropping overlooking the top of the falls. Be very careful—there is not much room up here, and the surface can get slippery on a wet day. The peaceful meandering of the Black River is certainly contrasted by the thunderous splashing below. On the other side of the river is a lookout and parking area, accessible from WI 35. So, if you decide not to view the falls from here, you can access them on your way out of the park.

Backtrack the 100 yards past the campsites and back to the main trail, taking a right.

The trail will now work its way closer to the banks of the Black River. But closer will mean wetter, and sometimes swampy areas of the trail will present themselves. If the water is shallow, the best hiking may still be in the middle of the trail rather than on the slippery sides. There are some ATV ruts, however, so be careful not to lose your footing.

Follow the trail past the historic Martin Pattison lumber camp on the banks of the peaceful Black River. Just beyond the camp, the trail will make a sharp turn away from the river and back up into the woods. But, the ascent is very gradual and the trail is still very wet. There are some wooden footbridges to help you traverse some very boggy areas, but they can get slippery, so be extremely careful. Eventually, the trail will pop you back out where you made your initial turn toward the trail shelter. Again, be careful of a Nordic trail, unmarked on the map, that leads off to the right (east) of the main trail. Ignore this and keep heading straight. The trail will pass down through the boggy valley and back up to the confluence of the Nordic trail/access trail and the original Logging Camp Trail that you took to get to this point. Take a left (west) and retrace the first mile of trail back to the parking area.

Once back at the parking lot, make sure to hike through the tunnel, under WI 35, to Big Manitou Falls. The prize falls of Wisconsin are a well-deserved reward for having completed a great hike and having had the opportunity to see and learn more of Pattison State Park than most visitors get to enjoy.

4

Copper Falls State Park

Total distance: 2.5 miles

Hiking time: 1 hour, 15 minutes to 1 hour, 45 minutes

Difficulty: 4.0

Vertical rise: 160 feet

Maps: USGS 7½' High Bridge, Wisconsin and Mellen, Wisconsin; DeLorme Wisconsin Atlas & Gazetteer, p. 95 (B-7)

While the most notable part of Wisconsin's geological past may be the most recent glacier, the state's geology had actually been affected by another unstoppable force: the flow and deposition of miles-thick layers of lava. Due to this diverse history, there are now places where leftover lava rests next to sandstone, shale, clay and granite deposited later. Quite conveniently, all the changes that have occurred in Wisconsin, from eons ago to the present day, are etched in history at Copper Falls State Park.

Here, at the junction of the Bad River and the Tyler Fork of the Bad River, great displays of geological past and present collide with tremendous force. Standing atop a wooden overlook, it's possible to feel the thunder of the water as it cascades over the red and black lava rock of the falls before passing through conglomerate, sandstone, clay, and shale. This rocky, exposed area, bordered by rushing water and an amazing mix of towering maple, hemlock, and birch, is almost unreal in its beauty.

As amazing as the area's geology is the state park itself. While it may have been tempting to run a road right up to the falls, this is a hiking park. The trails are incredibly well maintained and meticulously groomed. For the majority of this hike, you are actually on either a stone path or a wooden plank walkway. The rest of the trail is smooth gravel or packed dirt. But don't let this utopia of a trail fool you (as it does many). While relatively short in length, this trail makes up for it in vertical rise and fall. The valley of the Bad River is well over a hundred feet deep, and this trail, through a

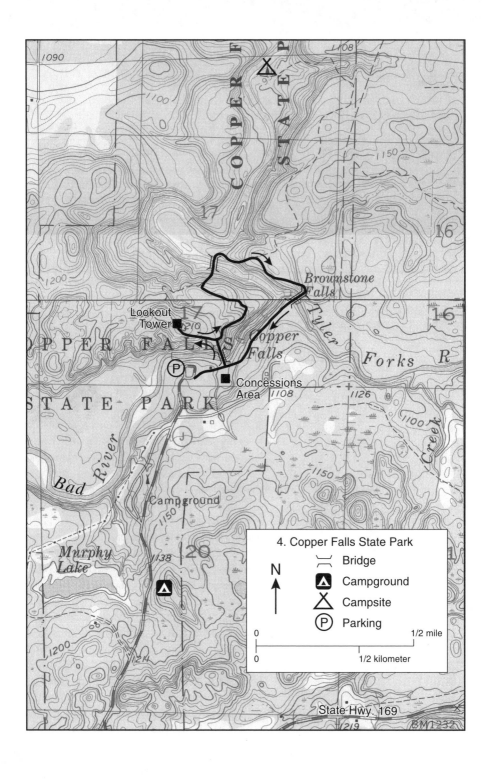

4. Copper Falls State Park

⏝ Bridge
◮ Campground
△ Campsite
Ⓟ Parking

N

0 _____ 1/2 mile

0 _____ 1/2 kilometer

The North Country Trail at Copper Falls State Park

series of steps, risers, and hills, takes you up and down the valley more than once. The stone steps aren't like the steps in your house, either. Like Morse code, they are an awkward combination of long and short, deep and shallow. And, on a wet day, the rock gets pretty slick.

But the hike is a beautiful one. It's the type that you do without saying much to a companion. On a sunny day, the shimmering water, the crashing falls, and the trees overhead just kind of envelop you to the point that there's just not much to say. And, on top of the stunning river valley—literally—is the panoramic view of much of Ashland and Iron Counties from the lookout tower, 0.25 mile and 227 steps (we counted) up from the trail. That's 0.5 mile round trip, but you'll understand why it's worth it if you go up.

How to Get There

From the south, take Main Street east out of Mellen to WI 169. Turn right (north) on WI 169 and take it for 1.6 miles just past Loon Lake. Turn left at the park entrance and continue past the park office to the north parking lot and picnic area near the falls.

From the north, take WI 13 south from Ashland for about 23 miles to WI 169. From there, turn north on 169 and follow the directions above.

From the east, take WI 77 west from Upson for about 11.5 miles to WI 169. Go north on WI 169 and follow the directions above.

For more information, contact Copper Falls State Park at 715-274-5123.

The Trail

If you plan on hiking to the top of the lookout tower, you probably want to do this hike clockwise. After parking, head past the concessions area to the trailhead. The Three Bridges Nature Trail will head left (north) over the river, or straight ahead on the east side of the river. Take a left and go over the bridge, taking the path just above

Copper Falls

Copper Falls. Steps will take you up to the level of the bluff, and soon you will be faced with the decision of whether to climb up to the top of the tower or not. To climb the tower, take the wooden steps up to the trail high above. The trail will wind westward along the side of the hill as it approaches the tower. And, as with any tower, you'll have several more steps before the top. It's a great view from up there, however, and in the fall there is a sea of brilliant color below.

As the sign at the bottom of the tower steps states, don't continue on the trail that brought you up to the tower. Instead, hike back down to the main trail and continue along toward the Copper Falls overlook. This marks a great spot for a break before moving on. There are several scenic stopping points and benches along the trail, offering good rest stops and picture-taking opportunities.

Continuing on, the trail will make a sharp turn west just opposite Brownstone Falls. Then, soon after, a long series of steep steps will take you down to the bridge next to Devil's Gate. Head across the bridge and up the other side along another series of steep stone steps. But, awaiting you soon after is both a bench for a rest and a boardwalk that heads out to an overlook just down from Brownstone Falls. If you've gotten lucky enough to nab the only backpacking site in the park, you'll head to the north, off the main trail.

Otherwise, heading back along the main trail, you will be shaded by a mixture of tall pines and maples before ducking back across the river at the cascades. From here the trail turns southwest and levels out as it heads along the river and back toward the parking area, parallel to the disabled-access trail. There are several areas for a rest and for pictures here, as well. Eventually, the trail will head down some stone steps across from Copper Falls, and you will emerge at the trailhead behind the smartly placed concessions area.

While this hike is not long, it definitely takes a while and can take a lot out of you. As a fellow hiker remarked slyly as we trotted down our first set of stairs: "What goes down must come up."

5

Rock Lake Trail

Total distance: 4.0 miles

Hiking time: 1 hour, 45 minutes to 2 hours, 15 minutes

Difficulty: 3.5

Vertical rise: Minimal

Maps: USGS 7½' Lake Tahkodah, Wisconsin; DeLorme Wisconsin Atlas & Gazetteer, p. 94 (C-3)

Each winter, thousands of skiers from around the world flock to take part in a famous ski race, the American Birkebeiner. While celebrating its 30th birthday in America in 2003, the race dates back nearly 800 years to Norway and the heroic efforts of a group of skiers who smuggled an infant prince to safety. These skiers were known as Birkebeiners due to the birch-bark leggings they wore. The rescue of the prince—who later became King Hakon Hakonsson IV—forever altered the course of European history.

This piece of distant Norwegian history has also altered the history of Wisconsin, with these thousands of modern skiers, from novice to world-class, descending on this very quiet corner of the state each winter to commemorate the efforts of the Birkebeiners. While they are no longer charged with the need to save a boy's life, they are often called upon to save their own. This grueling, 51-kilometer race, which takes hours to complete, pushes the human body to its limits as the trail winds its way up and down hills from Cable to Hayward.

Resembling a plate of spaghetti, the Hayward-Cable region is strewn with trails. In the summer and fall, these trails are very popular with both mountain bikers and hikers. (There is even an internationally known mountain bike race held here every fall, too.) Thus, in this area of exceptionally diverse forest and freshwater lake ecosystems, there also exists one of the most diverse and well-respected recreational trail systems in the world. And that's all in addition

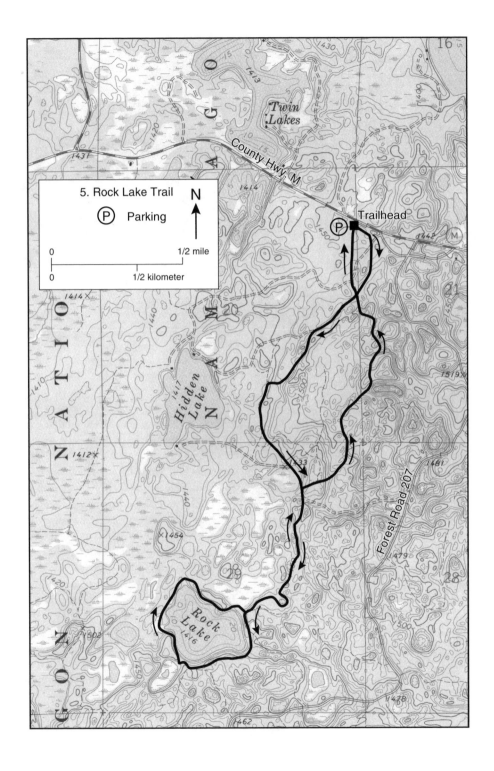

5. Rock Lake Trail

N

Ⓟ Parking

| 0 | 1/2 mile |
| 0 | 1/2 kilometer |

Trailhead

Rock Lake Trail

to some of the best fishing and canoeing found anywhere in the world.

In a sort of kid-in-a-candy-store way, the Rock Lake Trail system, located in the Chequamegon-Nicolet National Forest, offers most of the aforementioned candies in a single jar. Off the trailhead are miles of skiing, hiking, and mountain bike trails, meandering over glacial hills, down shallow valleys, and around pothole lakes. This hike takes you along one of these loops and around one of those lakes—Rock Lake. Approximately 4 miles long, it is not necessarily for beginners and probably not for kids. Yet the hike isn't overly strenuous due to hills or footing—although the trail can get muddy and there are a couple of climbs. Thus, with ample water, snacks, and breaks, hikers of most ability levels should be able to do this hike easily.

How to Get There

From the west or south, take County Route M out of Cable approximately 7.5 miles to the trailhead on the right, marked with a large sign.

From the north, take US 2 west out of Ashland about 6 miles to US 63 south. Turn left (south) on US 63 and follow it almost 20 miles to Cable. In Cable, turn left (east) on CR M and follow the directions above.

From the east, take CR M west out of Clam Lake and go approximately 12 miles to the trailhead parking lot on the left.

For more information, contact the Chequamegon-Nicolet National Forest, Glidden office at 715-264-2511.

The Trail

The trail begins just behind the kiosk at the northeast corner of the lot. Take it, following the 4K Loop next to the road before turning south. You will actually cross the return route of the 4K Loop while doing a sort of figure-eight; so stay to the right or pretty much straight.

The hike is very wooded, and you'll pass among a lot of birch, pines, aspens, and

A soft bed of needles blankets the trail beneath red pines at Rock Lake.

maples as you descend slightly toward Rock Lake. Soon after passing the first trail crossing, you will also pass an access road. Be aware that this area of the trail gets a bit jumbled with all the trails that crisscross here. There are several CAMBA (Cable Area Mountain Bike Association) trails, too. But all the trails are well marked, and by following the hiking trail signs you should have no problem.

Just after passing the access road, you will come to a turnoff for another trail. Follow the arrow and sign for the Rock Lake Trail to the left and continue on a steep uphill. At the top, the 4K Loop will turn left and head back to the lot, while the Rock Lake Trail will head right. Go right and past another access road. Soon you will come to the 7.1K Loop turnoff to the left; ignore it and stay on the Rock Lake Trail, heading down a valley before turning west toward the lake. This is a very scenic area, and the trees transition to fewer hardwoods and more old-growth pines towering overhead.

Soon you will come to the lake itself, and you will turn left at the lake loop trail, going clockwise around the lake (although you can go either way). Still hiking among pines, you will pass a small opening and fire ring before turning more westward. At the southwest corner of the lake, you will pass the turnoff for the 11.5K and 16K ski trails to the left. Stay next to the lake and follow the Rock Lake Trail. You will pass some more towering pines as you climb upward a bit, enjoying a great view of the lake, before descending to a boggy area and a short boardwalk on the western side of the lake. This is a great place to take a break and enjoy the lake before heading on the final push around the lake.

As you head along the northern edge of lake, you will pass more pines, along with some spruce. The trail will be bordered by the lake on the right and a deep valley to the left. Eventually, the trail will open up, just before heading back to the original turnoff, and another great look at the lake is available here. Don't be surprised to see a loon out on the water.

From here, hike up to the lake loop turnoff and head left (northeast). You will actually be doubling back, as you retrace about 0.5 mile of the trail. You will pass those big white and red pines again, as well as the 7.1K turnoff. At the 4 K turnoff, turn right and head northeast. Awaiting you will be the steepest and longest uphill stretch of the hike. It's sort of unexpected, considering the hike has been pretty tranquil and rolling so far. So, be ready for a taxing climb. Eventually, you'll level off and meet up with the 7.1K loop before beginning a steady downhill and a sharp turn to the left. You will meet up with the 2K trail and pass a CAMBA trail and an access road. Just stay straight on the hiking/skiing trail, and you will end up back at the lot.

This excellent trail system offers a great escape into the woods. Following this trail will take you to a remote, untouched lake—where we spotted a rare blue flag iris flowering on the shoreline—and among some towering, giant pines. While there is a confluence of trails here, they are well marked on the map and with trailside kiosks. The CAMBA trails may cause some confusion, but they are marked with signs, too. This is definitely a great day hike, as well as a great spot to go if you have bikers and hikers in the same cabin, or if you want to scout out some phenomenal skiing.

6

Willow River State Park

Total distance: 3.0 miles

Hiking time: 1 hour to 1 hour, 15 minutes

Difficulty: 3.0

Vertical rise: 130 feet

Maps: USGS 7½' Sommerset South, Wisconsin; DeLorme Wisconsin Atlas & Gazetteer, p. 70 (D-3)

Oftentimes rivers flow with as much history as they do water. Willow River's legacy includes two remarkable, yet very different wars. The Battle of the Willow River occurred in 1785 and pitted the Chippewa against the Sioux. The reason for the conflict: rights to rice lakes. Over one hundred years later another battle occurred and it, too, had everything to do with water and probably has a lot to do with you. When a local club of outdoorsmen sought to fence off the Willow River and claim it as their own, Frank Wesley Wade, a brave Civil War veteran, paddled right past. After being arrested, he kept paddling to the Wisconsin Supreme Court, and won. As the park newsletter states: "...the next time you go swimming, fishing, boating or are enjoying the beauty of one of Wisconsin's many lakes and rivers, be sure to think of Frank Wesley Wade and how he fought to make it all possible for future generations."

That's just how Wisconsin is: Nature is so deeply intertwined with what it means to be a resident—or a visitor—that public ownership is just as natural as a flowing river. And that is exactly the spirit you will find flourishing at Willow River, a relatively new park commissioned in 1967. Willow River staff and volunteers are working to restore the area to its original self. By removing dams, they have allowed the waters of the river to rush more naturally; by planting prairie grasses and flowers, they have caused old farmland to burst with color and come alive with insects and animals. And they welcome visitors to enjoy it all.

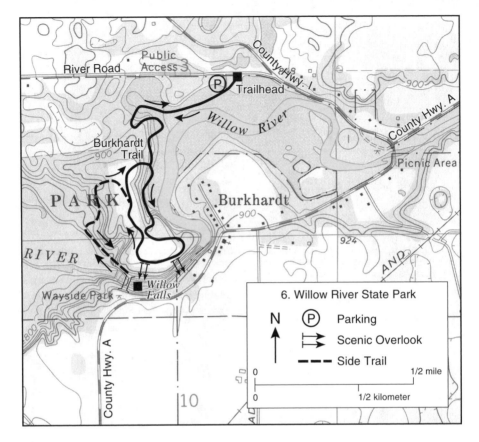

This hike takes you along the river and through those prairies. It also meanders through some of the woods in the park and up to the Willow Falls overlook. While there was a tall stairwell being built in 2003 to take you from the overlook to the bridge below the falls, there is also an offshoot trail that allows you to hike deep into the woods and downhill to the falls. Of course, this means another mile-long hike back up to the loop. Maybe by the time you read this, there will be stairs–although they can be pretty taxing, too.

How to Get There

From the east, take I-94 west to the US 12 exit. Turn right (north) on US 12 and take it about 1.6 miles to County Route U. Turn left on CR U and follow it 0.3 mile to where it ends at CR A. Continue straight on A, past the main park entrance, for about 3.1 miles to CR I. Turn left on CR I (west) and go 0.5 mile to River Road. Take a left on River Road, and the lot will come up pretty quickly on the left.

From the south, take WI 35 north out of River Falls, about 8.5 miles to CR N. Turn right on CR N and go 0.4 mile to US 12. Turn left (north) on 12 and follow the directions above from there.

From the north, take WI 64 west out of New Richmond 1 mile to CR A. Turn left (south) on A and follow it 8 miles to CR I. Turn right on I and follow the directions above.

Willow Falls

For more information, contact Willow River State Park at 715-386-5931.

The Trail

The Burkhardt Trail heads out of the parking area and down toward the river. The mowed grass can be pretty tall, but not too bad. You'll turn west and meander along the river in this marshy area full of tall grasses and wildflowers. It's a good place to look for birds, and there may be waterfowl on the slow water.

Follow the trail until it peels away from the water and into the woods. A short, steady incline through the woods takes you out into another very large prairie area. Turn left (southeast) where the trail comes to a T. This trail to the right is your return loop. Basically, while there may be some offshoot trails, this hike is shaped like a large hourglass. So stay left and loop around the edge of the prairie, ignoring the offshoots and the signs for Willow Falls.

Continue along the edge of the prairie with aspen, oak, hickory, and maple to the left and all sorts of wildflowers to the right. The area is in constant flux in the spring and summer months, and you may see pockets of the purple spikes of blue vervain, or pink phlox.

Eventually, you will work your way to the first of two overlooks. While you can't see the falls yet, this is definitely a good place to appreciate the vertical change of these bluffs compared to the river's level. This lookout, quieter than the falls overlook, is also a great place to stop for water, a snack, or lunch. Continue on the trail for only a few hundred yards to get to the falls overlook. This, too, offers a great look at the elevation change, but also at the falls and the river downstream. As of July 2003, the park staff looked to be about halfway done with a stairwell leading from this overlook to the water, more than a hundred feet below.

If you continue along the trail, however, you will find an offshoot to the left, which is

---

Willow River State Park

a trail leading all the way down to the bottom of the falls. If you want to hike this, it takes about ten minutes to get down and about fifteen to get back up, adding about 2 miles to the hike and taking you to almost 5 miles total. This is what we did, and it was pretty taxing on a hot day, but not unbearable.

Either way, from this turnoff point, continue north along the Burkhardt along the edge of the prairie and back to the T where you originally turned off to the southeast. Turn left (northeast) and backtrack along the same trail that brought you up. Head downhill, through the marshy area, and back to the River Road parking lot.

This great little hike is easily doable with children, but can be a pretty good day's trek for experienced hikers, too. In the winter, this area offers excellent skiing, and Willow River makes for a great destination any time of year.

7

Kinnickinnic State Park

Total distance: 2.8 miles

Hiking time: 1 hour to 1 hour, 15 minutes

Difficulty: 2.0

Vertical rise: Minimal

Maps: USGS 7½' Prescott, Wisconsin; DeLorme Wisconsin Atlas & Gazetteer: p. 58 (B-2)

River valleys are some of the most beautiful areas around. So, when you find yourself at the confluence of two rivers like the Kinnickinnic and the St. Croix, things are doubly breathtaking. This area of western Wisconsin, now essentially a far eastern suburb of the Twin Cities, has become inundated with people. In fact, a summer 2003 report cited the Hudson area as being one of the fastest-growing areas in the state. Thus, the incredible generosity and forethought of a few local landowners in the 1960s—assuring that this unique riverine landscape and its varied ecosystems were preserved as a state park—was more important than they may have guessed at the time.

While this piece of invaluable property could have easily ended up as huge lawns for a handful of private landowners, seeing the park crawling with people on a warm, sunny day truly makes you appreciate public lands. And, while this park does receive a lot of attention, the trails are not at all congested—probably due to the fact that the most popular hike is the short but steep downhill jaunt to the sandy shores of the St. Croix.

This hike takes you through the many habitats of the park, from the hardwoods near the overlook, out into the open prairie, and back again. We've called it the Prairie Loop, but it is actually a combination of three of the park's trails, pieced together to form a nice loop from the main parking lot. While this is not necessarily a long hike, nor

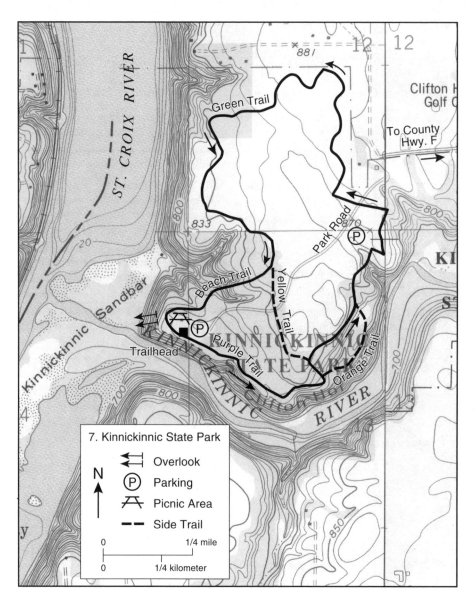

7. Kinnickinnic State Park

⇄	Overlook
Ⓟ	Parking
⛱	Picnic Area
– –	Side Trail

```
0                    1/4 mile
0                    1/4 kilometer
```

a very hilly one, meandering through an open prairie on a hot day can be pretty taxing. Expect to be out and exposed to the sun for the majority of the hike, and don't expect many shady stops or any water along the way. But expect to see some great plants and wildlife. Bring your bird and wildflower books, because you'll undoubtedly want them as you hike this trail.

How to Get There

From the east, take I-94 west to exit 2, County Route F. Turn right on CR F (east) and go 9 miles to 820th Avenue. (You'll see park signs.) Turn right and go 0.3 mile to the park entrance on the left. Follow the park road all the way back to the St. Croix Picnic Area parking lot.

From the north, take CR F out of Hudson and follow the directions above.

From the south, take WI 29/35 north out of Prescott about 1.2 miles to CR F. Turn left on CR F and go 4.1 miles to 820th Avenue. From there, follow the directions above.

For more information, contact Kinnickinnic State Park at 715-425-1129.

The Trail

It's easy to look at prairie hikes as uneventful. But if that's the case, you're probably not looking through the right lenses or you're not looking very hard. Prairies are among the most dramatic and diverse ecosystems around, with red-winged blackbirds battling for territories in the wetter areas, tall grasses tapping several feet underground for water in the drier areas, and insects hopping about like jumping beans just about everywhere. As a bonus, much of this hike follows the edge of woods and prairie, which is as good a place as any to stumble upon a rich diversity of plants and animals.

To start this counterclockwise hike, you first have to find the not-so-obvious trailhead. Once in the Saint Croix Picnic Area parking lot, hike to the picnic benches and grills in the southwest corner. As you drive in, this is directly to your left. Eventually, you will see a small sign marking the beginning of the Purple Trail and an opening in the woods. Here's your trail.

Head southeast through a pretty thick and older woods full of cedars, aspens, and oaks. This trail winds up and down, very gradually, along the edge of the Kinnickinnic River Valley. Eventually, you will come to the turnoff for the Orange Trail; go past that and up to the Yellow Trail turnoff to the right. Take this one and follow the Yellow Trail northward toward the small parking lot near the road on the left. This area of prairie, interspersed with trees, makes for good bird viewing. We came across a flock of grosbeaks calling back and forth, and we imagined it to be an ideal place to spot a bluebird's rusty chest.

After passing the parking lot, you will follow the Yellow Trail as it turns left (west) and goes across the park road. The trail is wide and well maintained, yet the grass can get tall and sometimes makes for tough hiking, especially for children. Soon after crossing the road, you will come to the intersection with the Green Trail; turn right and take it north. This is your last turn for a while as you begin the long segment around the open prairie. This portion of the hike definitely shows how the skiing must be quite good in the winter months. Its gently rolling terrain and wide path would be perfect for those not looking for rigorous hills and climbs.

As the trail winds westward you will meet up with more trees on the park's northern border. This makes for a good place to huddle into the shade and take a water or snack break. The view to the southeast is remarkable, with the tall grasses and flowers swaying in the breeze. The trail will continue southward from here before dodging across a tree line and along a long ridge and ducking back into the woods. Eventually, you will join back up with the Yellow Trail. Take it to the right (south) to the Purple Trail very soon thereafter. Take a right on it as it meanders through the woods and downhill toward the Beach Trail. You will pop out onto the paved Beach Trail; take a left and head uphill to the east and back to the lot.

In all, this trail is almost 3 miles and makes for a terrific hike. We're not certain why loops aren't the norm, because this is a great one. We did our best to cover some diverse terrain and take advantage of everything the park has to offer. The trails are exceptionally well marked, making it nearly impossible to get lost here. Enjoy the hike in this special, preserved piece of property in a county where land is in high demand.

Hoffman Hills State Recreation Area

Total distance: 2.7 miles

Hiking time: 1 hour to 1 hour, 15 minutes

Difficulty: 3.0

Vertical rise: 110 feet

Maps: USGS 7½' Rusk, Wisconsin; DeLorme Wisconsin Atlas & Gazetteer, p. 60 (A-2)

Take miles of hiking, skiing, and snowshoeing trails, with prairies, woods, wetlands, and an observation tower atop one of the highest points in the county. Subtract dogs, bikes, and any motorized vehicles, and you have just about the perfect park for silent sports. The only noticeable noise may be the birds in the summer, the crunch of leaves in the fall, or the yells coming from the sledding hill in the winter. Within a few miles of an interstate highway and well within reach of several mid-sized cities, Hoffman Hills is a great hiking retreat.

Although it has been an official recreation area only since 1980, Hoffman Hills seems as though it was planned as a park for a long time. The wide, well-maintained trails wind through the park's 700 acres, while a handicapped-accessible trail spans 1 mile through the wetland area. The relatively new observation tower also looks as though it was always meant to be there.

The Tower Nature Trail meanders through the park in a counterclockwise loop. The first half dips up and down small valleys while it makes its ascent to the tower. The trail is very well marked with small metal tower signs and offers a good sampling of what the area has to offer in terms of diverse habitats, elevation changes, and wildlife viewing. Don't be surprised to see a wide variety of birds, including woodpeckers in the woods and bluebirds in the tallgrass prairie, as well as deer and other wildlife.

This challenging, yet peaceful hike is a great destination whether you are new to

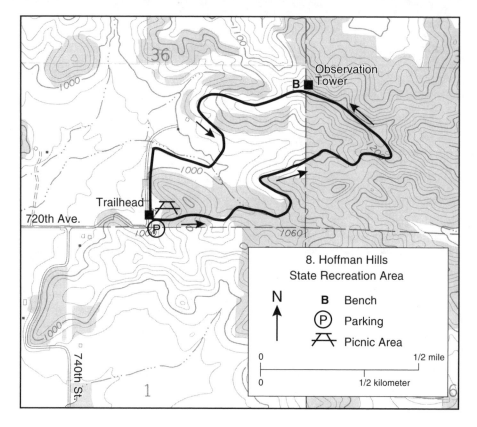

Trailhead
720th Ave.

Observation
Tower

B

**8. Hoffman Hills
State Recreation Area**

N

B   Bench

Ⓟ   Parking

⛉   Picnic Area

0   1/2 mile

0   1/2 kilometer

the area or want to stretch your legs on the way by. We estimate the distance at just under 3 miles, but the hills early on in the hike may make things feel longer overall.

How to Get There

From the north, take WI 40 south out of Colfax for about 5 miles to County Route E. Turn right on CR E and go 3.3 miles to 740th Street. Turn right on 740th (be careful, it comes up quickly) and take it 1.5 miles to the park entrance on the right, at the intersection with 730th Avenue.

From the south, take I-94 west from Eau Claire approximately 11 miles to WI 29/40. Take WI 40 north for about 3 miles to CR E. Turn left on CR E and follow the directions above.

From the west, take US 12/WI 29 east out of Menomonie about 3 miles to CR E. Turn left on CR E and follow it for about 5 miles to 740th Street. Follow the directions above.

For more information, contact Hoffman Hills State Recreation Area at 715-232-1242.

The Trail

The trail begins from the east side of the parking lot by hiking up the grassy hill to the right of the trail kiosk. You will be greeted rather abruptly by a significant ascent followed by a steep descent, making it hard to imagine skiing this trail. The trail will wind its way toward the group camp area among birch, ash, and red pine.

You will come out of the group camp

area and up into an area full of young maples, which is also covered in ferns in the summer. The trail will then bend from west to east and pass through a pine plantation before working its way first down, then up a long, steep ascent to the crest of the tower hill. Once atop the hill, you will have about a 0.5-mile break from climbing along the level ridge before you reach the tower. This area makes for a great place to take a break, have some water, snap some photos, or relax on the bench.

From the tower hill the rest of the hike is mostly downhill. The trail leaves the ridge to the southwest along a wide trail bordered by aspen and alongside a deep valley. Be sure to follow the tower signs, as there will be other trails joining and leaving the tower trail. After turning more southward, the trail will meander up and down through some small valleys before emerging next to the woods.

You will hike west along a prairie for about 0.5 mile. This area offers a great opportunity to look for interesting prairie flowers, and for bird-watching. The trail will bend south again, past the overflow parking lot and up into the woods along a slight ascent before descending into the grassy picnic and playground area next to the parking lot.

This trail offers a great variety of habitats and terrain and makes for a somewhat challenging hike. The hills in the first half of the hike may be too much for inexperienced hikers or small children. There are several good spots for taking breaks, and anytime you are making a long ascent it is a good idea to take several water stops. The view from the top is remarkable, and atop the tower it's even better.

9

Chippewa Moraine Ice Age Reserve

Distance: 4.5 miles

Hiking time: 1 hour, 45 minutes to 2 hours, 15 minutes

Difficulty: 3.5

Vertical rise: 120 feet

Maps: USGS 7½' Marsh-Miller Lake, Wisconsin; DeLorme Wisconsin Atlas & Gazetteer: p. 72 (C-4)

If you didn't know better, you would think that the Wisconsin Department of Natural Resources scientists and engineers got together and built a 4,000-acre model of exactly what a glacier leaves in its tracks. They would have included a sweeping, several-miles-wide moraine, and then they would have peppered the landscape with all sorts of little hummock hills and kettle lakes. On top of that, literally, they would have placed just about the most remarkable visitors center, overlooking the entirety of their masterpiece to the south, atop a long hill covered in prairie plants. Giggling like kids in a candy store, they would have thrown in some of the best trails in the state, exceptionally good trail markings, backcountry campsites accessible only by foot or canoe, and a heron rookery. They'd even be open year-round so that you could stop by and check out one of their pairs of snowshoes. It would be a sort of Ice Age paradise.

Well, they didn't do it because they didn't have to. All that was needed was legislation by Congress in 1964, which created the Ice Age National Scientific Reserves. Nine of these units are found around the state and seek to ensure the "protection, preservation, and interpretation of the nationally significant values of Wisconsin continental glaciation…" These reserves are all about getting people acquainted with their "glacial sides." Whether it's done by perusing the interpretive center, going on a guided hike, checking out a backpack full of nature identification materials, or simply tromping along the trails,

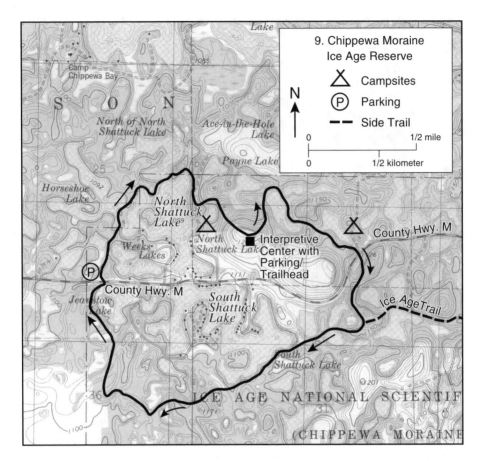

these reserves are inimitably successful at teaching as well as preserving.

But, getting out onto the trails reveals that much of what was preserved geologically is playing a critical role biologically. The dry hills and wet valleys of the hummocks and kettles support an incredible array of life, from tiny microorganisms, to all sorts of reptiles and amphibians, all the way up to black bears. The very fact that a loon called in the distance on our recent visit to this glacial wonderland is evidence of what can exist in protected areas.

The remarkable Ice Age Circle Trail leaves the nature center and begins a seemingly endless series of ascents and descents along the shores of several small kettle lakes. The trail is well marked and the landscape serene. This is definitely the kind of hike that leaves you speechless, when you just want to hike and take it all in, while contemplating why in the world you haven't ever been here before, your thoughts interrupted only by those pesky loons.

How to get there

From the north, take US 53 south out of Chetek for about 7.5 miles to County Route M. Take CR M east through New Auburn for about 8.3 miles to the Chippewa Moraine Ice Age Unit visitors center entrance on the left.

Crossing a corner of one of the many glacial lakes at Chippewa Moraine

From the south, take US 53 north to Bloomer. Take WI 40 north out of Bloomer for 11.7 miles to CR M. Turn right on CR M and follow it for about 2 miles to the Chippewa Moraine Ice Age Unit visitors center entrance on the left.

For more information, contact Chippewa Moraine Ice Age Reserve at 715-967-2800.

The Trail

The trail begins just off the visitors center parking lot to the north. The trailhead kiosk has maps, and the smart-looking veneer signs aren't just for the trailhead—they make the trail easy to follow all along the way.

Immediately into the woods and onto the trail you will come to a T intersection where you will head to the right (east), starting a clockwise route. The start of the loop and the return trail form an arc here atop a valley, making for a sort of natural amphitheater. Performing in the summer are thousands of ferns, blanketing the floor of

the forest, with a mixture of hardwoods towering overhead.

The trail dips down into the valley and heads immediately between two of the many lakes that you will visit on this trail. Look for waterfowl and deer in these lowland areas. You will then cross over the first of many very well-maintained bridges as you wind your way northeast alongside the eastern edge of the one of the first lakes. The trail will begin to ascend slowly, then more abruptly, next to another lake before winding around its southern tip and descending to where you will cross CR M. At the foot of this hill is the entrance trail to one of the remote campsites, right on the shores of this secluded lake.

After crossing CR M, you will begin another climb for about 0.25 mile. At the top of this hill you will pass out of mostly mixed hardwoods and into a more coniferous area, dominated by red pines. The trail will then pass by another lake before descending to

Northwest Hikes

The Ice Age Trail

the offshoot of the Ice Age Trail to the east. Stay right, on the Ice Age Loop, and continue westward.

This marks the beginning of a long stretch of trail that traverses bogs and wetlands, and meanders up and down alongside several kettle lakes and ponds. There are several places from which to view the lakes, and there are spots to take breaks at benches. The hills can get pretty taxing, so a couple of stops may be in order.

Eventually, the trail will turn more northward and the landscape will get a lot grassier and more open. The sun can get hot here as you make a few final dips and climbs back toward CR M. The trail will emerge just across the road from the gravel parking lot at the roadside trailhead. On days with lots of mosquitoes, this open area is a gift allowing for a break for water.

Heading back on the trail northward reveals a somewhat different topography. The trail seems more open here, and there are more conifers. Also, the strange, steam engine-like noises you might hear coming from the other side of the lake to the left are the fascinating sounds of the heron rookery. Almost like a science fiction dragon breathing and grunting, the noise of the rookery is both intriguing and a little worrisome.

The trail then passes over a bridge and portage area before beginning its final loop eastward. It was right around here where we heard the wail of a loon in the distance, a bit surprising for this far south. You'll pass yet another bridge and the entrance to another remote campsite, before skirting along the edge of Payne Lake. From here you will wind back up a long and steep ascent, exploring the other half of that fern-laden amphitheater to the top of the trailhead hill.

All in all, this truly beautiful hike amidst the glacial remains of the Chippewa Moraine makes for a great day hike. Meandering between these lakes and up and down their valleys is truly a unique hiking experience and one well worth the visit.

10

Brunet Island State Park

Total distance: 3.0 miles

Hiking time: 45 minutes to 1 hour

Difficulty: 2.0

Vertical rise: Minimal

Maps: USGS 7½' Cornell, Wisconsin; DeLorme Wisconsin Atlas & Gazetteer, p. 73 (C-7)

"Three Gifts of a Glacier" boasts a Wisconsin Department of Natural Resources informational pamphlet on Chippewa County recreation areas. And, with Lake Wissota State Park, the Chippewa Moraine Ice Age Reserve (also included in this book), and Brunet Island State Park, the boasting is very appropriate. While there are several areas in the state that pay homage to the most recent Ice Age, the Chippewa County area devotes a very respectable amount of attention to its glacial history. Most notable is a collection of several glacial lakes and their drainage, via many creeks and rivers, into the Chippewa River, whose ultimate destination is the Mississippi River—but not before some of its water is siphoned off and bottled as Leinenkugel beer.

An island park flanked by the Chippewa and Fisher Rivers, Brunet Island offers visitors a variety of options. While the bulk of the activity—beach, boat dock, campsites, and fishing pier—resides on the island, the best hiking is found on the "mainland." As a result of the last Ice Age, the park includes a wide range of plants, terrain, and wildlife. Activities at the park include several biking trails, canoeing, fishing, and swimming at a 200-foot sand beach.

The real gems of Brunet Island State Park are coniferous ones, though. Old-growth hemlock trees, a very rare find in Wisconsin, loom overhead and flank the trails throughout the park. While several of the trees were lost to a tornado a few years ago, there are still many left, both on the

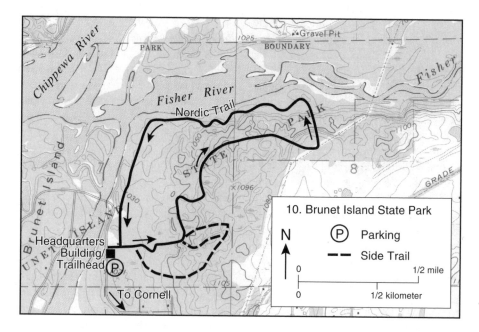

10. Brunet Island State Park

N

(P) Parking

- - Side Trail

0   1/2 mile

0   1/2 kilometer

island and in the Nordic Trail section. A ranger at the park notes that it may be one of the best stands of hemlock remaining in the state.

The best uninterrupted hiking trail at Brunet Island is found on the Nordic Trail. This loop takes you away from the park office to the east and up and down a series of small glacial hills and valleys and past several small ponds. The trail then turns north before heading along the shore of the Fisher River to the west. It is along this segment of the trail where you pass among the towering hemlocks before turning south and heading back to the park office.

How to Get There

From Eau Claire to the southwest, take US 53/WI 124 north. Stay on WI 124 when the two split, and follow it 2 more miles to WI 29. Take WI 29 east about 12 miles to WI 27. Head left (north) on WI 27, through Cadott, and about 15 miles to Cornell. At the stop sign, turn left on County Route CC.

Take the first right under the railroad bridge, a crossing point of the Old Abe bike trail, which is accessible from the park. Follow the entrance road into the park. Park at the lot next to the headquarters building on the right. The trail begins off this lot.

If coming from the south or southeast, take WI 27 out of Augusta (approximately 10 miles from Osseo and I-94). Take WI 27 north through Cadott, about 20 miles, and follow the directions above.

From the north and northwest, take US 53 south to WI 64, just north of Bloomer. Head east on WI 64 for approximately 25 miles to where it crosses the Chippewa River. The road to the park will be the first road on the left after the bridge.

From the north and northeast, take WI 27 south out of Ladysmith to Cornell, about 22 miles. Head straight through town, but do not turn left out of town. Instead, head straight under the railroad bridge, toward the river, and take the first right after the railroad bridge and before the river.

For more information, contact Brunet Island State Park at 715-239-6888.

The Trail

The trailhead is found just off the headquarters building parking lot. You will see a kiosk on the north side of the lot. This trail can be wet and passes several small ponds. Be sure to bring good waterproof footwear, and be prepared for bugs. Head east from the trailhead and begin a counterclockwise trip around the trail. There are two loops, a long loop and short loop. The long loop is about 3 miles and takes 45 minutes to an hour.

To follow the long loop, stay on the main trail through a rambling section among ferns and birch trees. An offshoot of the short loop will come up quickly on the right, or head straight for the long loop. You'll come to another map kiosk and the convergence of three trails. Straight ahead is the return of the short loop, to the right is a shortcut from the short loop, and to the left is the continuation of the long loop. Head left. The trail starts climbing from here and makes a few cutbacks as it heads up to its highest point. This area can take the wind out of you, and would be a bit of a challenge for children or those not in hiking shape, or on skis. But it isn't a grueling hill, and it's really the only one of note on the entire hike.

Through this area you will pass several small ponds as you meander underneath birch, aspen, oak, and a few hemlock. Eventually, the trail will make a left turn and head north toward the Fisher River. It passes between the Fisher and a picturesque large pond on the left. On sunny days, this may be the only sun you see on this tree-covered hike. As you follow along the Fisher, the trail traces the top of a long esker, or ridge of glacial debris, before heading back up in elevation and past the best concentration of hemlocks at the park. These cinnamon-colored giants loom over the trail, and on rainy, overcast days this area resembles a rainforest, making it hard to believe that you are in the middle of Wisconsin.

The trail then pops out of the woods into a power-line opening and makes a quick left, taking you south back toward the parking lot. This grassy edge habitat is great for bird-watching and for spotting browsing deer (and for picking up ticks—long pants are a must). Take this past the dumping station (we suggest circumnavigating that area to the right when you pass it) and back to the parking lot. This long loop trail makes for a very nice hike and is definitely the least-used asset of the park.

Brunet Island is one of the many hidden state parks found off the beaten path. This area is a phenomenal natural setting and offers hiking, skiing, fishing, and canoeing in unbelievable concentration. Not far from the interstate and the cities of Eau Claire and Chippewa Falls, Brunet Island makes for a great day trip or a spot to stretch your legs on a long trip up north or back down south.

11

Rib Mountain State Park

Total distance: 3.1 miles

Hiking time: 1 hour, 30 minutes to 2 hours

Difficulty: 4.5

Vertical rise: 515 feet

Maps: USGS 7½' Wausau West, Wisconsin; DeLorme Wisconsin Atlas & Gazetteer, p. 64 (A-3)

Literally like a diamond in the rough, Rib Mountain rests as a formidable stalwart of the glaciers. A huge mound of quartzite, the mountain has stood the test of geological time, and its peak is now the third highest point in Wisconsin at 1,939.5 feet. And as impressive as its height is its age–the mountain is dated at 1.6 billion years old!

Perhaps the most significant feature of Rib Mountain is located on its backside. The south side of the mountain holds a gem as valuable as the quartz below it: Maples and their golden sap. Here can be found one of the most impressive stands of sugar maple in the state. And it is among these beautiful trees and along the southern slope of the mountain that this hike will take you.

As soon as you start mentioning large hills, mountains, and trails that meander along the sides of them, you're probably talking some serious elevation change. During this hike, you will begin at the top of Rib Mountain, perched over 1,700 feet above Wausau. Before you know it, you will have descended to 1,330 feet and will be making the turn westward, back up the mountain. The return ascent seems easy at first. But before too long, you will turn straight north and begin a brutal uphill assault, climbing 320 feet in about 0.25 mile–almost a foot per stride. And on top of that, the trail is a hodgepodge of loose rock, making a walking stick a must rather than an option on this great, sweeping trail on the maple-shrouded southern slope of Rib Mountain. At the top you are rewarded with a phenomenal view

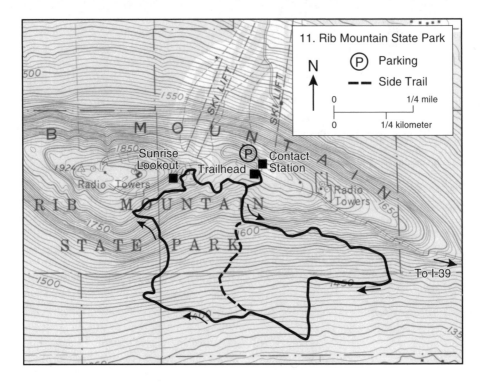

11. Rib Mountain State Park

N

Ⓟ Parking

-- Side Trail

0 _____ 1/4 mile

0 _____ 1/4 kilometer

atop Sunrise Lookout—perfect if you were able to crawl out of your tent and zip through this hike bright and early.

Definitely not for beginners, or for children, this hike is challenging. The wide path, used for snowshoeing in the winter, is a bit tricky due to the rocks hidden beneath fallen leaves, but it's not treacherous. As for the 320-foot climb, take it slow. There's no medal for getting to the top fast and you'll be wise to take two or three—or four—breaks on the way up. This great hike is a tough one, one of the most taxing in this book, but is an exceptionally pleasant way to explore Rib Mountain.

How to Get There

From the north or south, take US 51 to Wausau. Take the County Route N exit and head west to Park Road, 0.1 mile from US 51. Turn right on Park Road and take it for 1.9 miles up into the park. Park in the lot just next to the park office A-frame, or in the overflow lot just across the road.

From the west, take CR B south out of Marathon City about 2 miles to CR N. Turn left (east) on CR N and go 9.5 miles to Park Road. Turn left and follow the directions above.

From the east, take WI 29 west from Wittenberg for about 25 miles to the Wausau area. Merge with US 51 north and take the CR N exit. Turn left on CR N and take it 0.2 mile to Park Road. Turn right on Park Road and follow the directions above.

For more information, contact Rib Mountain State Park at 715-842-2522.

The Trail

If parked in the lot at the A-frame park office, head across the road on the north side of the lot and follow the arrow for the "parking

Birches and maples lush with summer growth at Rib Mountain

Squeezing between rocks on the way to Sunrise Lookout at Rib Mountain State Park

only entrance." The other option is to park over there, too. The trailhead is easy to find just off the northwest corner of the lot.

The trail is immediately pleasant to hike on. It's wide open and surrounded with trees. While you are headed downward, the hiking is pretty easy at the start. The return trail of this loop will come up quickly on your right. Stay left and continue down the first really steep section. The trail will get a bit rockier, making for some slippery footing at times. You will also pass the Middle Yellow Trail turnoff; skip this and stay left (east).

This section of the trail is a long, easy downhill taking you alongside the slope. This is where the maple forest really engulfs you. There are usually several pieces of small deadfall maple to grab as walking sticks for the upcoming ascent. Just watch that yours isn't nestled in a bed of poison ivy.

Eventually, the trail will come close to its easternmost point, where the Lower East Yellow Trail peels off to the east. Stay right

and go south before turning to the west along a fairly level stretch of trail. Soon the trail will turn directly south and drop about a hundred feet in just 0.125 mile before hitting its lowest point and turning northwest and beginning a very long uphill.

The climb is pretty slight at first as you pass the turnoff for the Middle Yellow Trail. Stay left again, technically taking the Lower West Yellow Trail. From here you will meander among a great many maples, climbing slightly, and even descending a little at one point. Soon you will turn right (north) and start heading straight up the side of the mountain toward Sunrise Lookout. It's a bit of a surprise after all the pleasant rambling you have been doing so far. Have your walking stick ready for support on loose rock, and go slowly. A couple of benches offer places to rest along the way, or you can simply stop every once in a while to catch your breath.

At the top, you will merge with three trails. The Red Trail will head to the left, the

Gray/Yellow will go straight, and the Gray will go to the right. Take the Gray Trail to the right along a narrower path than what you've been used to. This will take you toward the ridge of the mountain and up to Sunrise Lookout. The trail weaves between some boulders as it approaches the very rocky lookout. After making a bend in the trail and heading north, take the next right, which is a connecting trail to the lookout. Stay on this as it climbs first around the front of the lookout rock and then up around the eastern side of it, up some rock steps.

After resting at the lookout and taking some pictures, head northeast off the rock and follow the Yellow/Gray trail toward the road. But don't cross the road instead stay to the right and head east back toward Cobbler's Nob Loop. From here you will meet up with the original Yellow Trail at a bench. Take a left and head north a short ways to the parking lot.

Definitely one of the most scenic and challenging hikes in the state, this loop trail along the south slope of Rib Mountain makes for a great day's trekking. Enjoy the maples, especially in the fall, and don't forget to have a walking stick ready.

II

Northeast Hikes

12

Fallison Lake Nature Trail

Total distance: 2.0 miles

Hiking time: 1 hour to 1 hour, 15 minutes

Difficulty: 2.5

Vertical rise: Minimal

Maps: USGS 7½' Sayner, Wisconsin; DeLorme Wisconsin Atlas & Gazetteer, p. 88 (A-3)

Webster's Dictionary defines quintessence as "the pure essence or perfect type." If there were ever a quintessential northern Wisconsin lake-country lake, encircled by an almost perfect trail and covered by a thick northern hemlock and hardwood forest canopy, then that lake would have to be Fallison, and the trail would have to be the Fallison Lake Nature Trail.

On a cool northwoods evening, with the sun low on the horizon, the lake shimmers like black glass. To make matters unmistakably perfect, a loon would paddle alongside you as you hike, hooting lightly as if to guide you. The trail itself almost looks like a movie set. A mixture of young and old pines has left a thick carpet of auburn needles below, and the soft trail meanders between the tall trunks like icing surrounding the candles of a birthday cake.

In an area immersed in lakeshore development and paradoxically crowded remote roads, a visit to Fallison, tucked unassumingly off the road, is a refreshing change. The lake isn't right off the road; instead the trail makes a short climb and then a descent before you get your first glimpse. You then pass behind trees as your view improves. Then, you're guided into a bog along a long boardwalk before emerging, finally, to be rewarded with a view of the lake from the south shore.

This trail is a hiker's trail. While short, it takes a while to get around, but it's more than the distance that will keep you coming back. It's the solitude, the scenery, and the lack of any "stuff" other than nature itself.

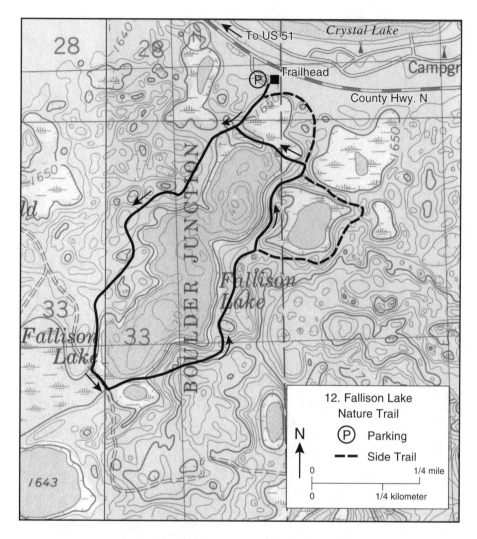

The area around the lake is a marvel of natural diversity, with rare hemlock, old-growth white pine, sphagnum bogs, eagles, ospreys, loons, beavers, and more. In fact, on our hike, we were constantly stepping over long-ago-felled trees that had been partially dragged to the lake by a busy beaver. As a remarkable addition to this hike, the Fallison Lake Nature Trail also has guidebooks at the trailhead kiosk covering the flora, fauna, and history of the area, making it a great stop for families or hikers interested in learning more while on the trail.

How to Get There
From the south, take US 51 north out of Woodruff about 4.5 miles to County Route M. Turn right on CR M and go 2.6 miles to CR N. Turn right on CR N, and the FALLISON LAKE trailhead sign will be 2.4 miles on the right.

From the north, take US 51 south out of Manitowish Waters for about 12 miles to

Pines at Fallison Lake

Fallison Lake

CR N. Turn left on CR N and go 4.1 miles to the Fallison Lake trailhead on the right. From the east, take CR N west out of Sayner for about 4.6 miles to the trailhead on the left.

For more information, contact the Trout Lake forestry headquarters at 715-385-2704.

The Trail

This hike goes mostly along the Blue Loop, although we cut off from the Blue and took the Green Trail back to the lot so that we could cut between the bog and the north end of the lake—a great view.

Start by heading right (southwest) out of the parking lot and trail kiosk area. You'll head down some riser steps, next to the bog, before climbing back up to a small ridge on the north side of the lake. The return loop for the Green Trail will come up quickly on the left; stay to the right and head counterclockwise around the lake on the Blue Loop.

The trail will take you away from the lake briefly, before turning back and giving you your first good glimpse from a boggy valley. From here, you'll climb a bit and pass a bench. This may be a bit soon for a break, so continue along the western shore, with a soft pine needle bed underfoot and towering pines overhead. Keep an eye out for loons paddling along the shore, or even for an eagle hunting in the area.

Soon enough, you will come to the southern tip of the lake and the trail will turn left (northeast) across a long boardwalk and over a large bog. Things are pretty overgrown here, making it tough to see much wildlife. It can also get pretty buggy. The trail will emerge from the bog and turn more northward, through a picnic area and past the hand pump. While things open up a lot here, and the trail is a little hard to find, simply stay near the lake, and the trail will follow along the shore. Make sure to look up, too, because you'll find yourself surrounded by one of the rarest sights in the northwoods: towering old-growth hemlocks.

Coming out of the picnic area, you will pass over a small bridge, offering a great look at the lake from the southeast corner. This is a great place to take a break, snap some photos, and do some wildlife viewing. Don't be surprised to see a beaver, working feverishly on some important building project.

The trail will then start to wind along the eastern shore of the lake. After a short climb and descent into a valley, you will find yourself at the connection of the Green, Red, and Blue Trails. We didn't go east into the open bog area along the Red and Green Trails. Instead, there will be several offshoot trails just up ahead along the Blue Trail that lead to the shore of the lake. A small peninsula makes for a great spot to view the lake.

From here, follow the trail to where the Green Trail heads west between the bog and the lake. This is definitely the way to go. There is a boardwalk leading to a short hillside that has a couple of benches looking out at the lake from the north shore.

Eventually, you will meet back up with the fork in the trail that you took originally. Head right (north) back toward the parking lot and trail kiosk. This hike, a short one, is perfect for kids or beginners. But it's a great one for experienced hikers, too, looking for some solitude and to stretch their legs.

13

Lost Lake

Total distance: 4.5 miles

Hiking time: 2 hours to 2 hours, 30 minutes

Difficulty: 3.5

Vertical rise: Minimal

Maps: USGS 7½' Long Lake Northeast, Wisconsin; DeLorme Wisconsin Atlas & Gazetteer, p. 90 (A-4)

The ideal northwoods getaway would probably be a small cabin on a quiet lake with great views, fishing, canoeing, wildlife, and a nice, cool canopy of trees overhead. Running water would be nice, and good neighbors essential. While getting a piece of the northwoods pie usually takes some pretty deep digging into one's pockets, you may not need to. In fact, you probably didn't know it, but you already own the aforementioned property.

Tucked deep in northeast Wisconsin is heavily wooded Florence County. Known for its trees, lakes, and trout streams, this is one of the most beautiful places on earth, let alone the state. The reason you are part owner of this property has to do with the fact that nearly half of Florence County is publicly owned. And, among the many campsites on picturesque, remote lakes, there is Lost Lake Campground, offering a true northwoods getaway.

In keeping with its name, Lost Lake is tucked away, far off the beaten path about an hour from either Florence or Eagle River. The small lake is flanked by arguably the most impressive remaining old-growth hemlock forests in the state. These giants erupt out of the wet lakeshore soil and tower overhead like space needles.

Topping off this perfect northwoods retreat are the trails. Lost Lake Campground just happens to be sitting right on the path of the Perch, Lauterman, Ridge, and Assessor's Trails—some of the best hiking in the Chequamegon-Nicolet National Forest. The trail highlighted here is the Ridge, and it

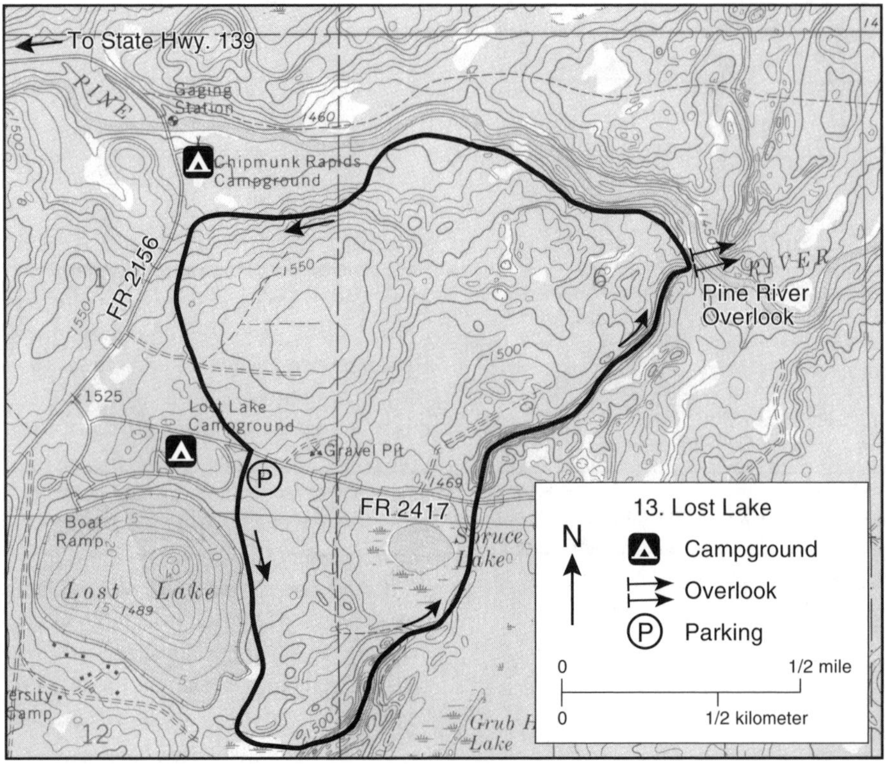
To State Hwy. 139
PINE
Gaging Station
Chipmunk Rapids Campground
FR 2156
Pine River Overlook
RIVER
Lost Lake Campground
Gravel Pit
FR 2417
Boat Ramp
Lost Lake
Spruce Lake
Grub Lake
13. Lost Lake
N
Campground
Overlook
Parking
0
1/2 mile
0
1/2 kilometer

starts right off your front step. It takes at least two hours, and may take upwards of three. Thus, it's definitely a day's worth of hiking and requires a good supply of snacks, or even a lunch, and lots of water. While well marked, the trail sees limited traffic, and there is some bushwhacking required in the more open areas of the trail. But, these are the places where the blackberries grow like wildfire in the summer. While not a trail for beginners, the Ridge Trail isn't necessarily hard due to footing or vertical rise—although there are some significant hills.

This rolling hike takes you deep into a national forest, offering great views of glacial remains, seldom-seen hemlock and pine trees, and a great escape while visiting Florence County.

How to Get There

To get to Lost Lake Campground from the west, take WI 70 east out of Eagle River for about 29.5 miles to the junction of WI 70 east and WI 139 South. Continue on WI 70/139 for 2.8 miles. Turn left on WI 70 east and follow it for 3.7 miles to FR 2450 (Dream Lake Road). You will see signs to Lost Lake Campground. Turn right on FR 2450, which merges with Chipmunk Rapids Road, and follow it for 3.7 miles past Chipmunk Rapids Campground. The next turnoff to the left will be Lost Lake Campground. Also, if you are not camping, drive past the campground entrance to the trailhead lot. Follow the gravel drive for about 0.5 mile to the Assessor's Trail trailhead parking lot on the right.

Lost on the trail at Lost Lake

From the east, take WI 70 out of Florence for 16.5 miles to FR 2450. Turn right and follow the directions above.

From the south, take WI 139 north out of Long Lake for 5.7 miles to junction of WI 70/139. Turn right on WI 70 east and follow the directions above.

For more information, contact the Chequamegon National Forest, Florence District Office at 715-528-4464.

The Trail

A map on the kiosk at the trailhead provides a good overview of the hike. Take the Assessor's Trail south out of the lot, taking you into the hemlock and pine forest of little undergrowth along the shore of Lost Lake. Be careful not to follow the Assessor's Loop. Instead, follow the sign to the Assessor's Pine, and then stay along the shore by the benches overlooking the lake. You'll continue back around the southwest corner of the lake, where there is a small bog—look for the wood duck nesting boxes. After hiking around the bog, you will find yourself in the midst of some of the huge hemlocks surrounding the lake as you come to a trail intersection.

One sign points left (northeast) and back to the Lost Lake Campground (it says 0.06 mile, but we think they meant 0.6) or, under the Ridge Trail heading, straight to the Pine River Overlook, Chipmunk Rapids Campground, or Lost Lake Campground 3.3 miles away. The latter is your trail.

Head southeast on this narrow trail, away from the lake and into a more mixed hardwood forest, with more undergrowth. You'll encounter fewer hemlocks now, and more maples. The trail will turn northeastward as you begin a somewhat taxing climb up to the top of the trail's namesake ridge. After the long climb, you will find yourself atop the ridge, probably a large uninterrupted drumlin, with deep valleys on either side. But soon after, you'll begin a long and gradual descent as you work your way down to FR 2417.

You'll find that at FR 2417—not much of a road—you have the option of heading west to Lost Lake Campground (0.5 mile away), or continuing on the Ridge Trail for another 2.4 miles. Head straight on the Ridge Trail, of course, and straight up another hill. Atop this ridge, you'll find almost no hemlock and a much brighter green mix of paper birches, tall aspens, and maple, with bright ferns underfoot in the warmer months. This narrow ridge will lead you toward the Pine River "Overlook." We say this with a bit of tongue-in-cheek, because in the lushness of summer there's not much of an overlook here.

You'll know when you've reached the river, however, because the trail will turn abruptly left (west) and head down along the edge of the river. This is the beginning of a lot more bushwhacking, so be prepared for some close quarters on the trail. Imagine your lawn's grass at home growing 5 feet tall, with not much of a path through it. That's what you'll find here. While tight, the trail is pretty easy to follow, and undoubtedly some other hiker has been through recently, making a path through the tall grass and berry bushes.

Eventually, you will turn southwest, away from the river, and make a long, slight ascent up an old overgrown logging road. At the end of this grassy climb you will head back into the familiar look of the woods and lots less undergrowth. The trail will be much easier to see and the hiking easier. You will come to a trail intersection. Head left and follow the trail into Lost Lake Campground or back to the trailhead parking lot.

14

Ed's Lake

Total distance: 3.5 miles

Hiking time: 1 hour to 1 hour, 30 minutes

Difficulty: 2.5

Vertical rise: Minimal

Maps: USGS 7½' Robert's Lake, Wisconsin; DeLorme Wisconsin Atlas & Gazetteer, p. 78 (A-2)

Being the first to find a remote lake and being able to name it certainly has its perks. Actually, whether or not Ed is to be thanked for this beautiful area, the wide, sweeping trails that flow over this wooded landscape have their roots in early 20th-century railroad trails that undoubtedly carted timber and ore throughout the area. For Nordic skiers, trails like these are gifts from a higher power. And hikers certainly benefit as well during the warmer months.

Ed's Lake sits unassumingly off County Route W, just between the now famous Crandon and Wabeno. While embedded in a relatively populated area of the north, Ed's Lake is almost eerily quiet—probably due to the fact that it sees more skiers than hikers. This solitude is also the reason that it was here—out of more than twenty hikes in northern Wisconsin—that we saw black bear sign like nowhere else. Several piles of scat led us along the trail and into a sunny opening, literally blanketed with blackberry bushes. Later, while contemplating a trail intersection map perched atop a wooden post, we found ourselves needing to brush aside several locks of coarse, black hair in order to see the map. While it was a directional guide for us, somebody else apparently valued this post for its back-scratching attributes!

Needless to say, this wild hike added some zip to our step and kept us talking excitedly about any and all odd topics—one of which had to do with the fact that one of us would run while the other would play dead in the face of a black bear charge. We won't

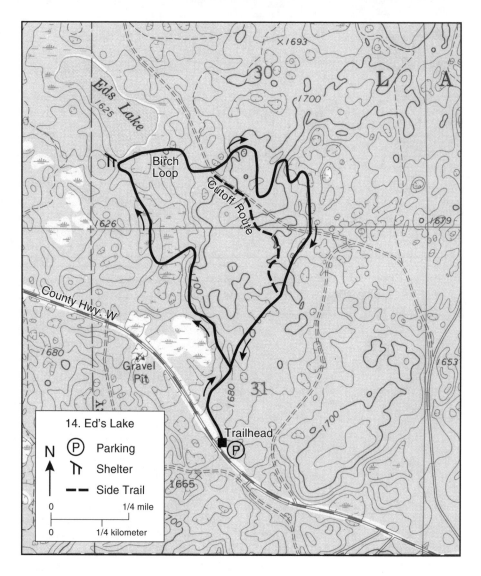

get into who plans on doing what. And it probably won't matter much, since we never seem to find these elusive creatures.

Ed's Lake National Recreation Trail is a sure bet for those wanting to try something a bit longer and more rolling than what you're used to and for those out scouting good Nordic ski trails for next winter. The impressive cherry-framed map at the trailhead marks the start of the Birch Trail, which heads west to the lake before looping back along an old rail bed. The namesake birches are more abundant along this trail than elsewhere in the state, and make for a beautiful white and brilliant green backdrop to a great trail.

How to Get There

From the northwest, take US 8 east out of Crandon for 1.6 miles to County Route W.

Turn right on CR W and go about 8.9 miles to the Ed's Lake trailhead parking lot, which is marked with a sign, on the left.

From the east, take WI 32 south from Wabeno 1 mile to WI 52 west. Take WI 52 for 3.2 miles to the Ed's Lake trailhead parking lot on the right.

From the north, take WI 32 south out of Laona for about 9 miles to Wabeno. Follow the directions above from there.

For more information, contact the Chequamegon National Forest, Laona District Office at 715-674-4481.

The Trail

From the trailhead kiosk, head left (northwest) on the Birch Loop. You will briefly share the trail with the Maple Loop before turning off to the left. It will become evident immediately why this is called the Birch Loop. The hills and small valleys are packed full of the papery bark and bright leaves of the birches. On a sunny day, the leaves dance overhead, blocking the sun and making for a cool hike through the woods.

The trail will wind up and down and eventually take a turn to the left (west), bringing you into a valley full of hemlocks and ferns. Quite different from the beginning of the hike, this change seems to fit as you climb up toward the Adirondack-style skiers' shelter atop the hill overlooking the lake. It's easy to imagine a group of skiers, out for the day, stopping for some hot chocolate and lunch in this little shelter.

Continue on the trail, downhill along the shore of the lake. There are several spots where you can hike in closer to the lake to look for wildlife. Don't be surprised to see a loon on Ed's Lake or to spot a deer on the shores. Eventually, you will climb away from the lake and will come to an opening in the woods, where you have the option of taking the long or short loop of the Birch Loop. We went left along the longer, 3.5-mile trail. It was the right choice, as we descended into a lush valley, packed full of young maples and aspens, making for a sight unlike any we've seen elsewhere on a trail. The grass overgrows onto the trail in this area, but it's not that bad and not for very long.

Eventually, you will emerge from the grass and meet up with the Maple Loop before you head southwest back toward the trailhead. Be careful here, because the trailside map kiosk places you in the wrong place, so don't rely on the nail marking a spot on that map! Continue southwest and past the return of the Birch Loop short trail. This section is a wide, flat trail that must have been a rail grade at one time. The trail is leveled off and cut into the hills, making for very easy hiking.

Soon you will pass the original Birch Loop turnoff. Head straight past it, and also past the turnoff for the Maple Trail as you head back to the trailhead parking lot, following a series of rolling hills. This great little trail is typical of the pleasant hiking found in the national forests, and makes for a marvelous hike.

15

Barkhausen Waterfowl Preserve

Total distance: 3.25 miles

Hiking time: 1 hour to 1 hour, 15 minutes

Difficulty: 2.0

Vertical rise: Minimal

Maps: USGS 7½' Green Bay West, Wisconsin; DeLorme Wisconsin Atlas & Gazetteer, p. 67 (D-8)

In many city parks these days, Canada geese are reviled like the plague, oftentimes trapped and moved, or sometimes killed. This hatred for honkers is absent at the Barkhausen Waterfowl Preserve. Instead, as you drive up to the almost dreamlike restored white farmhouse, now serving as the interpretive center, you are greeted by all sorts of long-necks ambling about honking, eating, and well, doing you-know-what.

At Barkhausen, the idea is to preserve the habitat in order to help ensure that the innumerable species of plants and animals dependent on wetlands and shore habitats have a place to live. Thus, geese take precedence over humans in a place like this.

Most of us who live in the Upper Midwest have undoubtedly marveled at a hooded merganser fluttering out ahead of our canoe, have watched an eagle or osprey pluck a meaty walleye out of the water, or have been amazed at the swooping flight of a great blue heron. But, have we really considered, from the comfort of our own lakeside cabin or home, how healthy their habitats are?

Unfortunately, shoreline habitat is diminishing quickly. Fortunately, the most successful preservation effort in all of the Great Lakes exists on the western shore of Green Bay. A sign posted in the Barkhausen interpretive center states that on this shore "...lies the largest coastal wetland on Lake Michigan, spanning two states and over one hundred miles in length. It is a major spawning area for fish and supports countless numbers of shorebirds, waterfowl, and

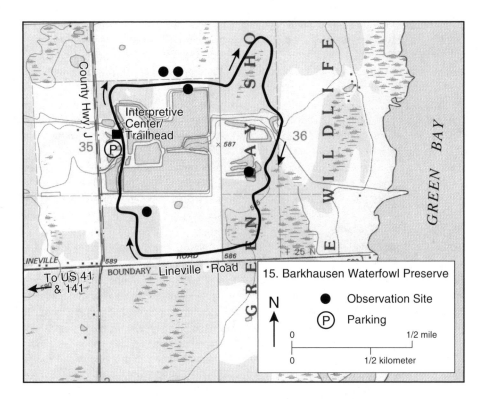

15. Barkhausen Waterfowl Preserve

● Observation Site

Ⓟ Parking

N

0   1/2 mile

0   1/2 kilometer

other animals. Its abundance and variety of wildlife can be found nowhere else on the Great Lakes."

Abundance and variety are the keys. At the trailhead, a pamphlet entitled "Birds of Barkhausen" includes a checklist of well over 300 bird species viewable at some time during the year. From the common house sparrow to the common loon, the diversity is incredible. And while this area marks the start of this hundred-mile-long wetland, Barkhausen still remains "Brown County's best-kept secret."

As commendable as the mission and success of Barkhausen are the more than 9 miles of skiing and hiking trails that allow visitors to explore the area. This hike takes you along the Meadow Ridge Trail, which starts at the interpretive center and winds its way past several ponds and prairies and into a wooded area as it sweeps along nearly the entire perimeter of the preserve. It is a very easy hike in terms of terrain, but the grass can be rather high, and on hot days the sun-exposed trails can make the hike a bit taxing. Fall hikes here are incredible, and the skiing is great for lovers of easy, flat terrain.

How to Get There

From the south, take US 41 north from Green Bay to the Lineville Road (County Route M) exit. Head right (east) to Lakeview Drive (CR J), less than 1 mile after exiting, and take a left, heading north. The entrance to Barkhausen is 0.25 mile on the right.

From the west, take CR M straight past US 41 to Lakeview Drive (CR J), about 1 mile after passing US 41. Take a left, and the entrance to Barkhausen is 0.25 mile on the right.

From the north, take US 41 south to the Lineville Road (CR M) exit. Head left (east) to Lakeview Drive (CR J), less than 1 mile after exiting, and take a left, heading north. The entrance to Barkhausen is 0.25 mile on the right.

For more information, contact the Brown County Parks Department at 920-448-4466, or visit them on the web at www.co.brown.wi.us/parks/parks/barkhausen/index.shtml.

The Trail

The trail begins just west of the interpretive center, and the trailhead is well marked with a large kiosk housing maps, bird guides, and a donation box. Head north, where you will pass between two ponds. The one on the left has a small study area for school groups and other educational programs offered here. After passing the water, the trail will get pretty woodsy, surrounded by several cottonwoods. After taking a turn to the east, you will emerge first next to a wetland restoration area and then into a more sandy prairie area. There is an observation blind off to the left, perfect for bird viewing.

The trail continues essentially straight along this route, with the trees on the right side of the trail and the prairie on the left. At the end of this stretch, the trail ducks back into thick woods, where you will leave the Mosquito Creek Trail and head left (northeast) looping through the woods.

Eventually, you will emerge out of the woods, where the trail will open up into a sandy area and you will pass right beside yet another long pond, which almost looks like more of a creek. After crossing this, you will meet a trail off to the right, which leads to an impressive observation blind nestled right on the water, perfect for a water break and snack.

Continue south on the trail toward Lineville Road. The Shores Trail will peel off to the left to cross the road, while you will continue right alongside it and past the Northern Pike Spawning Marsh, which is not quite visible through the thick grasses and tree line. But after turning north again, you'll reach another observation platform, which also offers great views of the large pond and out across the wetland areas to the east. The trail concludes by joining with and running alongside the park drive. Follow this straight north to the interpretive center and parking lot area. (Just listen for the geese!)

This hike definitely takes you through flat, lowland topography. But with bird book and binoculars in hand, especially during the migration seasons, you will undoubtedly find all sorts of exciting wildlife. It is always fun to find a great nature center and a great trail, but sometimes it's hard to find them both at the same place. Barkhausen Waterfowl Preserve offers this combination, along with and a good day's hike or ski trip.

16

UW Green Bay

Total distance: 4.1 miles

Hiking time: 1 hour, 15 minutes to 1 hour, 30 minutes

Difficulty: 2.5

Vertical rise: Minimal

Map: USGS 7½' Green Bay East, Wisconsin; DeLorme Wisconsin Atlas & Gazetteer, p. 68 (D-1)

College campuses are known for their aesthetics, and many were designed with the idea of incorporating their educational facilities into their natural settings. Whether through green common grounds, or sweeping sidewalks amidst tall trees, brilliant flowers, or ivy-cloaked brick, this has been the norm when it comes to campus planning. Imagine, then, a campus at whose doorstep is an arboretum.

An ecosystem surrounds the University of Wisconsin–Green Bay like a great green moat. In fact, from an observation deck overlooking one of the wetland areas, the campus buildings seem to grow out of and tower over the marsh's background, while wildflowers and prairie grasses paint the foreground. This almost surreal scene looks more like an idealistic "college of the future" rendering than a present-day college campus, but it isn't. This very real arboretum exists and flourishes, tucked next to an interstate highway and a large state university. And on top of that, it offers a great day's hike.

This trail takes you off a main campus road and into the woods as you wind your way through some old-growth hardwoods along a stream. Eventually, you pop out just next to WI 54/57 and into a prairie surrounding several ponds. The trail then turns west toward the waters of Lake Michigan's Green Bay, along a paved section and through more prairie. All in all, it is an easy hike in terms of footing, but can be rather taxing in the hot sun. It would serve as a good day's worth of hiking—particularly in

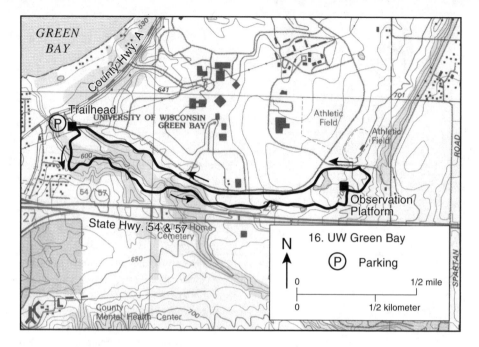

the spring and summer when there are all sorts of wildflowers to engage your botanical side.

How to Get There

From the north, on WI 57, exit at Scottwood Drive (County Route I). Continue about 2 miles to Nicolet Drive. Take a left on Nicolet and drive past the main parking entrance to South Circle Drive. Take a left on South Circle, and the trailhead will be immediately on the right. Pull-off parking is available.

From the east, take WI 54 toward Green Bay. Do not merge with WI 57 south. Instead, keep heading west on Scottwood Drive (CR I) and follow the directions above.

From the south and west, take US 43 either north or south and exit at WI 54/57, heading toward Sturgeon Bay. Take the CR A/University Avenue exit about 1 mile after getting onto WI 54/57. Turn right and head north toward the campus on CR A

(Nicolet Drive) for less than a mile. Turn right on South Circle Drive. The trailhead and pull-off parking are immediately on the right.

For more information, contact the UW Green Bay Cofrin Arboretum at 920-465-2272 or 920-465-5032, or on the web at www.uwgb.edu/biodiversity/arboretum/.

The Trail

This hike starts by heading past the arboretum kiosk, through the fence, and across the asphalt path. (We did this hike counterclockwise.) Head south into the small prairie and toward the woods. Soon after entering the woods, you will cross a bridge over the small creek running throughout the entire arboretum.

You are welcomed to the wooded area by a surprising variety of older hardwoods and a smattering of very large white pines towering overhead. For the most part, though, you will meander through a series of ups and downs amidst cottonwoods, hickories, and oaks, along with a few birches. The footing is very good, along packed dirt and wood chips. After quite a long stay in the woods, the trail will emerge briefly alongside the highway before taking you back down to the creek, where you will pass over to the north side once again.

After climbing a short hill, you are welcomed back into the open, with prairie surrounding the trail and a wetland and pond off to the right. Keep your eyes peeled for waterfowl, deer, and turtles in this area. The trail moves east before sending you winding northward to an observation platform nestled amidst prairie grasses and flowers. This is a perfect place to see the arboretum macroscopically, as well as to spot individual plants or birds. This area is as alive with color in the fall as in the spring and summer, and makes for a peaceful ski trail in the winter. The platform, just beyond the halfway point on this hike, makes for a great place to take a water break and have a snack or lunch.

The trail will now wind its way westward, beginning a long stretch back to the parking area. In the warmer months, keep a look out for all sorts of great wildflowers along here. The trail will be bordered by spiderwort, butterfly weed, Saint-John's-wort, and compass plant, while the sky will flutter with a great collection of birds and butterflies.

Eventually, the trail will wind back toward the woods and work its way back to the parking lot. All told, the hike is about 4 miles and, while mostly level, can take its toll on you on a hot day. It is definitely a destination worth visiting, whether in town to cheer on "The Pack," buzzing by on your way to Door County, or dropping off your student at one of Wisconsin's great public colleges. Hiking this trail, with the buzzing highway above, makes you wonder just how much you miss by taking the fast lane through life. How great that this university realizes that some of the best lessons occur out on the trail, from the leaves of trees, just as much as from the leaves of books.

17

Potawatomi State Park

Total distance: 3.5 miles

Hiking time: 1 hour to 1 hour, 30 minutes

Difficulty: 2.5

Vertical rise: 130 feet

Maps: USGS 7½' Sturgeon Bay, Wisconsin and Idlewild, Wisconsin; DeLorme Wisconsin Atlas & Gazetteer, p. 69 (B-5)

As the eastern terminus of the renowned Ice Age Trail, Potawatomi offers excellent hiking through a variety of habitats and over varied terrain. The park—named after an early Native American culture whose name means "keeper of the fire"—is now a great recreational area in all seasons, visited by hikers and mountain bikers from spring to fall and by skiers in the winter. There is even a downhill ski area within the park's boundaries.

No matter the time of year, cars whisk past Potawatomi on their way across the Sturgeon Bay Bridge en route to the heart of Door County. But this park, nestled off the beaten path across from the city of Sturgeon Bay and right on the water, is certainly worthy of a visit, whether as a side trip or as a destination in its own right.

This hike along the Tower Trail takes you from the observation tower and down toward Sturgeon Bay before winding back through the woods to the top of the ski hill and back to the tower. Standing atop a 150-foot limestone bluff, the 75-foot tower offers a bird's-eye view of the area. Much of Green Bay is visible to the west, as is Sturgeon Bay to the north. It's even possible to see Lake Michigan, across the peninsula, to the east. In the winter, the ice covering Sawyer Harbor is usually peppered with ice-fishing shanties, and in the summer the water is full of passing pleasure boats and enormous cargo ships.

This is a great hike, offering a glimpse of Door County up close and up high. And, if you are chipping away at the Ice Age Trail

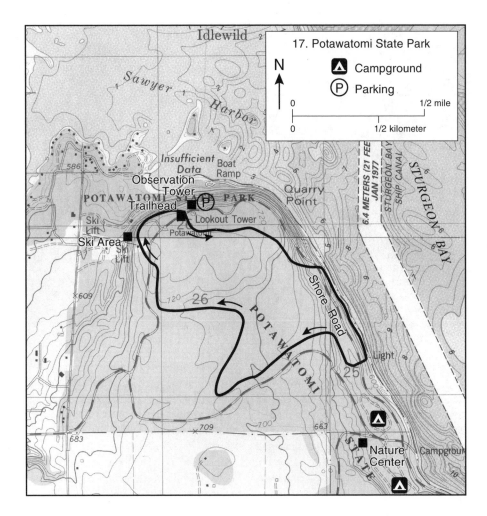

piece by piece, you'll certainly want to have hiked its eastern end point.

How to Get There

From the north take WI 42/57 south from Sturgeon Bay. About 3.5 miles after crossing the bridge, turn right (north) on Park Drive (County Route PD). Or, from the south, take WI 42/57 north. About 3.5 miles after the WI 42/57 junction, turn left on Park Drive (CR PD). Once on CR PD, go about 2.5 miles to the park entrance on the right.

It sneaks up quickly, and there are no signs aside from a small white board before the large entrance sign.

For more information, contact Potawatomi State Park at 920-746-2890.

The Trail

Once in the park, wind your way all the way past the campsites and up the hill to the lookout tower. This hike will go clockwise, so use the trailhead just across the lot, past the rock and plaque marking the beginning

Ice Age Trail, Potawatomi State Park

of the Ice Age Trail. You will enter the woods quickly and begin to meander downhill toward the water. The trail winds between tall hardwoods in a forest with little undergrowth. There are some steep descents, so watch your footing and be especially careful in wet conditions. The trail will cross the road and emerge at the water. Several short offshoots allow you to access the rocky shore. If you aren't in a hurry, this may make a great lunch stop.

The trail then continues along the wooded shore, sheltered by cedars, before it turns right (west) and leaves the Ice Age Trail. After passing the road again, you will head back into the woods and begin an immediate climb back up toward the tower. The trail will cross a bike path four times as it, too, meanders through the same woods. Take care to stay on the hiking path.

The trail will make a buttonhook turn past a stand of pines and head more northward as

it zigzags up toward the tower. The climb is relatively gradual, and you will also pass some very large white pines lurking in the shadows.

Toward the end of the hike, the trail will meet up with the road again. Although it looks as if you should cross the road, turn right (north) and hike the trail alongside the road until it pops out at the roadside. Cross the road toward the mowed grass path that ducks into the woods on the other side. Off to the left are the alpine ski hill and a great view of the lake far below. A narrow trail leads you up to the tower, and it is a short hike from here as it passes through a wooded bluff and takes you up to the northwest side of the lot where you parked.

A trip to Potawatomi offers miles of biking, hiking, and skiing trails, and gives you the opportunity to view Door County from the doorstep of Sturgeon Bay. And, if you're hiking the Ice Age Trail, a visit to its easternmost terminus is a must.

18

Whitefish Dunes State Park

Total distance: 2.8 miles

Hiking time: 1 hour to 1 hour, 30 minutes

Difficulty: 2.5

Vertical rise: Minimal

Maps: USGS 7½' Jacksonport, Wisconsin; DeLorme Wisconsin Atlas & Gazetteer, p. 69 (A-7)

Among the most exceptionally rare habitats found near lakes are the shores themselves. Rarer still are untouched, large sand dunes. These irreplaceable ecosystems support plant and animal life in unique diversity and abundance. Whether you're kicking along the sandy shores of Lake Michigan, or hiking up onto "Old Baldy," a trip to Whitefish Dunes State Park certainly offers a unique and varied hiking opportunity.

Like most of Wisconsin, the Door Peninsula was home to many early civilizations. In fact, while the beach at Whitefish Dunes may be peppered with sunbathers on a busy summer day, the crowding probably still pales in comparison to the congestion of early Native American cultures that called this area home for the summer. The incredible fishing in both Lake Michigan and Clark Lake, along with abundant game for hunting and farming-friendly soil, probably created a sort of utopia for those who lived here.

Today, in addition to human visitors, the residents of the park include a rich diversity of flowering plants, from wood anemone to wood betony. In the spring and fall, it is hard to hike along without being distracted by a patch of milkweed, a harebell, or, if you're lucky, a dune thistle.

This hike takes you immediately past a re-created Native American camp, which offers a good look at what things may have been like several hundred years ago. The trail then ascends up into the dunes through a valley before turning west and taking you to the top of Old Baldy, the tallest dune at 90 feet above lake level. You then wind

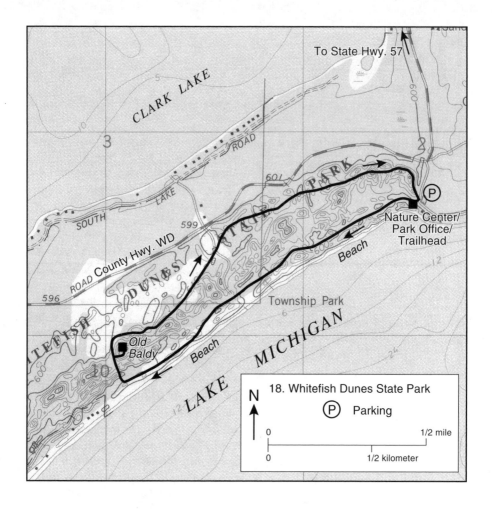

18. Whitefish Dunes State Park

(P) Parking

N

0 .... 1/2 mile

0 .... 1/2 kilometer

back through the flatter, sandy area of the park and into the woods before heading back to the trail's start. This is a great hike of minimal difficulty aside from the sometimes deep, sandy footing.

How to Get There

From the south, take WI 57 north from Valmy about 1 mile to Clark Lake Road. Turn right and follow Clark Lake Road about 3.5 miles to the park entrance on the right. It's a quick turn into the park after a sign tells you to stay in the right lane.

From the south, take WI 57 South out of Jacksonport for 0.2 mile to Cave Point Road. Turn left on Cave Point Road and follow it for 3.2 miles to the park entrance on the left.

For more information, contact Whitefish Dunes State Park at 920-823-2400.

The Trail

This hike, the Red Loop Trail, begins just to the right of the nature center as you approach it from the parking lot. Head west, behind the center, starting a clockwise loop.

Immediately to the right are several interesting re-creations of early Native American settlements. The exhibits are posted with informational signs. This is the only area like this on the hike, so it is worth taking some time here before moving on.

The trail, well marked with red blazes, then heads southwest up into the woods on a wide path. There is a gradual climb as you approach the beach access points, but the trail will then level off before making a long, easy descent. You'll pass the third beach access and a trail to the north; continue southwest to the turnoff for Old Baldy. This open area of the trail begins to offer good wildflower viewing in the spring and summer.

The turn to Old Baldy will take you up and down, and along several boardwalks, until you reach the main turnoff to the top of the dune—a short out-and-back trip that totals about 0.25 mile—and it is all along wooden boardwalks. Don't miss the opportunity to see this side of the peninsula, and the lake, from such a high vantage point. While the western side of the peninsula has many dolomite cliffs and hills offering big views, this isn't true on the east. From the top of Old Baldy, you can see well out into the lake and north to the shoreline and bay at Jacksonport.

After heading back down and resuming along the trail, you will turn northeast around the base of Old Baldy, where the trail will level off and become a bit more sandy. There is a picnic table here for a water break, snack, or lunch. The area is pretty open, however, so it may be a bit hot. A sandy prairie, the landscape is very unique. It is full of bird life, and there are a variety of wildflowers in this area.

The trail continues through this prairie, with some very deep sand for footing, until it suddenly ducks into the woods. The trail gets a bit narrower, the footing more solid, and the air cooler. Mixed hardwoods and some large pines greet you as you meander up and down rolling hills alongside County Route WD. You will eventually turn southeast, back toward the nature center, as you dip into a wet valley before emerging next to a fence leading back to the starting point.

Certainly not an exceptionally difficult hike, this is an exceptionally fascinating one. To be able to meander over and around rare Great Lakes sand dunes is well worth the trip to Whitefish Dunes. And, while many parks build observation decks, Old Baldy offers the top of its head for you to perch on while snapping pictures of the Lake Michigan shoreline below.

19

The Ridges Sanctuary

Total distance: 2.6 miles

Hiking time: 1 hour to 1 hour, 30 minutes

Difficulty: 2.0

Vertical rise: Minimal

Map: USGS 7½' Baileys Harbor, Wisconsin; DeLorme Wisconsin Atlas & Gazetteer, p. 81 (D-8)

Like all exceptionally beautiful places, Door County has drawn people for thousands of years. The first settlers, Native Americans, prospered from its mild winters, cool summers, and bountiful food supplies. Europeans took advantage of farming and fishing opportunities. And today, while some of the historic land uses still prevail, the peninsula's largest attraction is itself. People want to be here; they want to sit on decks amidst cool breezes and awake to the sun rising out of the blue water of Lake Michigan. But with all this desire for beauty comes demand for space. In an intrepid move by a group of conservation-minded citizens in the 1930s, some of this space was set aside and protected from the development that has grown like wildfire all over the peninsula.

A volunteer at The Ridges nature center stresses to visitors exactly what type of place it is by telling them: "It isn't a park, it isn't a recreation area, it's a sanctuary." And, there is definitely a feel to The Ridges unlike anywhere else in the county. This hike allows you to experience that feel.

You realize that The Ridges is different right away. The rules for visiting include no wheeled vehicles whatsoever (including strollers), no pets whatsoever, and no smoking. And, inside the nature center, large photographs highlight the current attractions, namely wildflowers in the summer. The list is almost unbelievable—including Indian paintbrush, Solomon's seal, loads of various lady's slippers, and many more—this

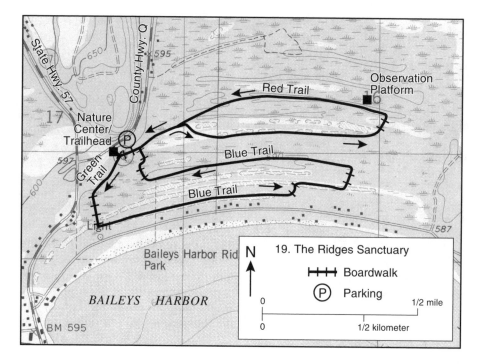

unique landscape offers a perfect haven for many rare and varied species of plants.

The namesake ridges themselves are like ripples in a bed sheet, marking the slow rise and retraction of Lake Michigan's water levels. Over time, 30 of these crests have formed. Hiking trails now traverse the ridges, while boardwalks breach the swales as you meander along in this unique habitat, home to nearly 500 species of plants.

This hike is the combination of the two longer loops through the sanctuary, taking the first loop south down a long boardwalk toward the water and east along a long ridge before looping back along the second one. This second loop heads through a pine woods along a ridge and loops back out past two observation decks, perfect for viewing birds and deer, before heading back. And here's a tip: For the best hiking and most solitude, get to The Ridges well before noon. It is a very popular spot, but

vacationing beachgoers usually don't get going too early, so you may have the place to yourself.

Note: Because The Ridges is a private, nonprofit sanctuary, a daily fee is requested to hike the trails. With no public monies, the entrance fees allow the place to stay in existence. In the summer of 2003, the fee was $5 for adults and $6 for a family.

How to Get There

From the south, take WI 57 north from Baileys Harbor to Ridge Road. Turn right (east) and the parking lot will be about a hundred yards on the right.

From the north, take WI 57 south from Sister Bay about 8 miles. Turn left on Ridge Road, and the lot is about a hundred yards on the right.

For more information, contact The Ridges Sanctuary at 920-839-2802 or find them on the web at www.ridgesanctuary.org.

Yellow lady's slipper, one of more than 100 species of wildflowers at The Ridges

The Trail

The hike begins as you bounce along a wide trail, covered with wood chips, out of the nature center area. Be sure to pick up a trail guide either from the center or at the kiosk as you're starting your hike. Take the first right (southwest) and head deeper into the woods. The trail guide tells you that this area is a lush and diverse boreal, or northern, forest. The cool lake winds create a microclimate—more reminiscent of northern Michigan—providing good habitat for boreal forest plants and trees. After a short while, in fact, you will pass the largest tree in the sanctuary, a towering, two-pronged white spruce, looming overhead.

The trail soon passes out of the woods and onto the first boardwalk. The longest one, this walkway stretches north and south and is flanked first by grasses and wildflowers, and then by trees on either side. Looking south, it appears to run right into the lake. Continue hiking toward the lake and past the Deerlick and Wintergreen Trail turnoffs. Keep your eyes peeled, however—it was along this part of the route that we came across several brilliant flowers, including a yellow lady's slipper.

Head left (east) and back into the woods at the Blue Trail turnoff. The footing is very sandy and is definitely a change from walking on sturdy, flat wood planking. You are greeted right away by a rare sight, a tamarack (American larch), which is a needle-losing evergreen. If you're here in the fall expect to see this tree ablaze in gold, or if here in the winter, don't expect to see many needles (leaves). You will continue past another huge tree, a 200-year-old white pine known as the "Lying Giant," and previously the "Leaning Giant," until it finally fell.

The trail meanders along this ridge for a long stretch, passing through the woods as you brush past grasses, encroaching trees, and flowers. The rare open area on the left is the site of an old potato garden. The sandy soil, not unlike the central sands region of Wisconsin, probably offered perfect growing conditions. As you get to the end of this long stretch, a bench provides a good break before heading north. In fact, the trail guide suggests simply sitting, with eyes closed, and listening to your surroundings, alive with activity.

The trail then continues north over a couple of boardwalks before taking you west to the Mountain Maple Trail. Turn right here (north) and up to the Red Loop Trail. Follow this to the right (east) and take the immediate right onto the Labrador Trail. Here you will head east and pass through an area full of pines. The trail closes in a bit, and the hiking becomes reminiscent of hiking a ridge top out west. Follow the trail all the way to the easternmost point and head north over a boardwalk. Around the corner will be an observation platform, perfect for having a snack and water, taking photos, or wildlife watching.

After a break continue west along the Red Trail (also called the Winter Wren). You will pass another platform, the Solitude Swale Deck, which was built for photography and bird-watching. The trail concludes by joining back at the original intersection of all loops and heads back up to the nature center. Depending on your level of curiosity, the hike may take an hour, or it may take all morning.

A visit to The Ridges, Wisconsin's oldest private nature preserve, is not a one-time deal. To view and contemplate all the diversity residing inside the sanctuary could be a never-ending mission. While the variety of species that make up the community at the ridges is certainly unique, rarer still is that a group of concerned citizens recognized the importance of preserving a place like this, and they did it. While the beaches, craft cottages, golf courses, and trinket shops are tempting, if you want to truly understand the land of the peninsula, a visit to Door County must include a hike, or several, at The Ridges.

20

Peninsula State Park

Total distance: 4.0 miles

Hiking time: 1 hour, 30 minutes to 2 hours

Difficulty: 4.0

Vertical rise: 180 feet

Maps: USGS 7½' Ephraim, Wisconsin; DeLorme Wisconsin Atlas & Gazetteer, p. 81 (D-6)

Peninsula State Park holds the distinction of having the most campsites of any park in the Wisconsin state park system. Telling your friends you have a site at Peninsula anytime between Memorial Day and Labor Day initiates the same jaw-dropping reflex as when you happen along a few spare Packers tickets from your uncle Carl. The reason is a good one. The park just happens to be one of the most beautiful gems in the state, glistening with miles of hiking and biking trails, a golf course, swimming, fishing, and boating. And it is also home to a resident summer theater group. The area is definitely the most congested in the summer, however, due to the traffic to Peninsula and to Fish Creek, its hometown. If Door County is Wisconsin's Cape Cod, then Fish Creek is its Hyannis Port.

While the present is full of activity, so was Peninsula's past. Formed by several advances and retreats of glaciers and ancient seas, the layers of exposed dolomite form the terraces of the shorelines and create microclimates and habitats for a diverse array of plants, animals, insects, and crustaceans. The same early Native Americans who settled near Sturgeon Bay lived here as well. A camp at Nicolet Beach served as base for fishing and hunting. And, as the park guide notes: "The last hereditary chief of the Potawatomi nation, Simon Kahquados, was buried in Peninsula in 1931."

Since its establishment in 1909, the park has seen a constant stream of visitors and campers, and has had a variety of uses.

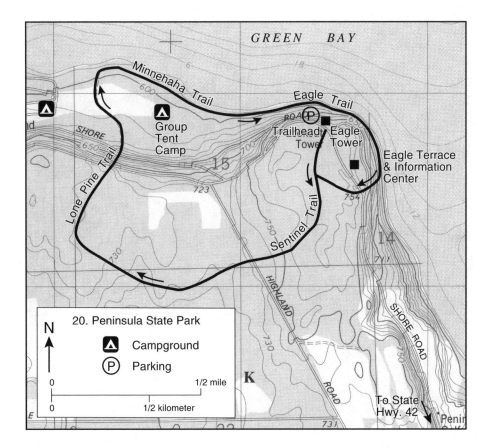

GREEN BAY

Minnehaha Trail

Eagle Trail

Group
Tent
Camp

Trailhead
Tower

Eagle
Tower

Eagle Terrace
& Information
Center

SHORE

Lone Pine Trail

Sentinel Trail

HIGHLAND

SHORE ROAD

ROAD

K

To State
Hwy. 42

Peni

20. Peninsula State Park

N

△ Campground

Ⓟ Parking

0   1/2 mile

0   1/2 kilometer

In the past it served as everything from a girls' camp to a WWI prisoner-of-war camp. But certainly the best way to appreciate the park is to come and explore it.

The trail detailed here, the Eagle Tower Loop, takes you deep into the varied and old-growth woods of the park before heading down toward the water's edge. It takes you along the limestone cliffs below the Eagle Tower before looping back up a serious climb to the tower parking lot. This busy park is definitely worth the visit, and by getting off of the roads and into the woods, you will find out why this area is such a treasure.

Note: This hike is quite level for the most part, but includes some very difficult sections in terms of both footing and vertical rise. This hike should not be attempted by novice hikers or anyone not in hiking shape. While children may do all right on the upper portion of the hike (the Sentinel and Lone Pine Trails), the Eagle Tower Loop section is not suited for most children. And, as always, consider leaving Fido at home for this one.

How to Get There

From the south, take WI 42 north out of Fish Creek. (Don't take the main park entrance unless you're camping, or bumper-to-bumper traffic is your idea of summer vacation fun!) Head out of town on WI 42 for about 2.5 miles. The road will wind downhill and there will be a northern entrance to the park, Shore Road, on the

Peninsula State Park

left—the sign will say PENINSULA STATE PARK GOLF COURSE. Take a left here and follow the road up to the Eagle Tower parking lot, about 1 mile after turning.

From the north, take WI 42 south out of Ephraim 3.5 miles to Shore Road. Take a right, and follow the road about a mile to the Eagle Tower lot.

For more information, contact Peninsula State Park at 920-868-3258.

The Trail

This clockwise loop starts on the Sentinel Trail just south of the Eagle Tower parking lot. After parking, cross the road and head into the woods, undoubtedly leaving all sorts of tower-related commotion behind, if you're here in the summer. The cool woods welcome you as you're able to strike up a good stride along a wide, packed dirt trail. The diversity and ages of the trees in this forest are incredibly fascinating. The tree species include hemlock, tamarack, maple, beech, birch, and towering red oak. This trail is very serene and is extremely inviting in every season. It's almost hard to believe that you're in a park that is packed with people, within minutes of one of the busiest areas north of Sturgeon Bay. Most of the time, you hear nothing but squirrels dashing about, leaves shaking overhead, or woodpeckers tapping away.

Shortly after beginning, you will pass the return loop of the Sentinel Trail on the right. Stay left and cross a park road, continuing in the woods for almost 0.5 mile before merging with a four-way connection of trails. To the right is the Sentinel Loop, straight ahead is the Lone Pine, and to the left is a connector trail. Take the Lone Pine Trail straight (northwest).

The trail will then cross a park road before entering a bluff full of red cedar, marking the beginning of your descent down to water level. This descent can be tricky. It is very steep and can get slippery. As you

Northeast Hikes

double back after the initial descent, a sheer rock face gives way to emerald ferns below, and the path strings between them before taking you to the next park road. Cross the road and head straight (north) alongside a road that leads through the campsites. Take this about 0.25 mile to where the trail resumes. This is right after campsite number 842, and there is a sign marking the trail.

From here, you duck back into the woods on the Minnehaha Trail and head east alongside the waters of Green Bay on a packed dirt trail bordered by cedars, and with many exposed roots. On the left you will pass the rocky shores of Nicolet Bay, and on the right you will pass the group tent camp area. Eventually, you will come to a bench and a merging of the Minnehaha with the Eagle Trail coming from the right (south) and heading left (east). Take a break here. You are in for a long, hard stretch, very unlike the mostly easy hiking so far. Lots of water and a snack or sandwich are in order.

And prepare yourself for a few people. The trail narrows, so passing is inevitable. For some odd reason, while this trail is by far the most rigorous in the entire park, you will see the most people on it, many of whom shouldn't be there. The once open trail shrinks and becomes rocky and slippery. The ascents are demanding, and the footing is very technical and challenging, so proceed with caution. But, with all these caveats, the trail offers incredible views of the dolomite limestone cliffs and is a really fun hike for experienced trekkers.

After your break on the bench, veer left onto the Eagle Trail. Almost immediately, wet and loose rocks, interspersed among tricky exposed roots, greet you to this trail. The first 0.25 mile is pretty level, with a few ups and downs. Soon you will pass the most dramatic cliffs and rock faces before entering again into the familiar cedar-lined trail resembling the Minnehaha. You will sweep below Eagle Terrace before making a turn right (south) and heading straight up the side of Eagle Bluff. While the trail will make a couple of cutbacks, it's not very forgiving. Take it slow and watch your footing. You'll be climbing a couple of hundred feet in less than 0.5 mile.

Eventually, you'll get to the last section of the ascent. It is more gradual and takes you northwestward, where you will pop out next to Eagle Terrace to the right. Follow the trail to the terrace for a good water break, a rest stop, and the view. Directly behind you, you should see a series of stone steps leading up to a map kiosk and a park road. Take those steps and head straight past the kiosk, through a connector trail, across another park road, and back into the woods, heading west and ignoring the tower and parking lot up to the right.

This small loop through the original woods makes for a great cool-down after the long ascent and will wind back to the original trail, the Sentinel, which you took from the parking lot. Upon merging with the Sentinel, take a right (north), and a short section of trail will take you back to your starting point at the lot, below the lookout tower.

There are some hikes that, upon finishing them, are true accomplishments, and this is one of them. It offers great scenery, varied topography, and a truly good workout. While the hike is mainly level and relaxing, it gets tricky and challenging very quickly, before giving way to a relaxing end to a good day's work on the trail.

21

Newport State Park

Total distance: 5.0 miles

Hiking time: 1 hour, 30 minutes to 2 hours

Difficulty: 2.5

Vertical rise: Minimal

Maps: USGS 7½' Spider Island, Wisconsin; DeLorme Wisconsin Atlas & Gazetteer, p. 81 (C-8)

While visited by thousands of people every year, Newport State Park is distinct from many areas of Door County by being quite a serene place. Aside from its beach, very much a Cape Cod–style sandy public beach, the park is not crowded. That isn't an accident. The offerings at Newport include long loop trails, suitable for serious hikers, mountain bikers, snowshoers, and skiers. In fact, the park guide notes that: "The recreational activities are part of the wilderness concept at Newport State Park." There are no drive-up campsites. Instead, to reach Newport's sites, you must pack everything in at least a mile and, in most cases farther, for a true wilderness camping experience.

The park has gotten even wilder of late. While there have always been rare sightings of black bears in Door County, this year a confirmed population of timber wolves was identified living in the northern end of the county, when a hunter mistook a wolf for a coyote and shot it. It is assumed—as of summer 2003—that there are about a half dozen wolves currently living here. Exceptionally good swimmers, and not afraid of ice, the animals are thought to have crossed over from the Upper Peninsula of Michigan by "island hopping." While this is definitely a success for the reintroduction of a native Wisconsin species, you may want to check with park officials regarding any recent news of wolves. Perhaps because of the unwarranted trapping and poisoning that drove all North American wolves to near extinction by the 20th century, wolves are generally very wary of humans and are ex-

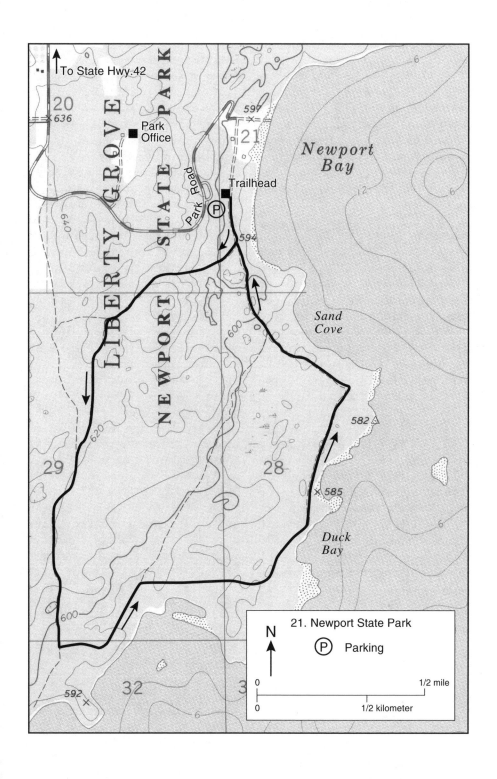

To State Hwy. 42

20
×636

LIBERTY GROVE STATE PARK

Park Office

Park Road

Trailhead

P

594

591

21

Newport Bay

12

6

6

Sand Cove

NEWPORT

600

620

29

28

582

×585

Duck Bay

6

600

592
×

32

3

600

N

21. Newport State Park

P Parking

| 0 | 1/2 mile |
| 0 | 1/2 kilometer |

tremely reclusive. Their fearsome reputation is largely undeserved.

This hike takes you from the beach area at Newport Bay and along the shore southward past Sand Cove and Duck Bay, before looping back into the deeper woods. You will come back north to the parking area, making for a great day's worth of hiking and landing you conveniently back at the beach—a great asset in the summer and a great view in the winter.

How to Get There

Take WI 42 out of Ellison Bay for 1.8 miles to Newport Drive (County Route NP). Turn right on CR NP and follow it about 2.0 miles to the park entrance. Head past the park visitor kiosk and past the first parking lot on the immediate right. Park in the second lot at the bend in the road. The trail begins off of the southeast corner of the lot.

For more information, contact Newport State Park at 920-854-2500.

The Trail

Head out of the parking area and down a connector trail to the main trail. Take a right, and head south for less than 0.25 mile before veering to the right on the Newport Loop. (The return route is straight ahead.) The wide trail, surrounded by birch and pines and thick undergrowth, meanders through the woods with little vertical rise or fall. This is one of those quiet woods that simply engulfs you and makes for a very relaxing hike. After about 0.5 mile, you will

come to a connector trail. Veer right, staying on the Newport Trail. Take this another 0.5 mile to where the Newport Trail joins with the Rowley's Bay Loop Trail.

After about 0.5 mile, you will come to a merging of four trails (although this is not shown in detail on the park map). To the right (west) is the Rowley's Bay Trail; straight ahead (south) is the trail to the campsites; and to the left (east) is the Newport Trail. If you're backpacking in for the night, your site may be straight ahead, or somewhere along the return loop. To continue on, take a left and head alongside the lake, passing several more of the remote sites. These campsites are so secluded that you often see only their paths disappearing into the woods, and you seldom hear people. Other than the occasional waft of campfire smoke, you'd never know campers were there. But they are, and they're enjoying some of the best, most scenic camping in the state—often on their own rocky beach or even on their own bay!

The trail will continue past Duck Bay and Sand Cove before meeting back with the original splitting-off point at Newport Bay. The beach lies straight ahead, while the parking area is just off to the left, to the west.

This hike is one of the most peaceful, remote, and relaxing hikes in Door County. While the county's roads and towns are full of visitors and crowds, Newport State Park is not. And, while the beach may be full, the trails will not be, making them a great treasure.

22

Rock Island State Park

Total distance: 3.5 miles

Hiking time: 1 hour, 30 minutes to 2 hours

Difficulty: 3.0

Vertical rise: Minimal

Maps: USGS 7½' Washington Island NE, Wisconsin; DeLorme Wisconsin Atlas & Gazetteer, p. 81 (A-8)

At the far northeastern tip of Wisconsin there exists a 900-acre, wooded island wilderness devoid of cars, roads, and even bikes. Is that enough to make you want to go? Not much more than about 1 square mile, Rock Island is actually covered in trails and is perfect for hiking, in addition to being a popular attraction for campers wishing to have a truly remote experience.

The island, undoubtedly as desirable historically for fishing, hunting, and shelter as it is today for tourism, was home to Native Americans long before European settlers saw its shores. The Potawatomi lived in small dwellings on the island and kept gardens in addition to gathering food. Excavations done in the 1960s and 1970s yielded tens of thousands of artifacts, helping to better understand the native people who inhabited this area. In addition to the Potawatomi, who were the main inhabitants, the Huron, Petun, and Ottawa cultures also called Rock Island home for short periods of time.

While no longer settled on the island, the Potawatomi were acknowledged when the first federally erected lighthouse in Wisconsin was built here in the early 1800s and named after them. Potawatomi Light still stands sentinel at the northwest corner of the island, above the dolomite cliffs and sandy shore.

Perhaps the most noticeable structure on the island, however, greets you upon your arrival. As you step off the ferry, you will find yourself at the dock of a massive stone boathouse, originally erected by Chester Thordarson, owner of the island between

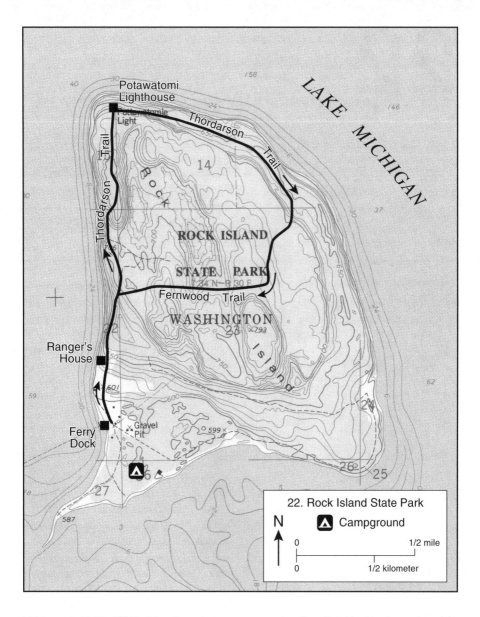

22. Rock Island State Park

N

▲ Campground

0   1/2 mile
0   1/2 kilometer

1910 and 1945. While his plans for an island mansion were never realized, this imposing boathouse was. It served as home to his 11,000-book library and was the site of many summer parties.

Although the partying in the boathouse is a thing of the past, a trip to Rock Island is exceptionally enjoyable. Yet, it can be tricky; while it rests on the tip of Door County, it takes two ferries to reach the island from Gills Rock on the mainland. If you're planning a day trip to Rock Island, we recommend getting there not much later than noon. As of 2003, the last ferry to the island leaves at

Rock Island

3:00, giving you only an hour before the last ferry back returns at 4:15. And if you miss the last one, you're stranded for the night. From what we've heard, it has happened!

How to Get There

First, take the Washington Island ferry from Gills Rock. Then, from the Washington Island ferry dock, follow Lob Dell Road/Detroit Harbor Road to Main Road for about 2.0 miles. Turn left on Main Road and follow it for 2.5 miles to Jackson Harbor Road. Turn right and take it for 3.5 miles to the Karfi Ferry/Rock Island State Park parking lot. A fifteen-minute trip across the lake gets you to the island. All told, the trip can take 1 to 2 hours from Gills Rock.

For more information, contact Rock Island State Park at 920-847-2235. For ferry information, contact the Washington Island Ferry Line at 1-800-223-2094 or at www.wisferry.com and the Rock Island Ferry (Karfi) at 920-493-6444.

The Trail

Upon hopping off the Karfi at the boat-house, head north along the shore up toward the ranger's house, the small stone house atop the bluff to the left. The trail begins just to the right of the house and meanders up the hill toward the huge, wooden park gate. After passing the ranger's house, the trail will pass by the wooden gate and into the woods. The majority of this hike follows the Thordarson Loop Trail, clockwise around the northern tip of the island.

Whether it's actually true or not, the trail at Rock Island just feels different. It seems wilder than most; it's almost as though you're in another part of the world and not in Wisconsin at all. The trail takes you through this wooded wonderland amidst maples and birches towering overhead, with a blanket of woodland plants at your feet. Be careful: This island is infamous for its poison ivy, so stay on the path and watch for the three-leaved menace.

This western leg of the trail will take you uphill most of the way. During the gradual climb, the trail will converge with a service road from the right, and you will eventually pass the junction with the Fernwood Trail return route from the east, on the right.

After a good, steady uphill you will level off and eventually, about a mile into the hike, you will emerge at the Potawatomi Light. Until now, while the lake has been close by, it hasn't been very visible. This is a great opportunity to take a break, explore the lighthouse, and visit the beach down below.

After stopping, continue on the Thordarson Trail east out of the lighthouse area and uphill. Again, you will climb gradually as you wind eastward along the northern shoreline. About halfway to the Fernwood Trail turnoff, you will come to a bench sitting high atop the northern shore and overlooking Lake Michigan and Saint Martin Island (Michigan) to the north. On a bright, sunny day, this opening makes for an almost surreal scene. The cobalt blue water bordered by emerald green trees and topped with pale blue sky looks almost like a brilliantly painted Hollywood background scene.

From here, the trail rambles up and down before meeting with the Fernwood Trail turnoff to the right (southwest). Take this right-hand turn; if you miss it, your hike will double in length and may triple in time. While you might think your gradual climbing should be done, it isn't. The trail will continue to climb very slightly, and soon you will find yourself immersed in the trail's namesake. Ferns blanket the ground of this cool, hardwood forest, making this remote hiking trail a serene adventure.

Eventually, the trail will reach a high point on the island and begin meandering down toward the original intersection with the Thordarson Trail. At the junction, take a left (south) and head back toward the dock area, once more passing the junction with the access road on the left. (But stay to the right.) You will again pass the wooden gate and the ranger's house before rambling down the grassy hill toward the dock.

If it's before 4 o'clock, you're doing well. If not, start asking around for extra sleeping bags and a fishing pole, because you're spending the night on Rock Island.

III

Southwest Hikes

23

Perrot State Park

Total distance: 1.5 miles

Hiking time: 1 hour, 15 minutes to 1 hour, 45 minutes

Difficulty: 5.0

Vertical rise: 475 feet

Maps: USGS 7½' Trempealeau, Wisconsin; DeLorme Wisconsin Atlas & Gazetteer, p. 49 (D-5)

The problem with learning about geology in school resides with books. There's simply too much reading, models, graphs, charts, and posters. In some unbelievably convenient way, the Mississippi River provides a lesson in geology unmatched by any textbook. It is here where you can actually witness, and feel, in layer upon layer of dolomites and sandstones, all the very reliable records of what happened here from the time of the ancient seas more than 600 million years ago to the second you put your foot on the trail. Undoubtedly, if we'd had our earth science lessons here, we'd all be geologists.

If you don't believe it, wait until you emerge from the woods atop Perrot Ridge and lose your breath from the view, and you simply sit and wonder. This phenomenal natural area has been called home by humans for thousands of years, from the first Native Americans to the French voyageurs to the loggers, and now to anglers, hikers, canoeists, skiers, and campers. And the great thing about drastic elevation change is that it's just about the most exclusively hiker-friendly place on earth.

On this hike you will leave the parking lot, just a few feet above the river, and you will meander along the bank before beginning a long and unrelenting uphill climb. After tackling the hill for a bit, it rises more and more until you think that you just may have taken the wrong trail. In fact, the higher you go, the more overgrown the trail gets, almost as though it hasn't seen but a few hikers who actually made it this far. Things

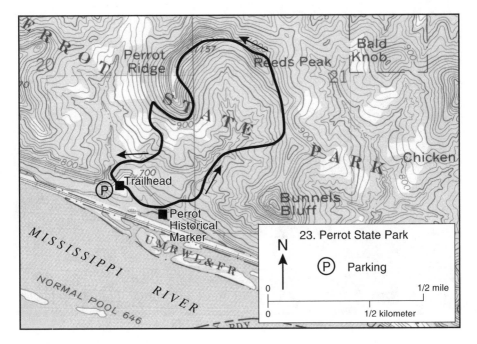

get pretty wild up there before you scramble to the top of the ridge and are blessed for doing so with one of the most remarkable views in the entire state, 507 feet above sea level. Then, you scramble down.

There are a few hikes in this book that are for experienced hikers only. This is, without question, one of those. This is a no-children hike. There is no water from the time you leave the river to the time you get back, thus it isn't really a dog hike either. (Besides, dogs can't see well enough to enjoy the view anyway.) Not only is the hiking very technical, but it's also dangerous atop the ridge, with narrow, rocky trails and drop-offs that could easily lead to a fatal fall. Be very careful.

How to Get There

From Trempealeau, take 1st Street west and go 1.8 miles to the park entrance. Follow the road past the historical marker to the next parking lot on your left.

For more information, contact Perrot State Park at 608-534-6409.

The Trail

The only way to hike this trail is counterclockwise, as far as we're concerned. Take the Perrot Ridge Trail out of the southeast corner of the parking lot down toward the river. You'll immediately head into the woods and curve your way south toward the water. You'll even head downhill a bit, only making for a bit more uphill. You'll soon emerge at the Perrot historical marker. A wood-chipped trail takes you diagonally across this area, across the park road, and up into the woods.

With your head down, the hill climbing starts immediately. But, while this is one of the most strenuous climbs in this book, the scenery along the climb is rivaled by few other trails. Huge, towering hardwoods loom overhead while a brilliant, emerald green blanket of ferns covers the many little

Taking a break on the crest of the bluffs over the Mississippi River at Perrot State Park

valleys as far as you can see. This area is pretty damp and cool in the summer and is so serene that you forget you're out of breath. Take several breaks along this ascent. There's no reason to rush—unless, like us, you're trying to get to the Trempealeau Hotel for a walnut burger before they shut the kitchen down for the night.

Local flavor aside, the trail continues upward until you come to an intersection with three other trails. Stay straight on the ridge with the Perrot Ridge Trail. You will immediately make a rather rocky ascent toward a towering rocky bluff, but you will duck behind it on the north side, and the trail will level off. As you emerge on the western side of this bluff, you will see that the trail continues to the right, into a very overgrown area. To the left and up this rocky, sandy bluff is another pseudotrail. Don't take this one. People undoubtedly have thought that they were at Perrot Ridge and turned up there, only to find that it wasn't the way to

go. So head to the right and into the thick, very thorny, overgrown trail.

You will meander along the ridge on a narrow trail as you climb, more gradually now, toward the ridgetop. You don't really see it coming as you scramble up the rest of the way, since the ridge actually curves to the south like a boomerang. But, you'll know when you're there. The river looks almost unnaturally far below, and that sort of top-of-the-Ferris-wheel feeling sets in. The view is remarkable, and a small bench at the tip of the ridge is positioned to let you take it all in. It is one of those places that is hard to believe exists in Wisconsin.

After a much-needed break, the descent lies ahead of you. Although you haven't been hiking for a few minutes, put your hiking cap back on, because things get tricky right away. The trail is rocky, sandy, and slippery and requires a lot of slow moving. (We even incorporated our backsides into the initial descent!) It

Southwest Hikes

The Mississippi

doesn't last long, however, and soon you will be working your way steadily downhill. You will come to a long set of riser steps that make things easier, although they are sort of awkwardly spaced and a bit rough on rubbery legs.

You will then merge with the cross-country skiing/mountain bike trail for a while. Take a right onto this trail at the bottom of the steps. It actually makes for a nice respite from the awkward footing and takes you along the grassy edge of the ridge foothill. Eventually, this trail will peel off to the right, and you will turn left and continue into the woods, downhill, and back to the parking lot, where several spectators will have assembled to cheer wildly and pat you on the back. (Okay, that probably won't happen, but it's fun to imagine.)

This hike, the shortest in the book, is by far not the easiest. Any time a mile and a half is slated to take longer than an hour, we tend to perk up—both because that means it's time to get focused, but also because it means we're probably in for some seriously good hiking. Both are the case on the Perrot Ridge Trail. This hike is breathtaking for both its beauty and its terrain, and is the kind that leaves you driving away saying, "Wow." Enjoy.

24

Black River State Forest

Distance: 4.0 miles

Hiking time: 1 hour, 30 minutes to 2 hours

Difficulty: 3.5

Vertical rise: 100 feet

Maps: USGS 7½' Hatfield SE, Wisconsin and Warrens West, Wisconsin; DeLorme Wisconsin Atlas & Gazetteer, p. 50 (C-4)

Imagine a backcountry trail, deeply embedded under a canopy of hardwoods and evergreens. Now give this trail some challenging and repetitive elevation changes, high hilltop vistas, and a blanket of woodland plants flowering underfoot. Unbelievably, this trail exists less than 5 miles from the busiest interstate highway in Wisconsin. But you'll be lucky (or unlucky) to hear a car, or a human, in the couple of hours you spend immersed in the Black River State Forest, hiking the Wildcat Trail.

If you come from the north, you are welcomed to the area by a bumpy and dusty, 5-mile drive along a gravel and dirt road. (We didn't realize until later that you can easily get to the trailhead via paved roads.) The terrain up to this point is mostly level, with a few climbs and dips. But the consensus, after having hiked to the lookout with its open view of Wildcat Mound to the southwest, was a resounding "Whoa." In fact, looking out from atop Wildcat Mound is like looking out at the Blue Ridge Mountains from atop a North Carolina peak, with soft green valleys leading up to curved hilltops.

To make matters even dreamier, this area of the forest is dedicated solely to the silent sports. The ATVs and snowmobiles have their own section. This area is for Nordic skiing—apparently for Olympians-in-training—and hikers. And, with a pass from the forest office, backcountry camping is allowed as long as you get off the trail 100 feet or more and into the wilderness a little farther.

This hike takes you alongside the road northward before heading northwest and up

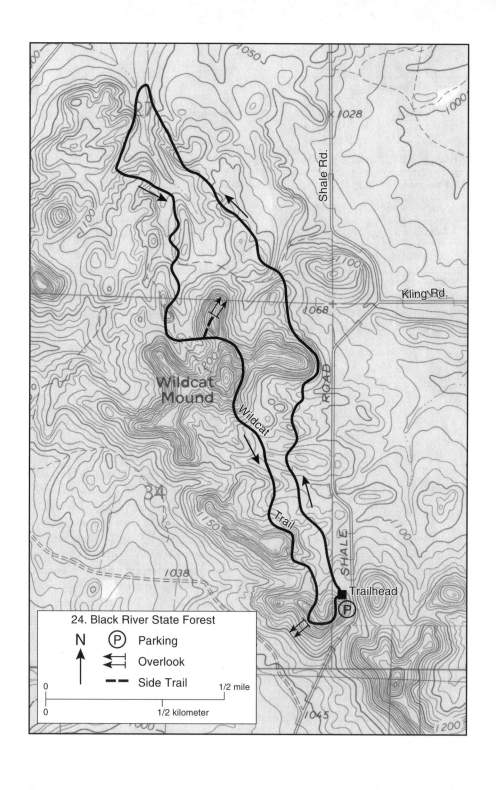

1028

1000

Shale Rd.

Kling Rd.

1100

1068

Wildcat
Mound

Wildcat

34

1150

Trail

1038

ROAD

SHALE

1100

Trailhead

P

24. Black River State Forest

N   P   Parking

⇄   Overlook

▬ ▬   Side Trail

0   1/2 mile

0   1/2 kilometer

1045

1200

into the sandy woods. You wind along a series of ups and downs before doing a buttonhook turn and heading south, up toward the first lookout and then through a series of hills and valleys before finally ending up at what we call "Whoa Hill." A note about distance: On the maps that we received, the distance was 3.5 miles, while the sign at the trailhead states 4 miles. We estimate the loop to be 4 miles, especially if you hike out and back to the overlook midway through the loop. So prepare for a long hike. There is no water on the trail or anywhere nearby, so come prepared—you will definitely need to replenish on this hike.

How to Get There

From the north, west, or south you will want to take I-90/94 to County Route O at Millston. Head east on CR O less than 0.5 mile to North Settlement Road. (Signs for Black River State Forest and Wildcat will be here as well.) Follow North Settlement Road for 3.3 miles to Shale Road. Take a left on Shale, and the Wildcat Trail trailhead will be about 1.5 miles on the left. Park on either side of the road.

From the east, you are better off taking WI 21 or WI 54 to the I-90/94 and heading north or south as needed to the CR O exit, and then following the directions above. The slippery gravel roads mentioned above can take a long time to drive, and they are pretty hard on your vehicle, so we suggest this option instead.

For more information, contact the Black River State Forest headquarters at 715-284-4103.

The Trail

Head through the gate and up the access road until you reach the trailhead. At a fork in the trail, you will come to the first of the many map kiosks that make navigating here very easy. Turn right and head north. This is the opposite direction from the state forest map, but a counterclockwise approach allows you to work into the hills rather than attacking them right away—and it leaves a picturesque lookout for the end of the hike.

As you approach the buttonhook turn, the trail will be mostly rolling and you will find yourself traversing a relatively old oak savannah. This opens up your view and makes it even easier to find that choice campsite in a clearing by a ridge. There is a bench in this area that makes a good spot for a water break. The turn southward is more gradual than it looks, but you will soon find yourself climbing your way up toward the first overlook area.

It's often tempting to skip the overlooks, especially when they are on offshoot trails like this one, but this is worth it. The trail closes in to a single-track path and meanders among some large oaks toward the end of the ridge. While it is a bit overgrown in the summer, the fall is a great time to come to this secluded point.

Continue back on the trail south. You will be hiking alongside a large ridge as you begin the roller-coaster succession of hills and valleys on the way to the Wildcat lookout. These are pretty taxing and make the idea of skiing rather hard to imagine. You will pass the shortcut trail—designed to allow skiers the option of skipping the largest climbs—but you'll want to stay straight ahead and work your way up to the lookout. Shrouded in trees at first, you'll emerge from the valley to find a great view awaiting you. Also waiting is a bench, a great place to have lunch and some water. The trip back to the road is a short one, and it's all downhill.

To finish up, take the trail away from the overlook area down to the "parking lot" as the sign calls it. It's less than 0.25 mile and makes for a less rigorous end to a good, long hike.

25

Roche-A-Cri State Park

Total distance: 4.5 miles (Acorn Trail 3.5 miles, plus observation platform, 1.0 mile)

Hiking time: 1 hour, 45 minutes to 2 hours, 15 minutes

Difficulty: 2.0

Vertical rise: 330 feet

Maps: USGS 7½' Roche A Cri, Wisconsin and Adams, Wisconsin; DeLorme Wisconsin Atlas & Gazetteer, p. 52 (D-2)

In the absence of the written word, paper, or books, it was hard to chronicle an important message in historic times. So, early Native American cultures used what they had. Those living on the banks of Carter Creek, at the site of Roche-A-Cri State Park, were blessed with a blank canvas on which to write. Roche-A-Cri Mound offered a 300-foot sandstone face as a place to record important events, mark the occurrence of a ceremony, or to pay homage to animals and hunting.

While it is hard to know exactly how long ago the petroglyphs and pictographs were etched into and painted on Roche-A-Cri Mound, they are estimated to be as much as 1,000 years old. Demonstrating how important it has always been to humans to record their past and immortalize themselves, the rock also bears the names and dates—as far back as the 1800s—of early Wisconsin settlers and Civil War troops, and graffiti from the 20th century.

It's easy to understand why people were excited to be in this area. Aside from the few feet of it used for painting and etching, the beauty of this sandstone hill is remarkable. And, the view of 10 surrounding counties from 300 feet above is even better. Only 10 years old in the spring of 2004, the Top of the Mound Trail and Stairway escorts thousands of visitors atop Roche-A-Cri Mound annually. This taxing climb is well worth it, especially on clear days. Crawling to the top and emerging over the wooded landscape below is like poking through the clouds in an airplane. The view, over 50 miles in every direction, is breathtaking—if you have any breath left, that is.

The bulk of this 4.5-mile hike is flat and rolling and very easy, aside from the length. It's a perfect hike for beginners and may be a good choice for children. The only caveat is the hike to the top of the mound. Almost a 1-mile round trip from the Acorn Trail, the hike up will take 10 to 15 minutes and really does take its toll. Only those in shape should go up this steep stairwell. But the view from the top is certainly worth the effort. After coming down, the trail winds around the mound and past the petroglyphs, just next to the parking area.

How to Get There

From the north, take WI 13 out of Wisconsin Rapids for about 30.5 miles to the junction with WI 21. Continue on WI 13 south for 1.6 miles to the park entrance on the right. Go past the park office for 0.2 mile to the parking lot on the left, across from the petroglyphs.

From the west, take WI 21 east out of Necedah 13.5 miles to WI 13. Turn south on WI 13 and go 1.6 miles to the park entrance. Follow the directions above from there.

From the south, take WI 13 north out of Friendship 1.6 miles to the park entrance on the left. Turn left and follow the directions above from there.

From the east, take WI 21 west out of Coloma for 14.9 miles to WI 13. Turn left (south) on WI 13 and go 1.6 miles to the park entrance. Follow the directions above from there.

For more information, contact Roche-A-Cri State Park at 608-339-6881.

The Trail

Head southwest out of the parking area and toward Carter Creek. At the creek, turn

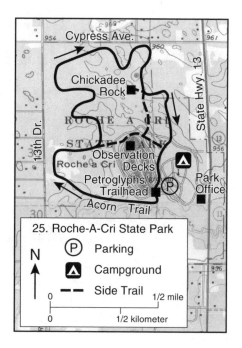

right, following the arrow pointing toward the kiosk. There will not be any signs for the Acorn Trail here, but this is the beginning of it. Soon after this point, you will pass an intersection with another trail from the left, but stay straight.

From here, the trail will begin its long ramble along mostly rolling terrain among oaks, pines, and maples. The trail is wide, flat, and a bit sandy; a great trail for skiing, too. Also nice are the many tree identification signs along the way. So, if you're still working on the difference between a white and black oak, you're in the right spot. The park is full of both species, and the signs make identification easy.

The trail is very tranquil and takes you far away from any commotion at the campsites or at the mound. Deep in the park, expect to see lots of birds and other wildlife. Don't be surprised to round a bend and find yourself sharing the trail with a deer.

Petroglyphs and pictographs at Roche-A-Cri State Park

Eventually, the trail will turn northward and pass through a pine plantation before turning east. Soon after, the Mound Trail will split off and head up to the mound. If you don't wish to hike 4.5 miles, taking this route would cut the hike in half. Otherwise, continue left (north) on the Acorn Trail as you get deeper into the woods and pass yet more tree identification signs. The trail will head east and then south up to Chickadee Rock before shooting east and south again and across the park road. Soon after crossing, there will be another offshoot trail to the right to climb the mound. This will be an out-and-back hike, and it will take at least a half hour to get to the top of the mound and back. If you decide to go, you will have 303 steps to climb before being rewarded with arguably one of the best views in the state.

Once back down, join back up with the Acorn Trail where you left it, and circle around the mound to find yet another incredible view, the petroglyphs. There is a good educational kiosk set up here to teach you about the etchings and pictures before you head down the wooden ramp and back to your car in the lot across the road.

This hike, in the middle of the Central Sands region of the state, is a great long, flat hike, good for beginners and children who can make a long trek. Even if you get tired, there are two outlet trails to shorten the hike. But, because of its flat terrain, the hike is very pleasant and not too demanding. The only demanding part will be if you choose to climb up to the lookout, a great choice but a taxing decision.

26

Jersey Valley County Park

Total distance: 3.1 miles

Hiking time: 1 hour, 15 minutes to 1 hour, 45 minutes

Difficulty: 3.0

Vertical rise: 110 feet

Maps: USGS 7½' Westby, Wisconsin; DeLorme Wisconsin Atlas & Gazetteer, p. 41 (C-4)

"Simplify, simplify," were the profoundly simple words of Henry David Thoreau. And, while we may not have the time, money, or gumption to head off to a lake to live deliberately, a trip to Vernon County's Amish Country may suffice. As you roll down the coulees and climb the ridges along these roads, passing waving Amish farmers in horse-drawn buggies, life does seem to get a bit simpler.

Particularly special is a little lake just outside of Westby with a phenomenal hiking trail looping around it. As we stood on the shores of the lake on one of those typical, oppressively steamy July days and looked across to see three Amish gentlemen fishing for their supper, we knew it was bound to be a unique place.

But it's not just this lake that is special; it is Vernon County's commitment to parks and forests that makes it quite different from most southern Wisconsin counties. While it's easy to find northern counties with large parks and forests, it is exceptionally rare in these parts. Overall, there are four parks encompassing nearly 1,000 acres, and there is a forest with 600 acres. Thus, we were happily rewarded after pulling onto County Route X and descending deep into Jersey Valley. Not only had we found a beautiful lake, but we had also found a way to make our day just a bit simpler—by hiking, of course.

This hike takes you over the large dam, more of a dike really, that is the large hill covered with wildflowers on the south side of the lake. While human-made, this lake doesn't look it. There is good marsh development,

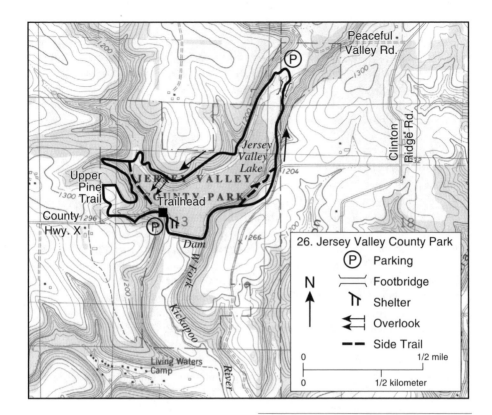

and the trees just seem to grow up out of the lake along the shores like those on a natural northern Wisconsin lake. Lakes like these were developed to control floods, a some-times catastrophic problem in these hilly areas. From the dam, you'll head up the east-ern slope of the lake on a heavily wooded hill-side before descending to the northern tip and a wetland. From there, you'll buttonhook back along the western shore and ascend to an overlook. You will then descend again to the boggy western tip before hiking through a pine plantation, across the park road, and down a steep ridge back to the parking area. All in all, this terrific hike will feel longer than it is and is actually pretty taxing. It's a great hike if you want to see wildlife, particularly turkeys and deer—we saw four—but may be a bit hard for a beginning hiker or for children.

How to Get There

From the west, take WI 27 north out of Westby for 2.5 miles to CR X. Turn right on CR X and follow it for 1.5 miles to where it enters Jersey Valley Park.

From the northeast, take WI 33 west out of Cashton for about 0.5 mile to WI 27 south. Go 4.1 miles to CR X. Take a left on CR X and follow the directions above.

For more information, contact the Vernon County Parks and Forests Department at 608-637-5485.

The Trail

There is no trailhead kiosk at the parking area, nor are there any maps. So, you will need to use these directions and our map, however the loop trail is pretty simple. To do the hike counterclockwise, begin by hiking past the shelter and up to the dam. This area is covered in wildflowers in the summer. Look for phlox, aster, cattail, and milkweed, which monarch butterflies seem to love. But watch out for wild parsnip—we saw lots of it here.

Continue along the dam until you turn north next to the sandstone outcropping and up into the woods. The trail starts to ascend very quickly, and before you know it you will be climbing for about 0.25 mile. The trail is wide and is actually more of an access road. There may be a trail that cuts off to the left; it works its way back to the main trail eventually, but we stuck to the wide one.

At the crest of the hill you will come to two red gates and an open area alongside a farm field. If there are some Amish fishermen here when you are, this undoubtedly will be the shady area where their bareback horses will be resting, awaiting the trip home. If you ever wondered what life was like during pioneer times, you'll definitely get the feel of it in Jersey Valley.

After passing the gates and following the trail to the left (north), you will begin to descend toward the northern tip of the lake. You will pass a small stand of rather large pines after having seen mainly maples, oaks, and walnuts thus far. Soon you will come to the bottom of the valley and a lush wetland area. The trail may fork; stay to the right and go over the bridge. The left fork will probably take you into the river (which you may want to do if you don't trust the bridge).

Once over the bridge, you will come to a grassy area that may be mowed. Stay left and head toward another gate. Once past the gate, the trail will take you up another ascent as you cut back and forth on the way up to the overlook. The trail is narrower on this side and may be a bit more overgrown. The "overlook" is pretty much an overstatement unless you are here from fall to spring.

Once the trees are leafed out, the valley is so overgrown that it is hard to oversee much. But the bench makes for a great resting spot and is probably just past the halfway point.

From the overlook, you will turn away from the lake and head deeper into the woods before starting a pretty steep descent down toward the western tip of the lake. You will emerge in an open wetland area. There may be a cutoff to the left, the Lower Lake Trail, but stay to the right and head uphill again. The trail will head straight west for a short time before making a buttonhook and coming back east, up along a ridge. This is where we spotted deer bounding away like jumping beans. Our senses were braced for each crash through the woods as these majestic animals were undeservingly roused from their afternoon naps.

From here, the trail will make another turn west and then curve southward, taking you through a tranquil pine plantation, with soft needles underfoot; this area is very unlike the rest of the hike. Soon after, the trail will pop out at the road. Head right, uphill on the road, and resume the trail just on the other side of the park sign on the opposite side of the road. From here the trail will turn east and begin a long descent back to the lot. Be extremely careful, however. The dropoff to the left (north) side of the trail is probably close to a hundred feet and is just off the trail. So, especially if you are with children, be extremely vigilant in this area. (To avoid this part, simply turn left and head down the park road instead of crossing it.)

The trail will take you right back to where you started at the parking lot, where you can soak your feet, drink some water, or have lunch in the shade of the shelter. A visit to Jersey Valley in the picturesque hills of Vernon County is certainly a great way to relax and to live simply and deliberately.

27

Wildcat Mountain State Park

Total distance: 2.5 miles

Hiking time: 1 hour to 1 hour, 30 minutes

Difficulty: 3.5

Vertical rise: 180 feet

Map: USGS 7½' Ontario, Wisconsin; DeLorme Wisconsin Atlas & Gazetteer, p. 41 (C-6)

Long before herbal supplements exploded in popularity in the West, the Chinese and other Asian cultures valued herbs as mainstays of medicine. Wisconsin, known for its picturesque dairy farms and milk and cheese exports, also just happens to be one of the largest exporters of ginseng in the world. In fact, it was deep in the heart of the coulees and hills of the Kickapoo River Valley that ginseng grew in wild abundance throughout much of the 20th century. Thus, when Edna and Edward Lord showed up at Wildcat Mountain to escape lung problems in the city, ginseng turned out to be just what the doctor ordered. Eventually, the Lords and others started the Kickapoo Mountain Ginseng Company.

And, it's this sort of hunter-gatherer legacy of the Kickapoo Valley, as well as the fact that its rambling hills aren't good for farming, that make it perfect for outdoor recreation. Wildcat Mountain State Park, originally 60 acres, now covers more than 3,500 acres and offers miles of hiking and skiing, as well as access to one of the most exceptional canoeing waterways in the whole state, the Kickapoo River.

This hike takes you from the site of Edward and Edna's farm, counterclockwise along the Old Settler's Trail. It starts just next to the park office building and heads past an amphitheater with just about the most incredible backdrop imaginable, a miles-long vista of the Kickapoo Valley and Ontario Township below. After visiting the Taylor Hollow Lookout, the trail dips down into the valley and meanders along several

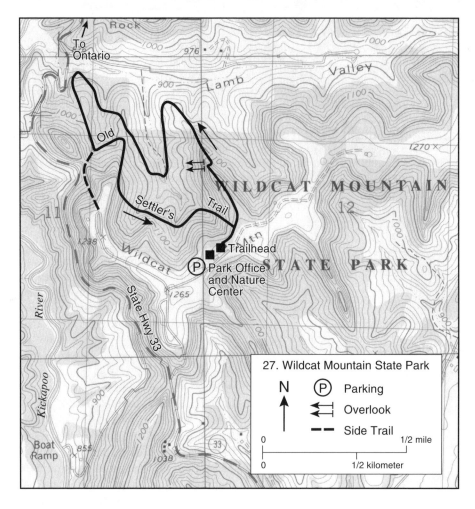

27. Wildcat Mountain State Park

N (P) Parking
⇄ Overlook
-- Side Trail

small coulees before looping around and heading back up to the cutoff to the lookout. The trail is relatively difficult. While the footing is quite good, there is a lot of climbing, making it a tough trail for children and possibly a bad choice for beginners. Still, if you're thinking of stretching your previous boundaries a bit, this hike might be perfect.

How to Get There

From the north and west, take WI 33 east out of Ontario for 3.0 miles to the park. Turn left on the park entrance road and follow it about 0.6 mile to the park office on the left.

From the east, take WI 33 west from Hillsboro for 12.2 miles. Turn right at the park entrance road and follow the directions above.

From the south, take WI 131 north out of La Farge about 10 miles to Ontario. Take WI 33 and follow the directions from the north and west above.

For more information, contact Wildcat Mountain State Park at 608-337-4775.

Wildcat Mountain

The Trail

Take the trail between the park office and the nature center and around the corner toward the amphitheater. Things start out rather uneventfully as you hike along the building, but they perk up pretty quickly. The trail then heads past the amphitheater amidst some towering pines and curves left (north) toward the Taylor Hollow Lookout. After taking in the great view overlooking the Kickapoo Valley and the town of Ontario, take the little trail heading southeast off the overlook. It will curve northward again and head down some riser steps into the valley.

You'll then pass a rock ledge and curve southwest, where you will be greeted by some old red pines as you descend into a little valley. But the trail will continue back up alongside another ridge, and the trees will transition back to hardwoods after you pass over a small footbridge. There is a rich diversity of trees, including maple, basswood, hickory, oak, and even a large stand of Norway pine—planted by local schoolchildren.

The trail will turn south, away from the pines, and begin its long ascent to the ridge where you began, a couple hundred feet above. You will pass one offshoot trail to the right, but stay to the left and continue uphill among hardwoods, along with ferns springing up and covering seemingly every inch of ground. There are many other woodland plants, too, including bloodroot, wild geranium, and jack-in-the-pulpit.

You will then pass over a bridge in a setting that looks almost like one of those postcards or calendars with green and dense woods, and picturesque trails bordered by ferns. A few steps later is a bench that makes for a good resting spot before making the final leg up the hill. At the top you will come to a split in the trail. Stay to the

High above the town of Ontario and the Kickapoo River valley at Wildcat Mountain State Park

right and turn back toward the amphitheater and visitors center.

This great hike, although very hilly, doesn't have the feel of an uphill assault. Instead, thanks to the many small valleys, you seem to ramble uphill. Of course, a hill's a hill, and this hike is relatively tough, but it's a great way to explore one of the beautiful green river valleys of southwestern Wisconsin's Driftless Area.

28

Wyalusing State Park

Total distance: 2.5 miles

Hiking time: 2 hours, 30 minutes to 3 hours

Difficulty: 5.0

Vertical rise: 260 feet

Map: USGS 7½' Bagley, Wisconsin/Iowa; DeLorme Wisconsin Atlas & Gazetteer, p. 24 (A-1)

While many visitors to Wyalusing State Park drive its roads to and from the campgrounds, bike trails, volleyball courts, and scenic overlooks, few actually hike down and up the wall of earth that made this area an attraction in the first place. As you hike down from the tops of the magnificent bluffs above the mighty Mississippi, you are also trekking backward in time. Indeed, while a visit to the Mississippi River can serve as a great fishing trip, it can also serve as a great learning experience.

Hundreds of millions of years ago, the first of several shallow seas began to blanket most of North America. Each recession of these seas left large deposits of sediment. These layers, like a seven-layer cake, grew over time. A result of this layering is found at Wyalusing. Not impenetrable, the "cake" was worn through in places, eroded by moving water that washed away the sediment, creating large bluffs and hills.

In fact, when standing at Point Lookout, you are actually at the beach level of the most recent sea, looking all the way down to the oldest layer, hundreds of feet below. It's like standing on the icing of the cake looking at the bottom of the pan. And, it's to that bottomland and back that this hike takes you.

Thus, this is the best place to decide whether this hike is for you. It is, by far, the most difficult trail in this book. While the two trails that form the bulk of this loop—the Bluff and the Old Immigrant—are described as moderate and easy by the park's trail guide, the issue of difficulty arises with the Indian Trail, the connector trail that gets you down the bluff, and the connector trail on the east, which gets you up. These are extremely difficult trails, with little visibility of the trail's surface due to encroaching plant growth. As if that weren't enough, the footing is slippery and sandy, and there are loose rocks. It was this trail that made us decide to always carry our neoprene ankle and knee braces in our hip packs—in addition to our small first aid kit—regardless of where we hike. This trail is not for kids, out-of-shape trekkers, dogs, or novice hikers. This is very technical hiking, and suitable for experienced hikers only.

How to Get There

From the east, take US 18 west to just outside of Prairie du Chien. Take a left (west) on County Route C. Follow CR C about three miles to CR X. Take a right on CR X, and the park entrance will be less than 1 mile on the right.

From the north, take WI 35 south through Prairie du Chien to the junction with US 18. Take US 18 east out of town to CR C. Take a right on CR C and follow the directions above.

From the south, take CR X out of Bagley about 6 miles to the park entrance on your left.

For more information, contact Wyalusing State Park at 608-996-2261.

The Trail

Moving clockwise, the trail begins by leaving Point Lookout to the west and meandering along a cool section of trail covered by mixed hardwoods. The trail is wide and there is little undergrowth, making visibility easy and hiking smooth. Follow this along for about 0.5 mile until you come to the connection with the Indian Trail. Take this to the

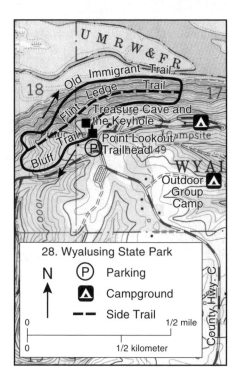

28. Wyalusing State Park

N

(P) Parking

🅐 Campground

-- Side Trail

0   1/2 mile

0   1/2 kilometer

right (north) and begin the rather tricky journey downward.

The trail will close immediately around you, and the footing will get less and less stable. And, although the park's map shows this trail as a simple arc downward, it is actually a collection of several cutbacks of trail, which zigzag their way down to the bottom. Along the way there will be areas where the trail has been shored up with wooden planks like sandbox supports, holding the trail's dirt in. While these are helpful, they are easy to trip over, and in their absence, the trail can get slippery. Some would say that downhill hiking is tougher than uphill. This hike will definitely help you in making your decision.

While it's hard to enjoy much of the scenery with your eyes attached by an imaginary line to your feet, by stopping from time

Confluence of the Mississippi and Wisconsin Rivers, Wyalusing State Park

to time you can begin to appreciate the geological past of this area and the force it must have taken to wear a several-hundred-foot gouge out of rock. The hill is home to all sorts of plant and bird life, and don't be surprised to find yourself sharing the trail with a deer. Like mountain goats, they clamber up and down these trails, too.

Eventually, you will pass the turnoff for the Flint Ledge Trail. While it comes up sooner and makes for a shorter loop, the Flint Ledge is a said to be even more difficult. And, it has even been closed due to washouts in the past! So continue left along the Indian Trail to the bottom, where you will merge right (east) with the Old Immigrant Trail. This brings you a nice break from the leg-numbing downward scramble as you amble alongside the backwaters of the Wisconsin River. You are now at the level of the water that looked so far down from Point Lookout, hundreds of feet above.

Pay attention for the turnoff to the Flint Ledge and Bluff Trails to the right (south). This may be a great time for a water and snack break. While it may be buggy and hard to stop, not fueling up could be a mistake. Also, keep your water handy, because you'll need to make at least one more stop on the way up.

The ascent is immediately taxing. Again, you'll wind your way upward through a series of cutbacks. Looking up, it appears to go almost straight up. Watch your footing here. This trail seems to be even less stable than the surface of the Indian Trail on the downward route. Eventually, you'll come again to the merging of the Flint Ledge Trail straight ahead (west) and the Bluff Trail to the left (south). Take the Bluff Trail, and you'll immediately come across a wooden bridge that appears to defy gravity by leaning, rather conspicuously, over the valley. A bit shaky (the bridge, that is), we traversed this thing one at a time. There was probably a way to go around it, too. Use your best judgment here, and remember that oftentimes volunteers maintain these trails. The bridge may need maintenance that they just haven't gotten to yet.

As you approach the end, the trickiest part of the trail emerges. The footing gets pretty loose and, to make matters worse, the drop-offs get steeper and closer to the trail. These areas should be easily traversable, but they really require a lot of attention. Soon you will emerge at Treasure Cave and the Keyhole, a hole in the rock that leads to an overlook. From this point, you have steps, boardwalk, and asphalt leading you to the end of the trail and back to Point Lookout.

It's definitely rewarding to sit atop the bluff now, having hiked down through history. Not only does this trail allow you to visit a part of Wisconsin's geological past up close, it also affords you the opportunity to hike what is said to be an actual Native American trail. Just imagine hiking up and down that trail en route to water, hunting, or gathering, or even carrying large amounts of supplies. It is a trail like this that makes hiking in Wisconsin so memorable and rewarding.

29

Mirror Lake State Park

Total distance: 2.5 miles

Hiking time: 1 hour to 1 hour, 30 minutes

Difficulty: 2.5

Vertical rise: Minimal

Map: USGS 7½' Wisconsin Dells South, Wisconsin; DeLorme Wisconsin Atlas & Gazetteer: p. 43 (D-5)

Many are familiar with Mirror Lake, thanks to the fact that it is situated right next to—in fact, almost under—an interstate highway. It is also neighbors with a crowded mega-casino and it is only minutes from the world-famous water slides of Wisconsin Dells. But, amid all this fabricated, human pro-gress is a beautiful lake surrounded by mixed conifer and hardwood forests.

Mirror Lake, named for its perpetually calm water, and its namesake state park are good examples of what brought people to this area for recreation in the first place. This region marks a sort of transition to northern topography, where hiking means pine-needle beds and sand underfoot and sappy-smelling, cool breezes overhead.

Because the lake is a designated no-wake zone, and the hikers and mountain bikers have their own separate trails, the hiking is pretty serene. While the buzz of tires moving down the road serves as a background reminder of where you are, once you're deeply into the trail, it's still hard to believe you're so close to "civiliza-tion." And, as is the case at many state parks, the hiking trails do not see nearly as much traffic as the other areas of the park.

This hike takes you away from the com-motion of the park's entrance and beach area and over to an area of hiking and skiing trails on the lake's peninsula. The hike me-anders along the shore of the lake before looping back through a warm, sandy prairie. Mirror Lake State Park is definitely a great destination, or a rest stop as you, too, whiz by along the open road.

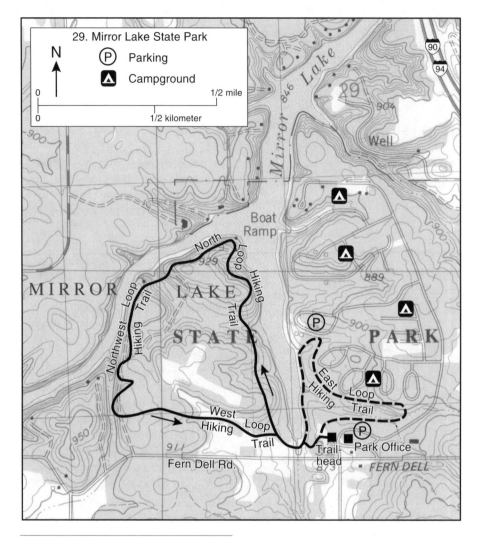

Map legend:
29. Mirror Lake State Park
N
(P) Parking
▲ Campground
0 — 1/2 mile
0 — 1/2 kilometer

How to Get There

From the north or northwest, take I-90/94 east to the Wisconsin Dells area. Take the US 12 exit and travel east on US 12 about 0.3 mile to Fern Dell Road. Turn right on Fern Dell Road and take it 1.5 miles to the park entrance on the right.

From the east or southeast, take I-90/94 west to the US 12 exit. Take US 12 east and follow the directions above.

From south, take US 12 west out of Baraboo for about 5.5 miles. Turn left on Fern Dell Road to the park entrance, which is 1.5 miles on the right.

For more information, contact Mirror Lake State Park at 608-254-2333.

The Trail

Park in the first lot connected to the visitors center and walk over to the trailhead on the

Deer at Mirror Lake State Park

other side of the visitors center building, to the west, across from the loop driveway. There will be a kiosk there marking the beginning of the trails. Head straight and veer left. The East Loop Trail will go to the right (north). A few steps later you will again meet up with the end of the East Loop Trail. Again, stay to the left, and you will pass by the southern tip of the lake and a marshy area. As you curve around the tip of the lake, you will hike past the Time Warp Trail and see signs directing you north for the Northwest and North Loops.

Immediately welcoming you will be huge Scotch pine trees and a few white pines, marking the area as distinctly coniferous. But, as you continue along, you will pass some big white oaks, along with large cherries.

The trail will continue along and will pass directly across from the beach area on the other side of the lake. You will turn to the left (west) and dip down into a small valley and up the other side before curving north again and out into an opening with an old, overgrown stone foundation. In the summer the trail is bordered by spiderwort and other flowers taking advantage of the sun.

From here, the trail will buttonhook to the west and pass by a large opening in the woods. In the summer, this area is full of the purple clusters of crown vetch, a non-native wildflower that loves openings and roadsides.

The trail will then climb out of this lowland area, transitioning from dirt to a remnant of an old cement logging road. You will come to the junction of the North and Northwest Loops. Stay to the right (south-west) and follow the trail on a long descent before winding back up and southward, past a large rock outcropping and into a pine grove.

The trail will then meander up and down and back and forth, before emerging into a sandy prairie and passing the return trails of the North and West Loops, as well as the Time Warp Trail. There is a good wildflower kiosk here, showing many of the flowers visible in the warmer months. Take the trail back past the southern tip of the lake and to the parking area.

This hike is a great escape into the wilds of the Dells area. There is a great variety of plant life and trees. Expect to see a good variety of birds as well. Also, keep your eyes peeled for deer—they are very common on this loop.

30

Devil's Lake State Park

Total distance: 5.5 miles

Hiking time: 2 hours, 30 minutes to 3 hours

Difficulty: 4.5

Vertical rise: 440 feet

Maps: USGS 7½' Baraboo, Wisconsin; DeLorme Wisconsin Atlas & Gazetteer, p. 35 (A-6)

The Baraboo Hills could be called the "Glacier's Last Stand." Fifteen thousand years ago a sheet of ice arrived here from the north, and stopped. Its advance brought with it sediment and rock that somehow plugged both ends of the Devil's Lake Gap, forming a lake. The lake is quite deep—more than 40 feet—and the surrounding bluffs 500 feet tall. In fact, the elevation change is so dramatic here that there are different climates! In the cool, shady lowlands there exist several northern species of woodland plants, in contrast to the warmer, high elevations favored by dry-loving prairie plants.

The park is home to 40 percent of the species of ferns and flowering plants found in Wisconsin, more than one hundred species of birds, and several varieties of amphibians and reptiles, including the very reclusive timber rattlesnake.

Perhaps the most pervasive summer residents, however, are the humans. The park's 406 campsites are almost always full. Take these campers and add a throng of daily visitors, and you get 1.3 million visitors annually, the most of any park or recreation area in the Wisconsin system. But, as busy as the park is, the majority of this hike can be done in the solitude of the woods and without much disruption. A recent June hike along this trail revealed very few people once we were off the beaten path.

The biggest caveat to hiking at Devil's Lake is the danger. Much more serious a threat than the rattlesnakes are the bluffs, some of which are hundreds of feet from top to rocky bottom. These exceptionally scenic trails can be treacherous. With

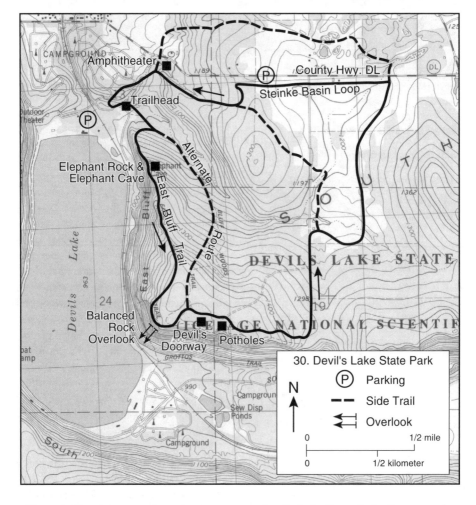

Map legend:

30. Devil's Lake State Park

Ⓟ Parking
- - - Side Trail
⟵ Overlook

N

0 — 1/2 mile
0 — 1/2 kilometer

Map labels: CAMPGROUND, Amphitheater, Trailhead, Outdoor Theater, Ⓟ, Elephant Rock & Elephant Cave, Elephant, Alternate East Bluff Route, East Bluff Trail, Bluff Woods, County Hwy. DL, DL, Steinke Basin Loop, Ⓟ, SOUTH, DEVILS LAKE STATE, Devils Lake, East Bluff, 24, Balanced Rock Overlook, Devil's Doorway, Potholes, Boat Camp, GROTTOS, ICE AGE NATIONAL SCIENTIF, TRAIL, Campground, Sew Disp Ponds, South, Campground

millions of visitors, there are bound to be accidents, and there have been, resulting in injuries and deaths. With a lack of signage and barriers on the bluff edges, a fall is easy. Yet it is also easy to stay clear of the edges. There is plenty to see from a few yards back, and a lot to lose up close to the edge! We do not recommend this hike for small children, and please, please don't take your dog on these trails. There simply isn't enough room, and we see more unknowing dogs on the brink of heat exhaustion than we care to.

Devil's Lake State Park offers more than 10 hiking trails to choose from and an incredible variety of scenery, geological features, and topography. This hike, on the East Bluff Trail and Steinke Basin Loop, seeks to combine a little bit of everything and offers a great look at this unique southern Wisconsin landscape. Also, this hike passes four of the five official points of interest found in the park. This trail is a long one, 5.5 miles, and again, is not intended for children or novice hikers. It combines rocky climbs with rolling, wooded stretches and

Rock stairs at Devil's Lake State Park

sunny, exposed prairie. It all makes for a great day's hike, but it is probably too much if you're not in shape. Also, you'll need lots of water for this hike—at least a liter per person—and a sandwich with some fruit. This is the minimum; take more if you think you'll need it, because you could be gone for 3 hours.

How to Get There

From the south, southeast, and east, take I-90/94 to the US 12 exit, south of Wisconsin Dells. Head south on US 12 for approximately 12 miles, past Baraboo, to WI 159. Turn left (west) on WI 159 and go 2 miles to WI 123. Turn right (south) on WI 123, and follow this to the park entrance about 0.5 mile away.

From the west and southwest, take US 14 to WI 78 east of Mazomanie. Follow WI 78 for 9 miles to US 12 just south of Sauk City. Take a left (west) on US 12, through Sauk City and follow it for approximately 18 miles to WI 159. Take a right (east) on WI 159 and follow the directions above.

For more information, contact Devil's Lake State Park at 608-356-8301.

The Trail

Enter the park via the main entrance on the north shore of the lake and head straight past the visitors center and past the large parking area on the right. Go over the railroad tracks and take the first right into the overflow parking area. You can park in any of these lots. The trailhead is located at the end of the second lot; look for the large, roofed kiosk. *Note:* The loop on the maps at the park will call a similar trail loop the East Bluff Woods/Steinke Basin Loop. In order to take this trail past the outcroppings and vistas of the east shore, we replaced the East Bluff Woods with the East Bluff Trail. This 1.1-mile section of the trail is extremely

difficult. Although much of it is paved with asphalt, the footing is very tricky, and spring water seeping out of the ground makes many of the rocks slippery.

Again, while there are several lookouts offered along the trail, they are not protected with barriers of any kind. There are several drop-offs, from 10 to well over 100 feet. Be very careful when taking pictures or stopping to rest. If this section is not appealing, you may want to replace it with the original East Bluff Woods Trail, where you will be farther into the woods and away from the bluff edge.

Thus, getting started, the East Bluff Trail (marked orange) begins soon after leaving the parking lot. It makes an immediate, and unforgiving, assault on the bluff by heading straight up a long set of riser-type steps. The trail is easy to lose, but by following the crudely paved asphalt path, you can usually find your way. Also, if you are here anytime between Memorial Day and Labor Day, you will be greeted by far more people than are fit to be on this trail, and leashed dogs that should have been left at home. So, while it's hard to lose your way, it's important to be careful while passing, and to watch for two-way traffic. The first—and much needed—break comes quickly at Elephant Rock and Elephant Cave. This is the first of many lookouts. The beach area is visible from here, as well as the west bluff and the north side of the lake. It makes for a good place to take a water break and take care of those initial gear readjustments.

Continuing on, you will climb gradually, moving away from the lake a bit and into the cool woods. At one point you will even descend a bit, then rise again and curve around a large rock outcropping. From here you will climb another long set of steps up toward your second destination at Balanced Rock, about a mile from the start of

The East Bluff at Devil's Lake

the trail. As its name implies, this several-ton rock sits like a ballerina's toe atop a cliff. Looming over the southeastern shore of the lake, this is definitely one of the most photographed, and populated, areas in the park. This makes for a perfect place to rest, hydrate, and snack before moving on.

Up to now, your hiking has consisted of a lot of scrappy, people-infested hiking...with breathtaking views. But, to open up the stride and see more of the park, take the shortcut trail over to the East Bluff Woods Trail (marked yellow) just a few yards away. Follow this to the right into the cool woods along a wide gravel path. You'll begin a long, gradual, 2-mile descent through mixed hardwoods and woodland plants. The hiking is good, and the terrain is a nice break from the cramped rock climbing. Follow the trail all the way down to where you will turn right (east) and hook up with the Steinke Basin Loop. This loop will take you through some marshy lowlands and back out into a sunny prairie opening. You will then enter a young pine grove offering cool shade and a much-needed bench to rest, hydrate, and have your last snack. Save some water, however, because the last stretch gets very sunny for almost a mile before returning to shade, so you'll want a drink later.

Heading out of the woods, you will meet up with the Ice Age Trail. Take a left and head west out into the exposed Steinke Basin, an ancient glacial lake bed. The trail will follow the edge of the prairie alongside County Route DL. From here, you will ascend a bit and reenter hardwood forest. This edge habitat is a perfect place to spot deer and turkeys. It's also a great time to chug some more water. From here, you're about a mile from the end. The trail meanders downhill through a valley, offering a relaxing conclusion to a long hike.

You'll come rolling out of the woods and across a bridge, where you'll pop out at the corner of the Northern Lights Campground.

Follow the trail past the amphitheater and to the park road. Take a left and follow the left edge of the road (against traffic) down to the bottom of the hill. The lot you parked in will be on the left at the foot of the hill.

Devil's Lake State Park is all about the lake. But exploring off the beaten path gets you away from the crowds, into an adjacent lakebed, through mixed forests, and allows you to really stretch out your hiking legs.

31

Governor Dodge State Park

Total distance: 5.25 miles

Hiking time: 1 hour, 45 minutes to 2 hours, 15 minutes

Difficulty: 3.5

Vertical rise: 190 feet

Maps: USGS 7½' Pleasant Ridge, Wisconsin; DeLorme Wisconsin Atlas & Gazetteer, p. 34 (D-2)

While the huge plow of ice of the most recent Ice Age could have decimated the rolling hills of southwest Wisconsin, it didn't. It stopped short. And, while there are several hikes in this book that traverse the terminal moraine—the final advancing point—of that glacier, no other hike is as deeply embedded in the Driftless Area as is the White Oak Loop at Governor Dodge State Park.

This park is truly a special place. This area holds the historical distinction of being the site of a lot of firsts. Some of the first early nomadic cultures moved here to enjoy the protection found in the fortress of limestone bluffs protruding through the earth like brick walls. These cultures and later camps of Fox, Sauk, and Winnebago Native Americans used the area as a summer home. Later came early European settlers, interested in mining the easy-to-find lead ore located just beneath the surface of the ground. It was these settlers—Germans, Irish, Welsh, Swiss, Norwegian, and more—who ultimately earned the name "Badgers," for their hard-working tenacity and drive to go into damp, dark crevices in search of ore.

This area is the heart of modern-day Wisconsin. In fact, the first Capitol—of the Wisconsin Territory, not the state—was in Belmont, 20 miles southwest of here. And the Territory's first governor just happens to have been General Henry Dodge (1786–1867). Dodge was instrumental in establishing peace among the Native Americans, longtime residents, and incoming settlers in the area.

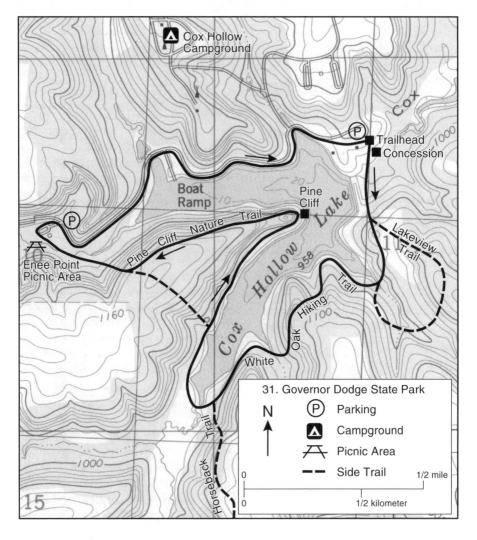

So hiking through Governor Dodge State Park is like taking a trip through time. It's not hard to imagine a small settlement of Sauk setting up for the summer below Enee Point, or a group of grimy, stooped Badgers crawling out of the mines after a long day of digging for ore. While different today, and now crawling with visitors, Governor Dodge State Park still draws people to its valleys for the fishing, swimming, hunting, bike and horseback riding, hiking, and rich history.

Without question, this is a somewhat difficult trail. There are knee-bending sections that take you over rock and up, down, and through all sorts of terrain. But it's worth it. It takes you away from the crowded beach areas and into the limestone-shrouded valleys off the beaten, or paved, path. This hike is not for beginners and is probably too long for most children. But it does have several spots for resting and, because it concludes with a mile-long trek along the park road, it

Southwest Hikes

Northern-type forest in the south at Governor Dodge State Park

ends on a less strenuous note. In fact, the trail pops out at Enee Point picnic area—after about 3 miles—making for a good lunch spot and resting area. Thus, while the hiking is strenuous due to terrain, it doesn't necessarily have to be difficult due to length.

How to Get There

From the east, follow US 18/151 South to Dodgeville. Take US 18 west (exit 47) toward Dodgeville and follow it for 1.7 miles to the intersection with WI 23. Turn right (north) on WI 23 and go 3.1 miles to the park entrance on the right. Turn right and follow the park road past the visitors center, turning right and following the road toward Cox Hollow Lake, and proceed approximately 2.7 miles to the parking lot at Cox Hollow Beach.

From the south, take WI 23 north out of Dodgeville and follow the directions above.

From the north, take WI 23 south out of Spring Green for approximately 12 miles to the park entrance on the left. Turn left and follow the directions from the visitors center above.

From the west, take US 18 east into Dodgeville to WI 23. Turn left (north) on WI 23 and follow the directions above.

For more information, contact Governor Dodge State Park at 608-935-2315.

The Trail

This trail, the White Oak/Pine Bluff Loop, starts just behind the concession building on the south side of the parking lot, up from the beach. The first leg of the trail is actually paved and takes you past the dam on the east side of the lake. Shortly after starting the hike and crossing the bridge over the creek, you can climb some riser steps to the top of the dam and hike south along the shore toward the woods.

Once in the woods, you will make a slight climb and come to the confluence of a couple of trails. The White Oak Trail is well marked, and a sign will direct you to veer right along the shore of the lake, sharing the trail with the Lakeview Trail. If you are here in the warmer months, there will undoubtedly be a lot of activity at the beach. As you hike along this trail, the beach noise will fade as you hike deeper and deeper along the White Oak.

The trail will meander along a backwater area of the lake before turning southwest a bit, where the Lakeview Trail will turn off. Stay right again and begin a slight climb uphill amidst rock outcroppings and roots. The trail will begin to transition now from predominantly walnut, birch, hickory, and of course, white oaks, to include more conifers. In fact, as you climb up again and are greeted by a large stand of immense white pine next to a huge limestone outcropping, you'd think the trail could have been called the White Pine Trail. As the trailside kiosk notes, these giants came south with the cool temperatures of the glacier and form one of the most remarkable stands of pine in the southern part of the state. Indeed, standing on the dam and looking over at Pine Cliff, you'd think you were in the middle of Vilas County on Wisconsin's northern edge.

Soon the trail will begin a long descent, and you will cross a boardwalk over a bubbling stream. The trail will follow next to the stream as you get closer to the southwestern tip of the lake, where the trail will briefly join the horseback trail. This area is an immense wetland and is full of spotted touch-me-not, whose stems hold a juicy remedy for poison ivy. At the map kiosk on the side of the trail, turn right (northwest) and through the wetland and back into the woods.

Governor Dodge State Park

The wide trail will start to climb up the hill, where a small trail will shoot off to the right, the Pine Cliff Nature Trail. No visit to Governor Dodge would be complete without taking this route. Thus, turn right (northeast) and follow the Pine Cliff Trail alongside the lake up toward Pine Cliff. Riser steps will take you up to the foot of Pine Cliff.

Once there, note the lack of signs leading to the right, up to the top of Pine Cliff. There is a reason for this. The park does not mark or maintain any trails leading to the top of the cliff. The staff considers this "trail" a volunteer trail, and there are not any guardrails atop the cliff. While there is ample room to walk around, the edges are undoubtedly unstable and dangerous. So use extreme caution atop the cliff, should you decide to climb it. And if you have children with you, it would probably be best to not go up to the top of Pine Cliff at all. Like the park staff, we do not consider the top of Pine Cliff a part of this hike.

Another set of riser steps will take you away from Pine Cliff, and the trail will level off and begin a long descent to the picnic area below Enee Point. You will join the White Oak Trail, which you left a while back, and head across a bridge before turning north and heading down a long series of steps. Soon the trail will emerge at the Enee Point parking and picnic area, a perfect place for lunch or a snack and some water. Unfortunately, there are no trail markings at this point. Equally disappointing is the fact that you will need to hike along the road back to the Cox Hollow Lake parking lot. It should be a pretty easy trek, and there is a mowed shoulder on the road. But, be advised that people tend to drive too fast in these parks, traveling way above the 25-miles-per-hour limit. So be careful and stay alert as you cool down on your way back to the lot.

Overall, this very scenic hike takes you over some very challenging and varied terrain amidst a variety of typical southern Wisconsin hardwoods and towering northern pines. Certainly one of the most unique hikes in the southern part of the state, it's definitely worth a visit.

32

Yellowstone Lake State Park

Total distance: 3.8 miles

Hiking time: 1 hour, 15 minutes to 1 hour, 45 minutes

Difficulty: 3.0

Vertical rise: 140 feet

Maps: USGS 7½' Yellowstone Lake, Wisconsin; DeLorme Wisconsin Atlas & Gazetteer: p. 26 (B-4)

Wisconsin is home to nearly nine thousand lakes. Of these, very few are human-made, but Yellowstone Lake is one of them. Known as the Driftless Area due to the lack of glaciation, southwest Wisconsin didn't receive the meltwater that formed the glacial lakes of the northern part of the state. So the 455-acre Yellowstone Lake was built in 1949. Today, after winding down into the Yellowstone River Valley, you are greeted by a wooded lakeshore surrounding a glassy body of water. The scene is so reminiscent of the northwoods that if you were taken blindfolded to the shore and left to smell the oddly abundant white pine in the air before taking a look, you'd never know you were deep in southwest Wisconsin.

Also unique are some of Yellowstone's summer residents. The 968-acre park is blessed by a uniquely high concentration of winged mammals: bats. Consequently, there is a noticeably low concentration of Wisconsin's state bird: mosquitoes! As the result of a project started in 1995, 31 bat houses now serve as the summer residences for over 4,000 brown bats that seek to decimate the park's population of mosquitoes.

Since Yellowstone is such a popular park for water recreation, the many very good hiking and biking trails here get relatively less attention. The hiking is mostly suited to experienced hikers or those of a moderate ability level. But, there are some short loops offering easy hiking for beginners and children. Thus, Yellowstone Lake

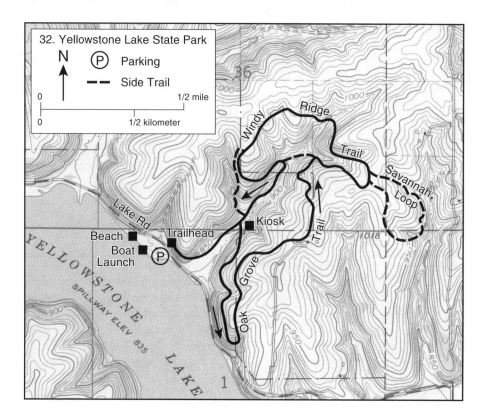

32. Yellowstone Lake State Park

N

Ⓟ Parking

– – Side Trail

0   1/2 mile

0   1/2 kilometer

Windy Ridge Trail

Savannah Loop

Lake Rd.

Kiosk

Beach

Boat Launch

Trailhead

Oak Grove Trail

YELLOWSTONE LAKE

SPILLWAY ELEV. 835

State Park makes a great destination for a day's worth of hiking, skiing, swimming, fishing, or for a weekend camping trip.

How to Get There

From Madison (and most points north, northwest, and east), take US 18/151 past Verona and toward Mount Horeb—about 25 miles or a half hour. Take the WI 78 exit and turn left, heading south toward Blanchardville, about 17 miles. In Blanchardville take a right on County Route F (don't take the first one; wait until you've gone through downtown). After about 8 miles you will begin a marked descent. Be ready for the turnoff to Yellowstone Lake, on the left toward the bottom of the hill. Take a left onto Lake Road or look for the large park sign. Overall it's about 45 miles from Madison and takes 55 to 60 minutes at a relaxed pace.

From the south or southeast, take WI 69 or WI 81 to Monroe, following WI 81 northwest toward Argyle. From Argyle, take County Route G about 8 miles to CR F. Take a right on CR F, and the park entrance will be about 2 miles on the right.

From the west, or from Dubuque, take US 151 to Belmont. Take CR G east out of Belmont about 19 miles to CR F. Take a left on CR F, and the park entrance is 2 miles on the right.

For more information, contact Yellowstone Lake State Park at 608-523-4427.

The Trail

Follow Lake Road past the park office to the large parking lot near the beach and boat launch. By parking on the left side of the road in the two adjacent lots, you'll be closer to the trailhead at trail's end.

This hike takes you along the Oak Grove/ Windy Ridge Loops. You'll undoubtedly notice that the trails' beginnings are not marked at all, and you'll be right. But, this is absolutely unlike what you find once on the trails themselves. There are easy-to-find and easy-to-read map kiosks at every single trail loop intersection, making it almost impossible to get lost.

From the parking area, hike south alongside Lake Road. The start of the Oak Grove Trail will be on the left side of the road about 100 yards from the lot. On the map, this is where the trail bends away from the lake from point A. After this, you're done with roads and you're off. Within the first few steps, the noise of boat motors seems to drift away, and you pass a wetland full of tall grasses. Take this trail to the first kiosk, point B, and turn right, heading straight up a very steep, 0.25-mile ascent built to take out the hiking kinks. As you crest the steepest part and get closer to the hairpin turn, some gnarly, old-growth burr oaks welcome you. Don't be surprised to scare up some wild turkeys munching on acorns under these woody giants.

The trail will continue along the side of this large ridge. At the top, a good view of the lake offers a nice break before heading on. You'll pass a trail connector with the Blue Ridge Trail; veer left and continue on the Oak Grove Trail. You'll make a descent into a valley with a curious mixture of old-growth oaks within a few feet of a stand of towering white pines. Hang a right and head right between them, onto the Windy Ridge Trail and up a challenging, sun-exposed hill. Add the Savannah Loop if you want, but it is very exposed, and the

Shooting star, Yellowstone Lake State Park

rough-cut, tall grass is hard to hike. Instead, veer left on the Windy Ridge, where a big oak welcomes you back to the woods and offers a nice spot to take a rest.

But don't get too used to it. While the woods provide some good shade for a few steps, you'll emerge from them to look down at a long descent out into open prairie. In the spring and summer, this area is covered on both sides by a sea of shooting stars. Continue around the valley to the other side. At the end will be nothing but woods. You'll come to a merging of trails. Take a left and head down a long and welcome descent to point C. Take a right at the bottom of the hill and head into a cool, marshy valley, with limestone outcroppings covered in trees that seemingly defy gravity by growing out of the rock. Continue past point B and head straight back to where you started at the park road.

Yellowstone Lake State Park is a great destination for a day's worth of pretty challenging hiking in one of the most scenic areas of the state. Close to the historic towns of Mineral Point, Monroe, Dodgeville, New Glarus, and Mount Horeb, there are all sorts of lodging, shopping and dining opportunities nearby, too.

33

Indian Lake County Park

Total distance: 4.5 miles

Hiking time: 1 hour, 15 minutes to 1 hour, 45 minutes

Difficulty: 3.5

Vertical rise: 200 feet

Map: USGS 7½' Black Earth, Wisconsin and Springfield Corners, Wisconsin; DeLorme Wisconsin Atlas & Gazetteer, p. 35 (C-6)

Aside from birds singing, leaves rustling, snow crunching, or wind whispering, Indian Lake is a pretty quiet place. It is this serenity, and an abundance of excellent trails, that keeps regulars coming back. This park is strangely overlooked, especially considering it is reachable in minutes from Madison. Several nearby state parks undoubtedly overshadow it. And, even though the parking lot may be partly full of cars upon arrival, we seldom see people on the trails.

Like the venues of many hikes in this book, Indian Lake is also a remnant of the most recent Ice Age—both its water and its hills are the result. It isn't too far from here that the glacier stopped. So, hiking these lushly wooded hillsides, amidst picture-postcard Wisconsin farmland, is like hiking along the final scoopful of glacial terrain. In fact, some trails—including this one—share their routes with the famous Ice Age Trail.

This is definitely a peaceful place worth visiting every season of the year. Whether you're rustling through crunchy fall leaves, gliding along freshly fallen snow, or ambling through a phlox-covered prairie, Indian Lake serves as a sort of publicly owned country retreat.

This hike takes you deep into the heart of the hardwoods and prairie before looping back to the parking area. From here you can add a short (1 mile round trip) hike to the small chapel built atop the bluff overlooking the parking area. No matter what your spiritual side favors, you will undoubtedly be amazed that a German immigrant and his son carted thousands of pounds of stone

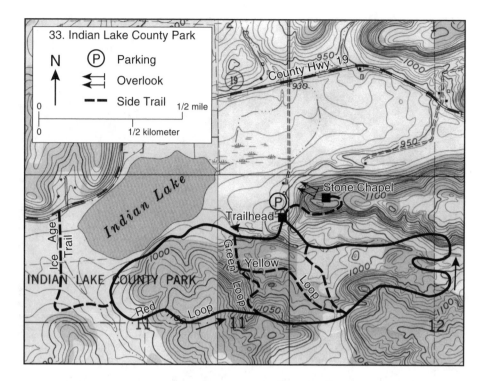

33. Indian Lake County Park

N

(P) Parking

Overlook

- - - Side Trail

0 ..... 1/2 mile

0 ..... 1/2 kilometer

County Hwy. 19

Indian Lake

Ice Age Trail

INDIAN LAKE COUNTY PARK

Stone Chapel

Trailhead

Green Loop

Yellow Loop

Red Loop

up the hill to build this chapel. Also breathtaking is the view from this hilltop, which overlooks Indian Lake to the northeast and is worth the trek up in any season.

How to Get There

From Madison, take US 12 west about 10 miles to WI 19 west. Take a left (west) on WI 19 and follow it to the park entrance about 2 miles on the left.

From the west, take US 14 east out of Mazomanie about 1 mile to WI 78. Take a left on WI 78 (north) to WI 19, about 1 mile. Take a right on WI 19 and follow it for about 8 miles to the park entrance on the right. (The first park entrance is the dog park and boat launch; take the second main entrance.)

From the north, take US 12 east out of Sauk City about 10 miles to WI 19. Turn right (west) on WI 19 and take it for about 2 miles. The park entrance will be on the left.

For more information, contact Dane County Parks at 608-246-3896.

The Trail

The Red Loop trailhead is located up the hill at the south end of the main parking area. Undoubtedly, there will not be any trail maps available, but there is usually a laminated map affixed to the kiosk. The trails themselves are extremely well marked by color-coded blazes and with signs.

Follow the Red Trail right (west) out of the parking area. The trail itself is wide, the sign of a good Nordic trail, and makes for good side-by-side hiking with a companion. The rolling hike meanders through mixed hardwoods, with a stand of huge hickories, white ashes, and cottonwoods ushering you along.

Trail at Indian Lake

You will wander along the southern shore of Indian Lake, passing a peaceful bench and overlook at one point before turning more southwest. The trail will lead you out of the woods and uphill into a grassy meadow, following the path of the Ice Age Trail. The Ice Age will veer off to the right (west) while you will continue on the Red Loop south along the western edge of the prairie, through a valley.

The trail will take a dramatic turn eastward and upward from here. You will be faced by a very strenuous uphill, difficult both for its vertical rise and its footing. The surface is basically a layer of loose rocks ranging from golf ball to softball size, making the footing very slippery. It's a long hill, too, so by the time you make it to the top you've earned a break.

From here you will follow the trail along the southern edge of the park and along the crest of the hill that borders the lake on this side. Here the trail is heavily wooded again, and you will be engulfed by towering shagbark hickories and cherry trees along this stretch. Don't be at all surprised to spook a deer or flock of turkeys that are dining in this woodland cafeteria.

Along this stretch you will converge with the Green and Yellow Loops. Just after joining the Yellow, the Red will turn off to the right (east) and make another assault on a large uphill stretch. Definitely less strenuous than the first, this climb is still pretty taxing. But you'll arrive high atop a ridge before beginning a long downhill into a deep valley on the eastern edge of the park. The trail will buttonhook to the east and then to the west, taking you out of the woods.

The woodland landscape changes quickly as you turn left (west) and pop out into an open prairie. In the summer, this area is covered in monarch-friendly milkweed.

The trail will pass below a warming house for skiers on the left. In the fall, the colorful trees blanket the edges of the amber prairie like a brilliant patchwork quilt. In the summer, this area is covered in wildflowers like phlox, Queen Anne's lace, and yarrow, and is bouncing with insects.

After passing below the warming house hill, you will duck back into the woods once again. A short climb back into the open will bring you through a service road gate and back to the grassy picnic area next to the parking lot where you began. To add the hike up to the chapel and lake overlook, stay right and head over to the large sign explaining the chapel's history and the trailhead for the Chapel Trail. Head straight up the hill and past that same service road. You'll pass a rare apple tree and begin to see more evergreens. The trail will zigzag up the side of this hill as you climb up several riser steps, and even a boardwalk of steps, on your way up.

The trail emerges just south of the chapel and you wind your way over to it through woodland plants. A very serene place, the chapel is open for visitors and is almost eerily amazing. Off to the right, (north), the trail dead-ends out of the woods and atop a remarkable bluff overlooking the lake bordered by thick deciduous forestland on either side of the valley. The ascent and descent are quick but challenging, and add a nice conclusion to a 4.5-mile hike.

Indian Lake County Park is a hiker's and skier's paradise. The trails are exceptionally well maintained, and there is good variety. The topography and range of vegetation are welcoming for human visitors as well as a large selection of migrating birds and mammals. Few places can be soundly and definitively characterized as serene, but this place is.

34

UW Madison Arboretum

Total distance: 3.0 miles (4.0 with Leopold Pines Loop)

Hiking time: 1 hour to 1 hour, 45 minutes

Difficulty: 2.0

Vertical rise: Minimal

Maps: USGS 7½' Madison West, Wisconsin; DeLorme Wisconsin Atlas & Gazetteer, p. 36 (D-1)

Aldo Leopold, in his seminal text on modern conservation, *A Sand County Almanac,* discusses his curious relationship with trees. In the chapter titled "Axe in Hand" Leopold talks about how, when given the choice, his axe falls first on the birch rather than the pine. Through a couple of pages he hems and haws over the reason for this and concludes by giving an uncharacteristically simple answer: "The only conclusion I have ever reached is that I love all trees, but I am in love with pines."

How appropriate, then, that in a few acres at the southwest corner of the University of Wisconsin Madison Arboretum is a stand of red and white pines, planted in the 1930s and called the Leopold Pines. These conifers are now rare giants and stand as living testimonials and fruits of the labors of the science of ecological restoration, a sort of hodgepodge of natural and social sciences coalescing and working toward the goal of helping a landscape heal and return to a more natural state.

When people like Leopold, landscaper G. William Longnecker, and botanist Norman Fassett first encountered the area that is now the Arboretum, it was a vast, barren landscape of cultivated fields and pastureland. It was the ideal place to initiate a wide-scale restoration effort and multiple scientific studies—studies that include nearly 200 scientific papers and are still ongoing. In fact, the 60-year-old Curtis Prairie, named for John Curtis, a pioneer in the use of fire as a restoration tool, is the oldest

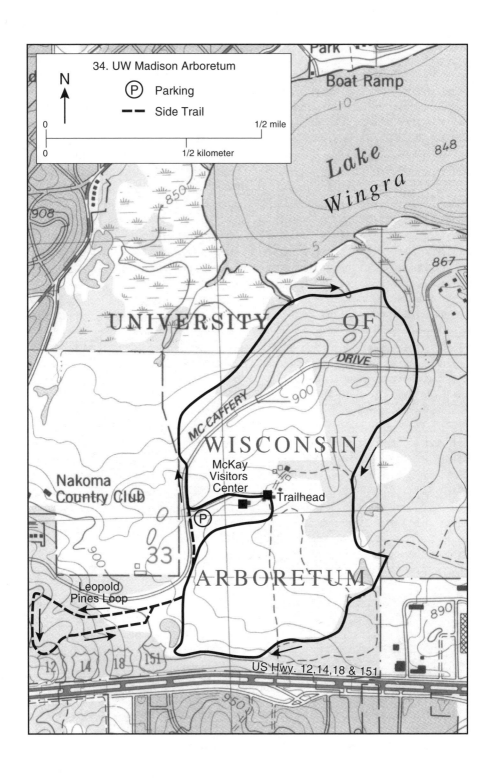

N

(P) Parking

- - - Side Trail

0   1/2 mile

0   1/2 kilometer

Park

Boat Ramp

10

848

Lake

Wingra

5

867

850

908

UNIVERSITY   OF

DRIVE

900

MC CAFFERY

WISCONSIN

McKay
Visitors
Center

Trailhead

Nakoma
Country Club

(P)

900

33

ARBORETUM

890

Leopold
Pines Loop

12 14 18 151

US Hwy. 12,14,18 & 151

950

and possibly the most important restored tallgrass prairie in the world.

But even with all this science going on, the place doesn't feel exclusive at all. On the contrary, involving the public in restoration efforts is part of the Arboretum's mission. With over a thousand acres, and 20 miles of hiking and skiing trails, visitors are encouraged to glide between those towering pines in the winter and hike amidst swaying grasses in the fall, or catch a glimpse of a rare songbird migrating through in the spring. Anchored at a state-of-the-art visitors center, there are also nature hikes and educational opportunities sponsored by Arboretum staff almost every week of the year.

While the founders of the Arboretum probably had no idea that this exceptional natural area, used and loved by the public, would be the result of their early efforts, they undoubtedly rest easy knowing that foxes and deer make their homes here, big bluestem grasses send their roots several feet into that old farm field, the science still goes on, and that the public is a part of it.

This trail, the Wingra Woods/Curtis Prairie Loop, gives you a good introduction to the Arboretum by taking you through mixed hardwoods, past a wetland and pond area, out into the Curtis Prairie, and over to the Leopold Pines. It is sort of a compendium of trails, but since this hike stays mainly on access roads (narrow, ATV-type trails) you are more likely to find them open all year, and this tends to be where the best skiing is in the winter, too. A fairly level trail, with few ascents of note, this hike is doable with children, but it can get long and hot on a sunny summer day. But there are several offshoot trails to get you back to the visitors center parking lot quickly if need be.

How to Get There

From the east, take US 12/18 (also called the Beltline) west to the Seminole Highway exit. Turn right and go about 0.5 mile to Arboretum Drive at the bottom of the hill. Turn right and follow this about 0.75 mile to the McKay Visitors Center parking lot.

From the west, take US 12/18 east to the Fish Hatchery Road exit, heading north. (This is a bit tricky—you need to be in the far right lane, and go under the Fish Hatchery Road bridge before taking the cloverleaf to the right. Watch for people exiting from the right.) Stay on Fish Hatchery Road for about 1 mile to Wingra Drive. Take a left on Wingra Drive and follow it about 0.5 mile to Arboretum Drive. Take a left and follow this 2.4 miles to the McKay Visitors Center parking lot.

From the UW Madison campus, take Mills Street from University Avenue 1.1 miles to Arboretum Drive (this is at the intersection of Mills, Wingra, and Arboretum Drive). Take a right on Arboretum Drive and go 2.4 miles to the McKay Visitors Center parking lot.

Note: Arboretum Drive is only a through street on Sundays. Otherwise, depending on whether you come from the west or east entrance, you will park on either side of the gate located between the two parking lots at the visitors center.

For more information, contact the University of Wisconsin Arboretum at 608-263-7888 or on the web at www.wisc.edu/arboretum/.

The Trail

To get to the trailhead, go out to Arboretum Drive from the north parking lot, between the Nakoma Golf Course and Longnecker Gardens. Follow the road for about 200 yards to the trailhead on the left side of the road. The trail will head into the woods along the golf course, before turning northeast into an open, grassy area and toward Lake Wingra. The trail will head back into the woods, Wingra Woods, toward Big

Spring, a bubbling freshwater spring supplying the lake. In the winter, this area can be brilliant green with watercress.

Continue along the trail amidst tall oak, maple, birch, and beech. Turn right at the K4 intersection (look for the small post) and head past the hemlocks, unusual in southern Wisconsin, and up this northern slope. You will pass a bench, a good spot for a water break and to enjoy the woods. Continue along this trail and to the road, where it will cross diagonally to the continuation of the trail across the road.

From here, you will head southwest, through Gallistel Woods, a large tract of oak with some maple and birch that have been planted. In this area, the trail will pass by the old stone shelter build by the Civilian Conservation Corps in the 1930s. You will also pass a few trail intersections, but ignore these and continue along this main trail until you come to the F6 intersection. Turn left and head past several large birch trees and past Teal Pond (a small offshoot trail takes you to it).

The trail will turn southeast for a bit before coming to an intersection. Turn right at L3, heading past another pond with a boardwalk loop. At the southern tip of the pond, you will cross a cement culvert and pass the intersection of L1. Stay on the main trail, heading west toward Curtis Prairie, visible in the distance. At the prairie, turn left at A8, which takes you along the southern edge and past a mixture of hardwoods and some older pines. Afternoon hikes in the summer are pretty well shaded in this area.

The enormous prairie is off to the north, a sea of grasses buzzing with all sorts of bird, insect, reptile, and amphibian life, not to mention the flowering prairie plants in the spring and summer. This prairie offers terrific cover to a large urban deer population, as well as foxes, owls, and hawks in search of all sorts of small mammals. As you hike along this prairie, you will be looking out at one of the rarest restored prairies in the world, which is probably why you came.

Soon you will come to another turnoff at B8. (Going straight wasn't even an option in 2003, due to timber thinning up ahead.) But this is a great place to turn, since it takes you around the pond and atop a small rise on the pond bank. This ascent gives you an even better look out on the prairie, perfect for birding and a good place to see waterfowl in the fall and spring. The trail will head over to an intersection (B3) with the main trail on the north side of the prairie at the intersection. From here you can head back to the visitors center to the right, making for about a 1-hour hike, close to 3 miles.

Otherwise, turn left at B3 and loop through the Noe Woods, a 41-acre oak woods, and back through the Leopold Pines. To do this, simply head to the E5 intersection and loop through Noe Woods to E8. Stay straight at this intersection and head back through the Leopold Pines past D7 and D8, where you'll emerge at the edge of the prairie at C4. Then head straight to C2, and left straight through the prairie to C1. Take a right and head back to the McKay Center. This will add another half hour to 45 minutes and about 1 mile.

35

UW Madison Picnic Point

Total distance: 2.2 miles

Hiking time: 45 minutes to 1 hour, 15 minutes

Difficulty: 1.5

Vertical rise: Minimal

Maps: USGS 7½' Madison West, Wisconsin; DeLorme Wisconsin Atlas & Gazetteer, p. 36 (D-1)

The perfect place on earth? This is the running question that surrounds Madison. It is for this reason that people come here, never to leave again. Thousands, if not tens of thousands, of residents have attained advanced degrees at the university only to become massage therapists, dog groomers, taxi drivers, and "consultants."

They probably showed up on campus some fall day, only to wind along Observatory Drive and up the steep hill to the namesake observatory high above Lake Mendota to see a multicolored peninsula sticking out into the glistening water below. They probably drove down the road until coming to a stone wall and gate, the entrance to that peninsula, called Picnic Point. After they hopped out of their cars, a warm, earthy smell of autumn and the sounds of waterfowl chattering away in the nearby marsh engulfed them. And soon after, they were dropping their classes and leaving theses unfinished because they just wanted to hike, canoe, kayak, and bike in peace.

And peace is what you will find at Picnic Point. While open to the public, the Point, as it's called around here, was once a wedding gift from a Madison man to his new bride. They built a house and are responsible for the large stone wall at the entrance. After a house fire, they moved to nearby Shorewood Hills and, by some incredible stroke of luck for the rest of us, sold the property to the University of Wisconsin. While an exceptionally popular place, the Point's trails are lightly traveled. People come here for the serenity and the scenery.

You'll find people reading, bird-watching, swimming, picnicking, canoeing, fishing, jogging, and strolling. On weekday afternoons in the fall, you'll even hear the sounds of the university marching band wafting through the air from a nearby athletic field.

Thus this is the Point, the peninsula that sticks straight out into Lake Mendota, the biggest of the Madison lakes, offering woodland and marshland habitats full of oaks, hickories, cottonwoods, cattails, and more. Sure, the ecologists who study this place will grumble about pesky honeysuckle, the lack of a diverse population of woodland plants, and receding shorelines. But nobody's perfect.

This hike takes you from the stone wall out to the tip of the point, offering a southern view over University Bay, the university, and downtown Madison across the way. There are several picnic areas along the trail where you can stop for lunch or simply sit and relax. The tip of the Point is located atop a high, narrow hill, about 20 feet above the shoreline. From here the trail doubles back about 0.125 mile before ducking along the north shore between the lake and a marsh. This side of the peninsula is known for its sandy shores and swimming, and is pretty popular in the warmer months. The trail then heads between an old beach house and the shore of the lake in the Caretakers Woods, before winding back south down to the parking lot.

How to Get There
From the east, take University Avenue to the Babcock Drive exit on the right. Take Babcock to Observatory Drive. Turn left on Observatory and follow it 0.7 mile to Walnut Street. Turn right and follow Walnut 0.3 mile to University Bay Drive. Turn right and follow this 0.3 mile to the parking area and

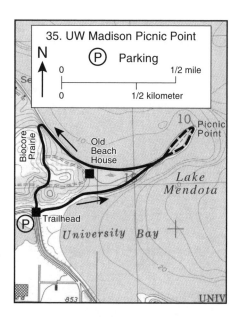

entrance on the right. Be careful as you cross the pedestrian and bike path.

From the west, take University Avenue to University Bay Drive. Turn left and follow it 1.2 miles (turning left at the top of the hill) to the parking lot on the left.

For more information, contact the University of Wisconsin Campus Natural Areas at 608-265-9275 or on the web at www.ies.wisc.edu/cna/ or Friends of the Campus Natural Areas at www.uwalumni.com/fcna/index.html.

The Trail
The wide gravel and packed-sand trail begins at the gate. Stay straight to do a counterclockwise loop, which offers better views across the lake at the outset. On your left will be an open grassy area for a while, but the trail will soon be surrounded and covered by large hardwoods. The trail is just inside the wooded banks of Lake Mendota, making the water hard to see at times. But there will be several openings further up the trail.

You will begin to pass the many picnic areas with fire pits along the trail. These are very popular in the warmer months. The trail will pass a couple of intersections with other trails, but stay on the main trail, keeping to the right when in doubt. You will make a slight ascent before coming downhill to the narrow (only a few yards wide) isthmus that connects the main peninsula to the tip of the point. There is a small beach here that is very popular in the summer. From here, you'll climb uphill again for 20 or 30 steps, before leveling off above the water. There is a hand pump out here in case you've forgotten your water or need a refill.

As you get closer to the tip, you will come to a place where the main trail goes straight ahead, while another trail shoots off to the right along the shore. Take this wood-chipped trail to the right, which takes you along the tree-lined shoreline of the point. From here, you will emerge at the tip, where there is another fire ring and a bench, as well as several trails that lead to the water. This really isn't the most scenic part of the peninsula, due to all the trees, so if you're considering having lunch, you may want to pick a spot on the way back.

Turning around, there is another side trail on the north shore that will lead to where you split from the main trail, or you can simply take the main trail back. Either way, head back past the pump and downhill to the beach. From here, don't head up the hill on the main trail. Instead, veer right and take the trail along the north shore of the lake, just on the other side of the lifeguard stand. This rather sandy trail takes you past some huge, towering cottonwoods and along the very sandy north shore to the old beach house. Once there, stay between the beach house and the lake, continuing on the footpath. The trail will get narrower now, and the footing gets a bit more difficult than on the wide main trail. But this is a great section of trail through the Caretaker's Woods. You will climb up away from the lake a bit as you get up on a ridge above the water. In the fall, a blanket of yellow maple leaves covers these woods in almost a neon brightness.

From here, you will emerge at the Biocore Prairie, a restoration project and part of the university's biology education program. Take a left and head south, where you will come to the intersection of two old roads. Stay straight, continuing south, and past the old orchard area on the left and into another woods full of large pines. At the next junction of roads, turn right and follow this final road all the way down the hill toward the stone wall and back to the entrance gate.

This hike, while very short, is a must if you are visiting Madison or if you want a great view of the lakes. Also, the varied habits at the Point attract a great diversity of migrating birds in the spring and fall, making this a very good birding spot.

36

Cherokee Marsh

Total distance: 2.5 miles

Hiking time: 1 hour to 1 hour, 30 minutes

Difficulty: 2.0

Vertical rise: Minimal

Map: USGS 7½' DeForest, Wisconsin; DeLorme Wisconsin Atlas & Gazetteer, p. 36 (C-2)

Madison is famous—and infamous—for its lakes. In a sort of love/hate relationship, citizens get the beautiful views, the dreamy sound of waves, and cool lake breezes in the summer. The only problem has been that those same breezes are accompanied by the distinct smell of algae. For decades these lakes have bloomed with algae due to the influx of fertilizer from farm runoff, in addition to the runoff of lawn products. The net result is lakes that are crystal clear and aroma free for about two weeks in March after the ice melts. After that, the algae is off and growing like wildfire.

To the city's credit, a lot has been done and plans are always in the works for how to deal with this stinky situation. But, nothing will compare to what was done in the 1960s with the purchase of a 1,000-acre wetland on the north side of town that served as the eventual impetus for a conservation park system. Cherokee Marsh borders the banks of the Yahara River, the waterway that connects all the Madison area lakes. Located at the headwaters of these lakes, the marsh has a great impact on what goes on down below. Like an enormous filter or sponge, the marsh's sedge mats suck in and cleanse water before releasing it downstream and into the lakes.

And this marsh is big. Standing atop a hill in the middle of park leaves you looking out across a vast landscape of marsh grasses and cattails. In the fall, the hardwoods are blooming with deep reds and oranges, and the skies are singing with the

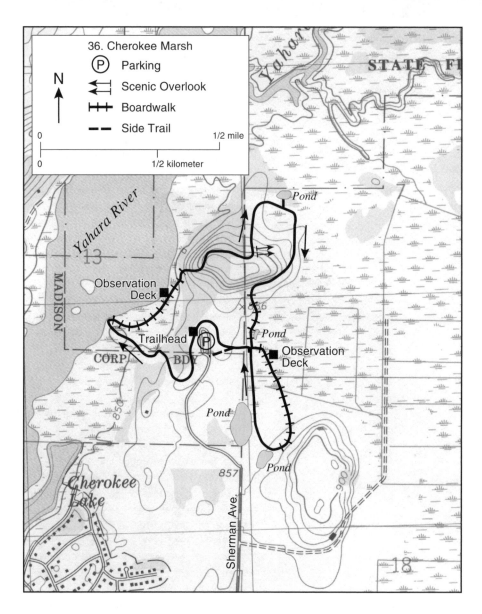

calls of ducks, geese, herons, and sandhill cranes. It is truly a beautiful urban retreat, only miles from downtown Madison, and its trails and boardwalks serve as a great way to get out and see a marsh in action.

This hike takes you from the parking area, through a large stand of hardwoods, and out to the river. Here you will leave turf behind as you hike along a boardwalk above the marsh and along the edge of the river. Back on the trail, you head up a fairly large hill, covered in hardwoods, before emerging on its open eastern crest, overlooking the marsh below—bordered by the state and interstate highways and the Dane County Airport. From here you loop away from the river and through the marsh, passing a couple of ponds before returning to the parking area. Not a long trail, this hike is one of those destinations that you keep in the back of your mind as a place to visit on your way through town or on a lazy weekend. Because it's not too tough, it's a great place to bring kids for the day and to expose them to the wonders of a marsh. Be careful on the boardwalks, however—a fall from one would not be pleasant.

How to Get There

From the north, south, or east take I-90/94 to the Waunakee/Sun Prairie exit, WI 19 toward Waunakee. Go 3.5 miles on WI 19 to WI 113. Turn left (south) on WI 113 (Be careful. This is a tricky intersection.) Take WI 113 for about 5 miles to Sherman Avenue. Turn left (north) on Sherman, and go 2.7 miles to the Cherokee Marsh parking lot at the end of the gravel drive.

From inside Madison, take Northport Drive to Sherman Avenue. Turn right on Sherman, and go 2.7 miles to the Cherokee Marsh parking lot at the end of the gravel drive.

For more information, contact the City of Madison Parks Department at 608-266-4711 or at www.ci.madison.wi.us/parks/.

The Trail

We suggest doing this hike clockwise. From the parking area, an access trail runs along the western edge of the lot and leads south out toward the prairie you drove through on the way in. It passes by some aspens before turning northwest and into the woods. The trail makes a descent and takes you to a park access road. Turn left on the road and take it to the where the trail resumes about 20 yards down. The trail then heads to the right (west), through a large hickory stand, to the edge of the Yahara River.

From here, you will turn up to the north along an old, gray but sturdy boardwalk. Pay attention to your feet though, because a misstep could leave you wet and probably injured. This is a great place to see wildlife, and the view of the wetlands is incredible. On a fall day, with the hardwoods along the shore in full color, this area is one of the best spots around. In fact, it's hard to believe you're in town.

The boardwalk leads you to an observation deck on the edge of the woods, which makes for a good spot to have lunch and relax while watching wildlife or shooting photos. From here, the trail will meet back up with the access road, where you will take it to the left for a few steps before resuming the trail on the right. The only real climb of note lies ahead of you, as you hike up a hill covered with oaks and hickories toward the overlook. You'll emerge from the woods atop the hill, where there is a bench on a cement pad.

Take the offshoot trail to the left (north) down toward the small pond below. The trail will leave the woods at the foot of the hill, and you will begin a long, exposed loop on the edge of the marsh. Prairie fills in from the marsh back up to the woods, so the area is alive with bugs and birds, and don't be surprised to scare up a deer down in this area. You can also take the short offshoot trail to the pond off to the north, which is usually alive with frogs.

The trail will loop south and pass an intersection with a trail that heads down from the overlook to the east. Pass this and head westward. Then take the trail south, where you will pass another trail intersection. Go past this trail and stay left, passing a small pond on the left. (A small boardwalk takes

Cherokee Marsh

you past the pond.) You will then come to a four-way intersection. Take the trail to the left to do a loop that will bring you back on the trail straight ahead. You will hike out onto the marsh again along a long boardwalk. Another observation deck is located out here as well. You'll leave the boardwalk at the southern tip of the loop and turn back north, away from a small pond, before passing a larger pond and an observation platform, which is used for the hundreds of school groups that come each year to Cherokee.

Soon you will arrive back at that four-way intersection. Turn left (west), and the trail will take you back toward the parking lot. An offshoot trail will go directly to the road; otherwise, turn north at this bend in the trail and you will head up to the parking lot trailhead area where you started.

Definitely a great trail system anytime of the year, Cherokee Marsh is the crown jewel of the Madison Park System and is well worth a visit to see a living sponge at work.

37

Magnolia Bluff County Park

Total distance: 2.9 miles

Hiking time: 1 hour, 15 minutes to 1 hour, 45 minutes

Difficulty: 3.0

Vertical rise: 145 feet

Maps: USGS 7½' Orfordville, Wisconsin; DeLorme Wisconsin Atlas & Gazetteer, p. 28 (C-2)

Unless you live there, you are probably familiar with Rock County only through the lens of your car windshield while traveling the Interstate between Beloit and Janesville. But, when driving along this road, you are driving through a uniquely historic area, glacially speaking. It is here where the most recent Wisconsin glacier saw its southernmost advance. This area is now a wide-open landscape—basically a watershed full of fingerling creeks and rivers feeding into the Rock River, whose ultimate destination is the Mississippi.

While once home to ancient Native American peoples who roamed the area, Rock County is still a great place for hiking and exploring—Janesville itself hosts one of the few urban legs of the Ice Age Trail. But there also exists a tranquil, hidden county park whose sole purpose seems to be its excellent trails...and an incredible overlook atop a 50-foot bluff.

Magnolia Bluff is unique—so much so that it possesses its own climate. Due to the dramatic change in elevation between the north and south sides of the bluff, a microclimate exists. Within this zone is the only naturally occurring stand of white birch in the county.

Unique, too, is that this park is less than a half hour's drive away from one of the most populated areas of the state. This trail would serve very well for those training for a backpacking trip. Its challenging terrain and varied woodland plants and trees make Magnolia Bluff County Park a worthwhile day trip.

How to Get There

From the north or east, take WI 213 south out of Evansville about 2.5 miles to WI 59. Take

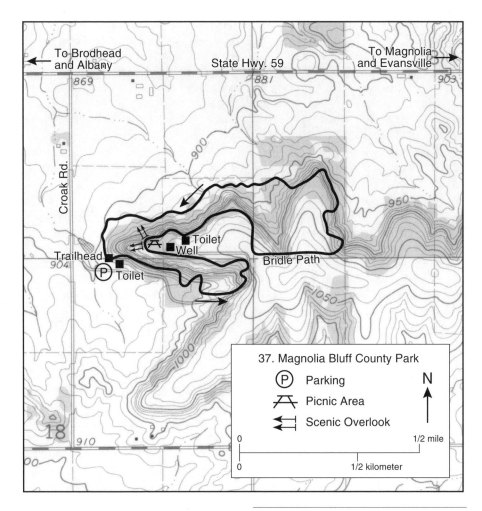

37. Magnolia Bluff County Park

(P) Parking
🛆 Picnic Area
◁— Scenic Overlook

N

0   1/2 mile
0   1/2 kilometer

WI 59 right (west) 3 miles to Croak Road. Take a left on Croak Road, and the park entrance will be about 0.5 mile on the left.

From the south or southwest, take WI 104 north out of Brodhead. After about 6 miles, it will merge with WI 59. Take the next right (east) on Finneran Road and the next left (north) on Croak Road. The park entrance will be 0.5 mile on the right.

From the west, take WI 59 out of Albany 3.5 miles to Finneran Road. Follow the above directions from Finneran.

For more information, contact the Rock County Parks Division at 608-757-5450.

The Trail

A 3-mile trail in the middle of a Wisconsin farming county seems like a piece of cake, especially after parking and looking around at the homey, well-kept park setting at the trailhead. But this trail challenges hikers with both length and tricky footing.

The trail begins by making an immediate climb eastward up the side of the huge sandstone bluff that is Magnolia. On fall and winter days, much of the rock will be visible. Sandy soil, a by-product of the broken-down rock, makes for challenging footing as you meander upward through mixed hardwoods and among woodland plants. A slight descent and a turn of the trail to the right will eventually lead to a pretty tricky climb through a rocky outwash with exposed roots—making the idea of skiing up this section seem comical. But, once up, the trail will hairpin to the left and traverse westward above the bluff you passed at the beginning. The views southwest over Rock and Green Counties are now barely visible through the trees. Especially in the summer, this area greets you with sun and makes for a pretty tough bit of hiking after that climb. But, the jewel of the park awaits and is a perfect place for a break.

The trail emerges from the woods and into the upper parking and picnic area, and beautiful trees. Like giant stewards of the bluff, a grove of oaks awaits you and escorts you to the bluff's edge. Their shade and picnic tables make for a good water break and an opportunity to take a picture. On a clear day, the view extends for several miles, with much of Green County (Wisconsin's Switzerland) lying sleepily below like an emerald carpet in the summer and a multicolored patchwork quilt in the fall.

With your back to the bluff, the trail continues just to the left of the closest oak tree. It skirts the edge of the north side of the bluff, back into the cool woods. After meandering along this trail, overlooking a large dropoff to the left, the trail will merge for the first time with the bridle path. *Note:* Hikers should always yield the trail to horses by stepping off to the side and allowing the riders to pass. The signs, direct you to continue straight and follow the trail around to the beginning of the bridle path, making a sharp left turn (east), past the first sizable birch stand and a gnarly, twisted oak. Just beyond this area, the trail will descend, and you again pass a trail junction. Stay on the Long Route and continue hiking straight past a large stand of white pines on the left and a farm field on the right. The trail will make a steep descent into the woods, where the footing gets a bit tricky due to the shared access with horses.

Greeting you after the next ascent is yet another habitat. A large prairie emerges on the left for a few hundred yards, before the trail meets with a large stand of birch and aspen and ducks into the woods again. From here the trail leads to the northeast corner of the park and the site of the horse hitching area. This corner makes for a good water/snack break before making the final push. Study your map and be ready for the only slightly tricky area of trail coming up. Note where the equestrian trail will make a hairpin turn to the right and head back to the hitching post area, while the hiking trail cuts right across the hairpin and heads northwest, straight down into the north valley.

This last stretch of trail gets extremely sandy, demanding a heads-down hiking approach. Follow the signs until the last junction of the hiking trail with the horse trail. Be careful. While not marked on the paper maps available at the trailhead, the trail marker actually points left (south) for hiking/skiing, and straight (west) for horses/hiking. You want the left turn. The trail will now be at the foot of the bluff, offering good views of the rock in the fall and winter. After skirting along this western edge, you will quickly see the parking lot and you will pop out into the grassy park area.

The Magnolia Bluff trail is much more challenging than it looks. The views and the varied terrain make this trail a great find in southwestern Wisconsin and the hidden jewel of the Rock County park system.

IV

Southeast Hikes

38

Ice Age Trail, Waupaca/Portage

Total distance: 1.75 miles

Hiking time: 45 minutes to 1 hour, 15 minutes

Difficulty: 2.0

Vertical rise: Minimal

Maps: USGS 7½' Blaine, Wisconsin and King, Wisconsin; DeLorme Wisconsin Atlas & Gazetteer, p. 53 (B-6)

Toward the end of this hike, the trail crosses Emmons Creek for a second time. The area is almost like a fairy tale scene. The crystal clear creek glistens, probably full of trout, the banks are covered with grasses and flowers, and cool trees overhead provide shade like umbrellas. Just before the bridge, off to the left, there's even a small bench. A Leopold bench! Named for its creator and the father of modern conservation, Aldo Leopold, this style of bench is a simple, six-board structure designed for leaning back and contemplating things. No Leopold bench should ever be finished, stained, or painted, and this one isn't. They're meant to season, age, rot, and crumble back into the earth from which they came. It's the kind of cyclic thinking that the prescient Leopold understood and embraced long before terms like "ecology" and "environment" and "organic" were tossed around like salads.

On the back of this bench, sitting appropriately on the bank of Emmons Creek, is Leopold's name and his life-span, 1887–1948. You can just imagine him sitting there, thinking thoughts few of us can think and seeing things most of us overlook. His gaze into the natural world was so deep that, without him, we may not be hiking on this trail today. He pleaded with us to consider developing an ethic, to embrace nature as a higher power to which we are beholden and would never seek to harness and hurt. While many people may not know who Leopold was, they now think some of his thoughts without even knowing it.

This little loop hike, part of the Ice Age Trail, takes you past an unassuming hayfield

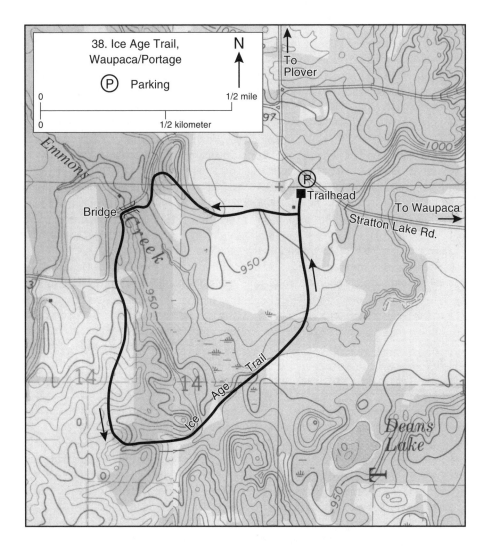

and deep into a woods on the shores of Emmons Creek. Two things will make you not want to hike this trail. The first may be its short distance. The second may be the hayfield. Don't let either discourage you. We think that the 1.7-mile reported length is probably a bit short, and the hayfield is much more monotonous than the rest of this beautiful hike. In fact, this trail meanders through what may be one of the most unique habitats found anywhere in the Upper Midwest. Shortly after crossing the

creek for the first time, you will look around to find yourself deep in the heart of an oak savannah, and not just a small one, either. This savannah will ramble on and on, giving you a rare glimpse at what Wisconsin may have looked like just as the French voyageurs were first hopping out of their canoes on the shores of Lake Michigan. No wonder Aldo's bench is here; he's probably resting there right now, not only thinking about the way it was, but contemplating how it is and how it could be still.

How to Get There

From the northeast, take WI 22 west out of Waupaca for 5 miles to Stratton Lake Road. Turn right (west) and go about 4 miles to the trailhead parking lot the left, just before the bend in the road.

From the northwest, take WI 54 east out of Plover 15.5 miles to County Route D. Turn right, south, on CR D and take it 3.5 miles to the junction with Stratton Lake Road. Continue straight on Stratton Lake Road for 1.1 miles to the trailhead parking lot on the right, just after the bend in the road.

From the south, take WI 22 east out of Wild Rose for 10.4 miles to Stratton Lake Road. Turn left and go about 4.0 miles to the trailhead parking lot on the left.

For more information, contact Hartman Creek State Park at 715-258-2372.

The Trail

From the parking lot, head south among some tall prairie grasses to the fork in the trail. The return trail, the Ice Age, will be on the left; stay to the right and do a counter-clockwise loop. The trail will head out into the open, so on a hot, sunny day this could be pretty warm. You'll head toward a tree line, around it, and then you'll turn northwest and up into a woods along a single-track trail.

This very nice woods is full of red and white pines overhead, a blanket of ferns underfoot, and an amazing abundance of poison ivy encroaching on the trail. If you're not certain what this plant looks like, you will after hiking this trail! For some reason it has spread like clover. At one point, it was the only plant we could find for several feet in every direction. We were glad for long pants and kept right on hiking.

Soon the trail will turn southwest along a road and head down toward the creek. You will actually need to hop out of the woods and cross the creek using the road bridge. Be careful on your way back into the woods on the other side, however. There are a lot of trails immediately next to the creek, probably from trout anglers; go about 20 steps up the road, and the continuation of the trail will be marked on the left.

Head south and past a large fern bed. The forest will begin to transform into more oaks as you hike, until you eventually emerge into a seemingly never-ending stand of oaks, with tufts of grass carpeting the ground. The surreal scene is magical, and is incredible in the fall when the oaks and grasses change color.

The trail will meander up and down these hills of oaks for quite a while. None of the hills are too taxing, yet on a hot day you'll want to make a couple of water breaks. Eventually, the trail will lead you down into a sandy valley with fewer oaks and some random pines. There are many more wildflowers here, too. Soon you will meet up with the Ice Age Trail, coming in from the right (south). You will join with it as you hike through a marshy area, over a series of boardwalks, and across the creek.

After crossing the bridge, you will emerge from the woods and out into a very impressive prairie, covered with black-eyed Susans in the summer. Also, look for flannel plant, yarrow, blue vervain, knapweed, and lots of milkweed dancing with monarch butterflies. Head north, past the prairie and the hayfield, back up to the parking area.

This great hike is a tranquil escape into a rare landscape, full of oaks. If you happen to hike with young people, remind them to come back in 50 years to see the stand of even bigger oaks growing on these hills alongside the Ice Age Trail. And remind them to see how Aldo's bench is holding up. It might be time for a new one.

39

High Cliff State Park

Total distance: 3.0 miles

Hiking time: 1 hour, 15 minutes to 1 hour, 45 minutes

Difficulty: 3.5

Vertical rise: 185 feet

Maps: USGS 7½' Sherwood, Wisconsin; DeLorme Wisconsin Atlas & Gazetteer, p. 55 (C-6)

A band of limestone stretches from Niagara Falls, New York all the way through the upper Great Lakes, to Door County and then south, eventually forming the eastern shore of Lake Winnebago. By a twist of geological fate, the Fox River Valley could have been more like Niagara Falls than you might think. This band of rock marks the sedimentary deposits of countless billions of calcium-rich organisms that died and layered, like calcium deposits in a teapot, the bottom of an ancient sea that covered much of North America—eventually forming limestone. To walk the bluffs at High Cliff is to hike over this sediment that was deposited millions of years ago.

Valued highly for its use as a building material, the lime was extracted as a powder by taking huge blocks of limestone and feeding it into a giant kiln. Exactly this type of operation once flourished at the foot of the cliff at High Cliff State Park. Imagine taking huge chunks, several tons each, out of a quarry a thousand feet above water level and somehow negotiating them into the kilns below. Only the skeletons of these kilns remain, crumbling structures at the foot of High Cliff and the start of this trail.

But European settlers weren't the first visitors to this area, and other skeletons exist at High Cliff to mark their existence. In fact, there are mounds of them. Accessible as an offshoot of this hike are the Native American burial mounds found atop the cliff. Many of the mounds are marked by educational kiosks posted in front of them, allowing hikers to learn about the history of these remarkable burial structures.

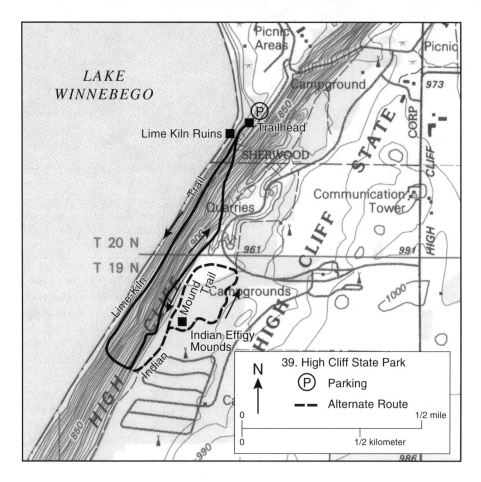

This fascinating area offers a look at how such different peoples utilized a distinct geological feature in such different ways, and how they left it. This hike takes you past the lime kilns and along the shores of Lake Winnebago before swooping straight uphill toward the foot of the cliff. From here you can climb some steps and add on the Indian Mound Loop (which offers views from atop the cliff), before heading back down the steps and meandering up and down along the foothills and valleys of the cliff. Definitely a taxing hike with some technical footwork—especially toward the end when your legs get rubbery—the trail is both level and wide along the shore and atop the cliff, but covered with roots, narrow, rocky, and slippery along the foothill section. Nonetheless, this hike is well worth the trip, and the Indian Mound Loop offers a unique opportunity to view and learn about mounds, and provides an outstanding view across Lake Winnebago from atop the cliff.

How to Get There

From the north, take WI 55 south from Kaukauna about 6 miles to Spring Hill Drive. Take it for 1 mile, turn left on State Park Road and go a half mile to the park entrance. To get to the trailhead parking area, go past main office and take a left at the stop sign. Just past the nature center/museum/general store, take a right into the long parking lot and park toward the end. The trailhead is next to the lime kilns.

From the south, take US 151 out of Fond du Lac for approximately 16 miles to WI 55. (WI 55 will stay north, while US 151 will head due east.) Take WI 55 for about 11.5 miles to Spring Hill Drive. Turn left on Spring Hill and follow it for 1.8 miles to State Park Road. From there, follow the directions above to the parking area.

From the west, take WI 114 from Menasha about 7 miles to State Park Road. Take a right on State Park Road and take it to the park entrance on the right, about 3 miles. From there, follow the directions above to the parking area.

From the east, take US 10 to WI 55 south. From here, follow the same directions as from the north above.

For more information, contact High Cliff State Park at 920-989-1106.

The Trail

The Lime Kiln/Indian Mound Loop begins by heading southwest out of the parking lot and past the old lime kiln ruins. Eventually, you will get to where the return loop meets with the trail. Stay to the right, along the shore of the lake, for a counterclockwise loop. The beginning stretch is mostly level with some rolling changes in elevation. If anything, you are descending a bit. Almost all of this hike is wooded, and you are greeted right away by a mixture of hardwoods, especially towering maples and elms. You will come to a shortcut trail to the left (southeast), but stay on the long loop section along the lake.

After passing a series of boardwalks, the trail will come to a turning point where there is a bench overlooking the lake. This makes

for a good resting stop before heading up the hill to the foot of the cliff above. While you may not be tired yet, this may be a good time to fuel up. Head straight up the hill, a pretty taxing climb among some monstrous old-growth cottonwood trees. Toward the top, the trail will bend a bit to the northeast, and this is where you veer to the right to access the Indian Mound Loop.

The trail will head up a rocky ascent and squeeze between the cliff wall on one side and a huge separate spire of limestone on the other. Steps will take you up the final 30 feet to the top of the cliff. Straight ahead will be the campground. Take a left (northeast) on the trail atop the cliff and hike about 100 yards to the beginning of the Indian Mound Loop. Turn right and hike this loop counterclockwise as well. This very tranquil area offers a pretty open forest floor, and you can easily see the mounds, despite the many shagbark hickories growing up here.

Follow the loop back around to where it will curve west past the upper parking lot and to the upper cliff trail. Take a left here and head southwest to where you came up the steps from the Lime Kiln Loop. This stretch will offer you all sorts of overlooks atop the cliff. Be very careful and stay on the trail. There are no protective barriers up here, and there is nothing but a sheer drop-off, close to 100 feet, between you and the ground below. You can see plenty from the trail, which makes venturing out onto the cliff unnecessary anyway. At the steps, hike back down to the original turnoff for the return of the Lime Kiln Loop. Take a right and head northeast.

From here the trail gets markedly more tricky and taxing. A series of valleys take you down and up several times, each climb seeming like the last. At one point, the trail will follow along a long boardwalk of steps downward, only to have you climb back up

High Cliff State Park

some more trail afterwards. The trail is pretty slick back in here due to the moisture that gets trapped between the lake and the cliff among all the trees. And, because the trail get narrower and overgrown with more vegetation, loose rocks and roots get tougher to see. But this is a great end to a hike with very diverse terrain and scenery. Eventually, the trail will ramble downhill one last time as you meet back up with the original trail, and you will head northeast, past the lime kiln ruins, and back to the parking lot.

This trail is definitely one worth visiting to see the westernmost extent of the geologically significant Niagara Escarpment. The views and the history of the area are both unique and exceptional and make for a great day's hike.

40

Point Beach State Forest

Total distance: 4.0 miles

Hiking time: 1 hour, 15 minutes to 1 hour, 45 minutes

Difficulty: 2.5

Vertical rise: Minimal

Maps: USGS 7½' Two Rivers, Wisconsin; DeLorme Wisconsin Atlas & Gazetteer, p. 56 (C-4)

While it is easy to forget, many Wisconsinites still make their living on the waters of Lake Michigan. Between shipping, sailing, and commercial and charter fishing, the waters of the lake are alive with activity. It may be that the reason we don't hear much about these activities is because they are much safer now than ever before. The Rawley Point Lighthouse is surely one of the many reasons that this is the case.

There has been a lighthouse here since 1853, but it hasn't always assured safe passage in the waters more than 100 feet below. Before 1894, 26 ships were caught up on this point. Today, like almost all lighthouses, the light here is affixed to a steel tower and is automated—turning on before dusk and turning off just after dawn.

Climbing over the dunes next to the lighthouse reveals a sight not unlike the Cape Cod National Seashore. A vast, sandy beach stretches in both directions, bordered first by bounding sand dunes and then by mostly coniferous forest. It is in this border habitat, in fact, that the rare dune thistle struggles to survive. Be sure to stay on the sandy paths and away from the vegetation out on the dunes—you may be crushing a threatened plant species. And, if you're thinking about hanging up your hiking boots to go whizzing along fragile sand dune habitats on an ATV, please reconsider. Motorized vehicles, along with shoreline homebuilding, are all contributing to the destruction of this rare habitat and the rare species residing there.

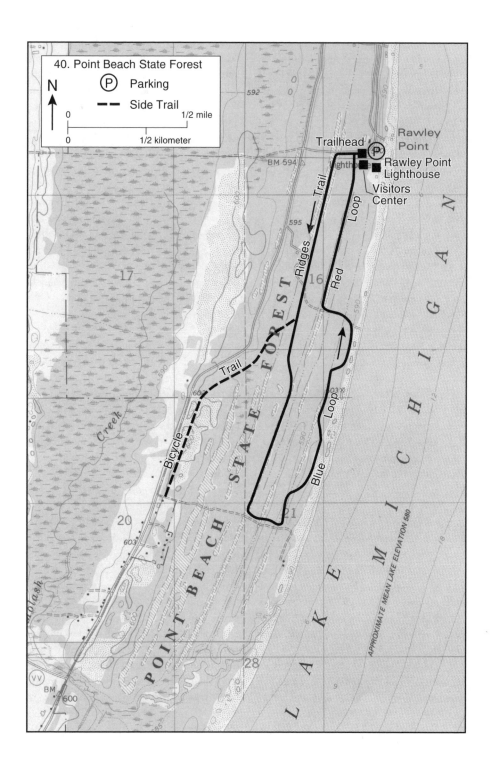

40. Point Beach State Forest

P Parking
- - - Side Trail

N

0 _____ 1/2 mile
0 _____ 1/2 kilometer

Rawley Point

Trailhead

BM 594 △

Lighthouse

Rawley Point Lighthouse

Visitors Center

Ridges

Trail

Red   Loop

Trail

Bicycle

Blue   Loop

Creek

POINT BEACH STATE FOREST

LAKE MICHIGAN

APPROXIMATE MEAN LAKE ELEVATION 580

17

16

20

21

28

603

592

595

600

BM 600

VV

Point Beach offers a look at Wisconsin Great Lakes history, as well as a great opportunity for beach bumming, Wisconsin style. This hike loops through the park from the visitors center and heads south to the Molash Creek, where it turns toward the lake and then north along the dunes toward the lighthouse. It makes for a nice visit to the coastal habitat of Wisconsin and also makes for a good, long hike or ski.

How to Get There

From the north, take WI 42 south from Kewaunee for 16 miles to County Route V. Turn left (east) on CR V and follow it for 2.5 miles to CR O. Turn right (south) on CR O to the park entrance on the left.

From the south, take I-43 south from Kewaunee for 16 miles to CR V. Turn left, east, on CR V and follow it 2.5 miles to CR O. Turn right (south) on CR O and follow it to the park entrance.

From the west, take CR V out of Mishicot and go 6.8 miles to where CR V ends. Turn right and take CR O south. Take CR O for 1.7 miles to the park entrance.

For more information, contact Point Beach State Forest at 920-794-7480.

The Trail

If you pick up a map at the visitors center, you will see that there are Red, Blue, and Yellow Loops. This hike combines half of the Red Loop along with all of the Blue Loop. By cutting the Red in half, you do not need to cross any roads, you stay clear of the crowded camping areas, and you only need to share the trail with bikes for a short while. This combined loop makes for about a 4-mile hike.

If possible, park in the small parking lot just past the visitors center. It is frequently crowded, but oftentimes people are inside the office for just a few minutes, so don't give up right away.

After lacing up, take the entrance road back past the visitors center, staying on the left-hand side of the road. You will pass the return trail first; go past that and up to the second access point for the Red Trail on the left. Take a left and head south along this smooth crushed-gravel trail. You will share this leg of the trail with cyclists, so stay to the right and be aware that they may be passing. The trail is quite wide, however, and congestion should not be a problem.

You are greeted by several red pine and spruce, as well as an occasional towering white pine. The trail, which rests atop a slight ridge, passes next to a sometimes boggy area to the east. About 0.5 mile into the hike, the bike trail will split off to the right, while the Red Loop will veer left. Shortly thereafter the Red Loop will make a sharp left turn as it heads back to the visitors center. Veer right and continue on the Blue Loop. The path is no longer gravel, and you now amble over soft pine bedding.

The trail will approach a park road leading to the indoor group camp. While the Yellow Loop crosses the road, the Blue will veer left, toward the lake. A series of plank footbridges gets you across the several strands of bogs before you climb a bit and turn toward the edge of the dunes. The trail will emerge from the woods and follow between the dunes and woods for about a mile before turning back into the woods. This is a good spot to explore the dunes, and there are several benches atop the hills to look out at the lake and take a water and snack break.

Continue into the woods, where the trail will close in a bit and get more overgrown and grassy. Less than 0.25 mile after heading back into the woods, the trail will merge with the return of the Red Loop. Take it to the right (north) and head back to the visitors center road. Take a right at the road

Rawley Point Lighthouse, Point Beach State Forest

and back to your car, the lighthouse, and the beach.

This hike through a mixture of habitats and along the sandy shores of Lake Michigan is perfect if you're on your way by or looking for a day's worth of hiking. Between the hiking and biking at Point Beach, you could stay very busy for a weekend, exploring this unique Wisconsin landscape.

41

Kettle Moraine State Forest, Parnell Observation Tower

Total distance: 3.5 miles

Hiking time: 1 hour, 30 minutes to 2 hours

Difficulty: 4.0

Vertical rise: 120 feet

Maps: USGS 7½' Cascade, Wisconsin; DeLorme Wisconsin Atlas & Gazetteer, p. 47 (C-5)

With 30,000 acres comprising the Northern Unit of the Kettle Moraine State Forest, you would never know that it receives nearly one million visitors a year. The success of this area has its roots in a group of interested citizens, part of the Izaac Walton League, who sought to preserve this unique natural area close to Milwaukee. In fact, the group's leader, Raymond Zillmer, thought that Kettle Moraine would draw people here just as the great national parks draw people to the West. And he was right. Unfortunately, Zillmer's original plan to have a several-miles-wide park stretch like a ribbon through Wisconsin, encompassing the most recent glacier's path, was never fully realized. Fortunately, Kettle Moraine State Forest was.

Today the area offers picnicking, biking, camping, skiing, hiking, horseback riding, hunting and fishing, snowmobiling, and all sorts of wildlife and plant viewing. There is an incredible diversity of life residing in the forests, prairies, and wetlands throughout Kettle Moraine North, offering a never-ending list of sights to see.

While it might be possible to pick 50 hikes from among the 130 miles of trails in the Kettle Moraine itself, this hike seeks to show you a good example of what the area has to offer. This loop hike takes you up to the 60-foot Parnell Tower, and along the Parnell Esker, one of the best and longest examples of the remnant of a meandering stream that flowed through a tunnel in the glacier, leaving sediment in its tracks. The trail is located toward the north end of

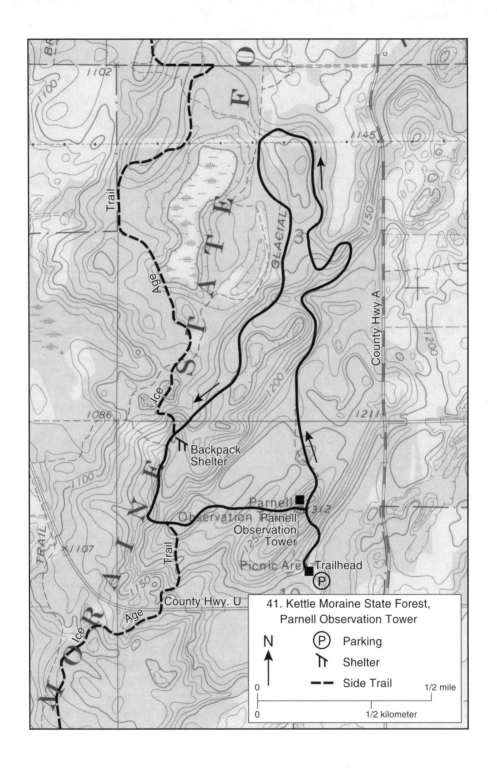

41. Kettle Moraine State Forest,
Parnell Observation Tower

N

(P) Parking

⼈ Shelter

- - - Side Trail

0   1/2 mile

0   1/2 kilometer

Kettle Moraine North, offering a good view of the rest of the forest to the south. This loop, which joins up with the Ice Age Trail for a while, also includes one of the backpacking campsites available in the park. These Adirondack-style shelters are available with reservations and are extremely popular for their seclusion. Anyone looking for a backcountry camping experience, but not ready for the wilds out west, would find these shelters perfect for a weekend getaway.

And, while hiking this trail will serve as a great introduction to the park and this area of Wisconsin, a visit to the Ice Age Visitors Center, located a few miles southwest on WI 67, is a must. In addition to information and exhibits related to the area, several educational programs are offered throughout the year, ranging from canoeing to learning about wolves to nature storytelling.

How to Get There

From the south or southwest, take US 45 north out of Kewauskum to WI 67. Turn right on WI 67 and take it north for about 13 miles. Turn right on County Route U and follow it for 2.3 miles to the Parnell Tower parking lot on the left, just before the junction with CR A.

From the north, take WI 57 south out of Kiel. Follow WI 57 for about 17 miles to CR U. Turn right (west) on CR U and follow it for about 7 miles to the Parnell Tower parking lot on the right.

From the east, take WI 67 south out of Plymouth for about 6 miles to CR A. Turn left (south) on CR A and take it for about 2 miles to CR U. Turn right (west) on CR U about 0.25 mile to the Parnell Tower parking lot on the right.

From the west, take WI 23 east out of Fond du Lac about 15 miles to CR U. Turn right (south) on CR U and follow it about 8 miles to the Parnell Tower parking lot on the left.

For more information, contact the Kettle Moraine State Forest at 414-626-2116 or the Henry S. Reuss Ice Age Visitors Center at 920-533-8322. On the web at www.iceagetrail.org/ is the Ice Age Park and Trail Foundation, a great source of information about the Ice Age Trail.

The Trail

After pulling off CR U and rounding the corner of the entrance drive, a huge parking lot awaits. The trailhead is located at the far western end of the lot.

The trail begins rather brutally by taking you immediately up the first set of wooden riser steps toward the observation tower. After about 0.25 mile, the return route of the trail will appear on the left, from the west. If you are backpacking your gear into the shelter site, you'll undoubtedly want to take this trail for the quickest route to the shelter. If not (or if you're training for that trip out west), continue straight ahead toward the tower and up another long set of risers— which never seem to fit a human's stride, by the way. Soon the tower will emerge in an opening. By heading up to the top, you can see for miles in every direction. The incredibly lush woods of the forest blanket the hills around you.

Head back down and continue north through young maples that offer cool shade in the summer, vibrant color in the fall, or stand like quiet stick people in the winter. The trail will wind its way, mainly downward, as it passes through the forest and meanders through glacial rock debris. As you hike along, the ridge you are on top of will become more prominent, as will the dropoff, too. A shortcut trail will meet up with the main trail from the left (west). Ignore this and continue on the main trail. This densely wooded area is covered in birch, cherry, oak, and maple, and in the warmer months, the floor is carpeted in wild geranium, mayapple, and bloodroot. In this setting, and along this narrow, packed trail, this hike takes you far away from civilization as you merge with the woods themselves.

Eventually, the trail will buttonhook to the left (west), and you will be met by a knee-bending descent into a deep valley. The trail will then curve back north before heading due west and out into an open prairie, full of phlox in the summer. If the hike has been buggy, this makes for a great place to stop for a water break. The open exposure to the sun keeps the mosquitoes as much at bay as possible. But watch out for the wild parsnip here. It comes very close to, and even encroaches on, the trail.

The trail then ducks into a small pine plantation before heading back into the hardwoods and ambling alongside a ridge to the left. You will then climb up and down as you begin to head southwest toward the junction with the Ice Age Trail. A steep, rocky ascent will take you out into an opening and a trail to the backpacking shelter, which is visible to the left. If you took the long route with your pack on your back, you're home. If not, this marks a great place

for a break. If the site is occupied, a bench with an overlook of the park to the south is just up the trail. Either way, this is a good time to have that last snack and water break before pushing to the end.

The trail will meander down into a wooded valley, now with less undergrowth, before making a long, steep ascent. You will reach a ridge that will take you back to the start of the trail. The Ice Age Trail will cut off to the right (south). Eventually, the trail will pop out just above the first set of risers from the beginning of the trail. If your legs feel kind of rubbery and uncertain on the way down, you'll understand why we had you hike up to the tower at the beginning and not at the end—not lovers of towers, we've missed a lot of them thanks to end-of-hike delirium and lactic acid buildup in the legs. Take a right (south) and head back down to the lot.

This relatively rigorous hike takes you deep into the heart of the Kettle Moraine State Forest and, we think, absolutely epitomizes why those Milwaukeeans fought to preserve this unique and precious area of Wisconsin. Fittingly, the shelter on this loop is dedicated, marked by a modest sign, to Raymond Zillmer himself. We imagine that spending eternity on the trail is just the way he would have wanted it. Who wouldn't?

42

Horicon National Wildlife Refuge

Total distance: 3.4 miles

Hiking time: 1 hour to 1 hour, 30 minutes

Difficulty: 2.0

Vertical rise: Minimal

Maps: USGS 7½' Waupun North and Waupun South, Wisconsin; DeLorme Wisconsin Atlas & Gazetteer, p. 45 (D-7)

Looking out over the fiery-colored fall vegetation sprouting out of the Horicon Marsh on a cool October day with tens of thousands of geese dotting the sky above like bomber squadrons, you'd never guess what this place used to look like. At the turn of the century, the Canada goose population had been gunned down to almost nothing, and the marsh, after an unsuccessful attempt to dredge and transform it into farmland, was a vast wasteland suitable for neither farmer nor goose.

Recent annual censuses have recorded more than a quarter of a million geese in the 32,000-acre Horicon Marsh, which is actually protected as both the Horicon National Wildlife Refuge and the Horicon Marsh State Wildlife Area. This internationally recognized bird habitat area is also the largest freshwater cattail marsh in the United States, and there are lots more than honkers in this amazing habitat. More than two hundred species make the marsh home at some point during the year. Included are waterfowl and shorebirds like herons, mallards, sandhill cranes, teal, cormorants, and coots, in addition to all sorts of songbirds and raptors, along with hundreds of species of mammals, snakes, amphibians, and insects. To name them all would take many pages.

Three animals of note, the egret, the red fox, and the redhead duck are the appropriate honorees of this hike. In fact, Horicon is the biggest nesting area for redheads east of the Mississippi. This trail is actually a combination of the three loops, arranged

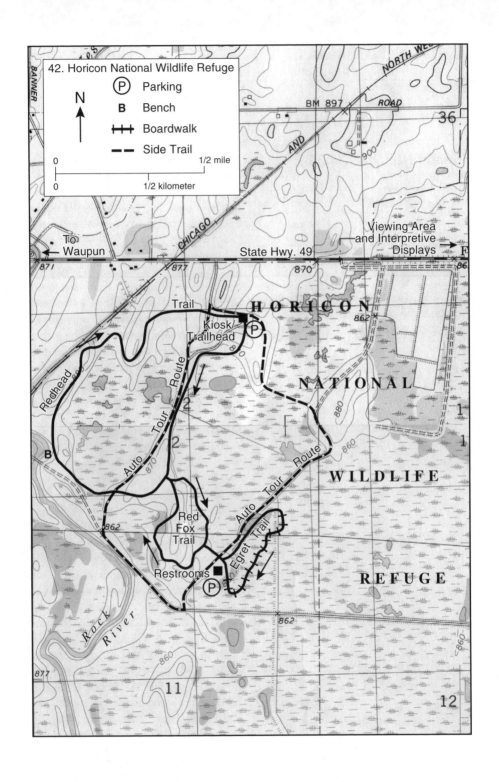

like a snowman. The longest, the Redhead, starts by taking you into the marsh and around a large pond before sweeping along the edge of an incredible prairie restoration on the Red Fox Trail–alive with color in the summer months. From there you join the Egret Trail and emerge from a hardwood stand to hike right through the marsh on top of one of the most scenic and amazing floating boardwalks around. From here you can get right up close to wildlife either flying by or wading below. The hike rounds up by tracing its way along the other side of the prairie and rambling up and down small hills alongside the woods on the banks of the Rock River, before turning back to the parking area. It's a great hike that takes about an hour with blinders on, or much longer with binoculars, camera, and wildlife identification books in tow.

How to Get There

From the south, take WI 26 north out of Burnett for 4.9 miles to WI 49. Turn right (east) on WI 49 and go 1.4 miles to the parking lot on the right. (Be careful, it comes up quickly soon after you pass the bike trail crossing.) Follow the drive to the lot, veering left at the fork in the drive.

From the west, take WI 49 east out of Waupun for about 2.8 miles and follow the drive to the lot, veering left at the fork in the drive.

From the east, take WI 49 out of Brownsville about 9.2 miles to the parking area on the left. Turn left onto the drive and follow the drive to the lot, veering left at the fork in the drive.

From the north, take US 151 South out of Fond du Lac for 14.3 miles to WI 49. Turn left (east) on WI 49 and go 1.9 miles to the parking area on the right. Follow the drive to the lot, veering left at the fork in the drive.

For more information, contact the U.S. Fish and Wildlife Service office at the Horicon National Wildlife Refuge at 920-387-2658 or the Wisconsin Department of Natural Resources Horicon Service Center at 920-387-7860. The Marsh Haven Nature Center (a nonprofit visitors center) is also a good place to get marsh-related information. Contact Marsh Haven at 920-324-5818.

The Trail

At the parking area, start hiking at the trailhead kiosk on the south side of the lot, heading south and starting a clockwise loop. After climbing a short hill along a wide, crushed-limestone trail, you will reach the crest to find one of many great views along this trail. In front of you will be standing water, and you will be greeted by the sight of egrets in the warmer months. The view stretches in every direction. You will skirt the edge of this pond area by heading west to the auto tour road and then south alongside it. There is a rich diversity of wildflowers in this edge habitat, including milkweed and vervain. The trail will veer left into a small woods before emerging and coming to the intersection with the Red Fox Trail. Take this to the left, staying on a clockwise route.

This trail runs along a short hillside and skirts the edge of an immense prairie restoration. In July, you'll be rewarded with a multicolored blanket of black-eyed Susans, wild bergamot, blazing stars, prairie dock, and a sea of prairie coneflowers and compass plants. This open habitat will transition dramatically as you cross the auto tour road and join up with the Egret Trail at a small T-shaped boardwalk. Head left (northeast) alongside the road and into the woods, full of large oaks and various woodland flowers.

You will emerge from these woods to find yourself at the marsh's edge. There is

Horicon National Wildlife Refuge

an access trail to the left, but stay to the right and head south toward the boardwalks. The trail, once solidly supportive beneath you, will transition to a still solid but now floating surface. This phenomenal boardwalk takes you past hopping frogs, honking geese, and any number of birds munching on duckweed. A large overlook gazebo provides a great spot for photos and wildlife viewing.

From here, you'll wind back north toward the Egret Trail parking area, restrooms, and the road. This may make for a good breaking point for water and a snack. This trail can be pretty taxing on a hot summer's day, so a break or two will be needed. Continue on the Egret back to the T in the trail and take it left, across the road, and back to the Red Fox Trail. Veer left on the Red Fox this time, along the southern side of the prairie, and up a hillside. Looking northeast from here, you are treated to a great view of the marsh and much of the area that you have just covered.

The trail will now meander along and through a couple of large stands of oaks, old and new, before taking you back to the intersection with the Redhead Trail. Take a left at this intersection and head west, across the auto tour road and toward the Rock River. The prairie along this section of trail is still in development, and it appears that a war with sumac and wild parsnip is in full steam. But the terrain makes for good hiking, and a bench alongside the slow-moving Rock River makes for a nice break before making the final push home. Eventually, the trail will pass by an old stone fence and foundation before crossing the auto tour road and winding around a hillside and east to the parking lot.

This hike is a great way to get up close with all sorts of wildlife, wildflowers, and the immense cattail marsh at Horicon. On a hot day, these 3.4 miles will feel more like 4, but it's well worth the trip. In the fall, you will be rewarded with a dizzying array of waterfowl, and be treated to an almost unending chorus of geese as they randomly take flight and land in shifts and flights all day long. A rolling hike, this is definitely suitable for children capable of a longer hike, or you can always lop off a segment to make the hike shorter.

43

Lake Kegonsa State Park

Total distance: 2.5 miles

Hiking time: 1 hour to 1 hour, 30 minutes

Difficulty: 1.5

Vertical rise: Minimal

Map: USGS 7½' Stoughton, Wisconsin; DeLorme Wisconsin Atlas & Gazetteer, p. 28 (A-3)

For thousands of years, the lakes and rivers of what is now the Madison area have attracted humans. The Winnebago Native Americans who once lived in this area named the lake Kegonsa, which translates to "lake of many fishes." And, when you see the lake covered with ice shanties in the winter, or the shoulder-to-shoulder anglers at the bridges in the summer, it appears that many fish still reside here. If you imagine Kegonsa without the cars and campers, or boats and motors, you can see why the native people would have found this area desirable. While the landscape has changed since then, there were undoubtedly similar shady woods and open prairies full of the game that the Winnebago and other nomadic cultures needed to make it through the long, cold winters and hot summers. In fact, the mark of one of these cultures lies indelibly in the area of the White Oak Trail, in the form of effigy mounds, or sacred burial sites, often in the shape of animals.

Today, the park offers swimming, boating, skiing, and hiking along the shores of Lake Kegonsa, one of the four Madison area lakes known, appropriately enough, as the Four Lakes. These lakes, like much of the surface waters of Wisconsin, are the remnants of the last Ice Age and the Wisconsin glacier. Damming of a large riverway was caused by glacial debris, resulting in this string of lakes, which are connected by the Yahara River.

This hike takes you around a very successful, and young, prairie restoration and through a very old hardwood forest area, made up primarily of giant white oaks. As

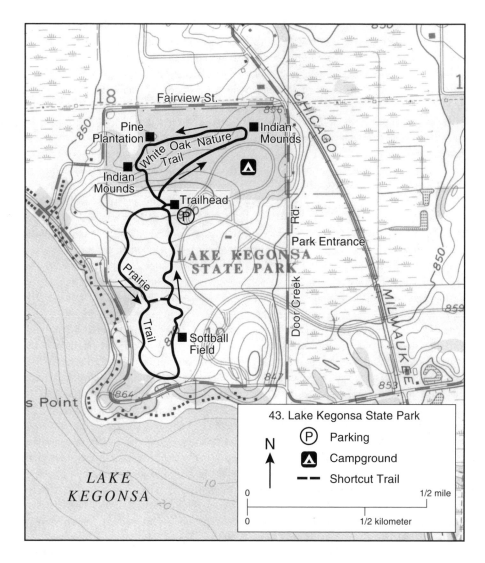

with most multipurpose watersport parks, the park's trails see less traffic than the water, making this trail an ideal hiking spot no matter how busy the season.

How to Get There

From Stoughton, take North Page Street north out of town 2 miles to Williams Drive. Take a right on Williams Drive and stay on it for 4 miles until it comes to Williams Point Drive. Take a left on Williams Point Drive and the first right (approximately 1 mile) on Door Creek Road. The park entrance is immediately on the left.

From Madison, take US 51 south to County Route B just before Stoughton. Take CR B for just over 1.5 miles to Williams Drive (this is a four-way stop). Turn left (north) on Williams Drive and follow the directions above.

From the north, south, or east and coming from I-39/90, take the CR N exit and head south toward Stoughton. Turn right on Koshkonong Road (approximately 1 mile) and take it for about 0.5 mile to Williams Drive. Turn left (south) and take it for approximately 2 miles. Turn right on Williams Point Drive and follow the directions into the park above.

For more information, contact Lake Kegonsa State Park at 608-873-9695.

The Trail

This hike is a combination of two loops, the Prairie and White Oak Nature Trails, both done counterclockwise. If it's hot, we suggest doing the Prairie Loop first before ducking into the cool shade of the White Oak Loop. Because the Prairie Loop skirts the edge of the prairie, the trail is shaded by the bordering trees for much of the afternoon.

Upon passing the park office, drive past the small parking lot on the right and take the next road to the right instead. This will lead to another small lot on the immediate left, or a third lot around the corner to the left at the trailhead. There are restrooms and water here, and this is also the beginning of the ski trails.

Looking to the west from this last lot, you will see a large painted welcome sign and three trails (left, straight, or right). Take the trail to the left and head straight to a sign describing the prairie plants found in the area; this is the beginning of the Prairie Loop. Turn right (west) and begin the loop. Immediately, all sorts of prairie plants will emerge, including big and little bluestem, rattlesnake master, butterfly milkweed, and phlox. For a young restoration, it is very successful and thriving. There are often matted-down areas of bluestem under trees, marking deer bedding sites.

The trail travels along the western edge of the prairie, heading south just a couple of hundred feet from the lake, although it is hardly visible in the summer months. The first leg of the hike is a gradual downhill. Looking east across the prairie from here offers a great glimpse of what a truly healthy prairie ecosystem looks like. In these grasses are hundreds of species, including 60 species of birds, reptiles, spiders, butterflies, and mammals.

The hiking (and skiing) is relatively easy and would be a good one for kids. The grass is usually cut short and is easy to walk through. After a long and slight descent, you will turn and merge with a shortcut trail. Don't take this; instead, turn to the right and continue along another slight decline. The trail will then make a U-turn and head back north, passing a large stand of mixed hardwoods, mainly walnut, great for shade in the summer and brilliantly colored in the fall. After passing the softball field, veer right and past the other end of the shortcut trail on your left, but continue on the main trail to the right. This will take you along the park road and past various prairie plant species and back to the beginning of the loop at the plant sign. Take a right (north) and head back to the parking lot area. This is a good spot for a water or snack break before heading on.

The White Oak Nature Trail is straight ahead. There are very informative and worthwhile guidebooks available at the trail's start. Grab one before heading off into the woods. The trail starts by making a downhill turn east—notice the banked curb for skiers. The change from the prairie is amazing. The park staff is as interested in preserving and restoring the woods as in managing the prairie. And, while there is currently almost 90 percent canopy coverage in the woods, they hope to lessen that to a healthier 75 percent. This will enable many of the desirable ground-dwelling woodland species of plants a chance to get growing again.

The trail passes the light gray bark of several white oaks as it meanders eastward, past a couple of campsites, before making a U-turn left and eastward up a hill toward the effigy mounds. If you're not looking, or you don't have your trail guide, you'll miss them—they're off to the right. The trail then makes a slight dip and heads past some of the larger trees in the woods, past a pine plantation, and begins its final ascent toward the end of the trail. The last uphill climb is a bit challenging, but the footing is easy and the end is near. A bench at the top is worth stopping at to look back over the valley you just traversed. It's a great view, and you may spot a deer or a wild turkey creeping out the other side. The trail's end and parking lot are just a few yards from here.

This hike offers a great look at the efforts of the Wisconsin state parks to take an active role in preserving and restoring ecosystems to their native states. The combination of science and history found along these trails is enlightening, and the hike is very relaxing while moderately challenging.

44

Kettle Moraine State Forest, Pike Lake

Total distance: 4.7 miles

Hiking time: 1 hour, 45 minutes to 2 hours, 15 minutes

Difficulty: 3.5

Vertical rise: 230 feet

Maps: USGS 7½' Hartford East, Wisconsin; DeLorme Wisconsin Atlas & Gazetteer, p. 38 (B-3)

The original proposal, over 50 years ago, was for a wide swath of land to mark the terminal moraine of the most recent glacier and to meander through Wisconsin as one long, narrow state park. While Kettle Moraine State Forest was eventually established, and an Ice Age Trail is inching toward completion, the long, Appalachian Trail–style park was never realized. But satellites of the original park idea were formed and survive, like blips on a screen, in the form of Kettle Moraine State Forest.

While a detached island, the Pike Lake Unit of the Kettle Moraine exemplifies why places like this were desirable park areas. Its large lake, itself a kettle, is surrounded by a park area with a beach, parking, a shelter, camping, and a newly built observation tower–offering views for miles atop 1,350-foot Powder Hill, itself a kame.

Much of this loop trail borrows its course from the Ice Age Trail. The trail starts at the beach area parking lot and heads straight up Powder Hill along the Ice Age Trail route to the turnoff for the Powder Hill tower. A 0.5-mile out-and-back hike takes you to the top of the tower and offers phenomenal views of much of Washington County and Pike Lake below. From here the trail leaves the Ice Age Trail and heads east through mostly hardwood forest and past the campsite area, before turning north and then west for a long stretch back through woods and some prairie to the trailhead. The trail is very hilly at first, and moderately hilly throughout. And, while the beach is bustling on warm summer weekends, the trails see

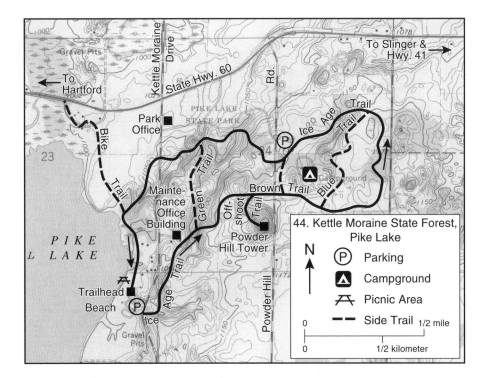

44. Kettle Moraine State Forest, Pike Lake

N

- P Parking
- ⬛ Campground
- ⛱ Picnic Area
- – – Side Trail

0 ——————— 1/2 mile

0 ——————— 1/2 kilometer

limited use, making them great destinations if you're in the area looking for a great hike.

How to Get There

From the west, take WI 60 east out of Hartford 1.6 miles to the park entrance on the right (Kettle Moraine Drive). Follow this drive for about a mile, past the visitors center, to the beach parking lot on the right. The trailhead is directly across the drive from the parking lot to the east.

From the east, take WI 60 west out of Jackson for about 8.0 miles to the park entrance, Kettle Moraine Drive, on the left. Follow this drive for about a mile, past the visitors center, to the beach parking lot on the right. The trailhead is directly across the drive from the parking lot to the east.

From the southeast, take US 41 north out of Menomonee Falls 9.5 miles to WI 60. Turn left (west) on WI 60 and go 3.5 miles to the

park entrance, Kettle Moraine Drive, on the left. Follow this drive for about a mile, past the visitors center, to the beach parking lot on the right. The trailhead is directly across the drive from the parking lot to the east.

From the north, take US 41 south out of Allenton 7.5 miles to WI 60. Turn right on WI 60 and go west 3.5 miles to the park entrance, Kettle Moraine Drive, on the left. Follow this drive for about a mile, past the visitors center, to the beach parking lot on the right. The trailhead is directly across the drive from the parking lot to the east.

For more information, contact Kettle Moraine State Forest, Pike Lake Unit at 262-260-3400.

The Trail

After crossing the road from the pleasant lakeshore and beach, you are engulfed by both the woods and Powder Hill. The trail begins its ascent immediately as you head alongside the park road and wind along the west side of the hill. The trail, wide and covered with wood chips, will take you up past the park maintenance office, past the intersection with the Green Trail, and up some more. Eventually, the trail will come to a bench and an offshoot trail to the south, which will head up to the tower. The hike up there is short but brings with it more hills. But, when it comes to towers, the Powder Hill tower is pretty remarkable. New and sturdy, this tower offers a great lookout across the many kames that dot the horizon.

After trekking down from the hill, head east, staying on the Brown Trail. The Ice Age Trail will turn off with the Orange Trail at this point. From here, you will pass Powder Hill Road, join with the White Trail, and hike just along the edge of the camping area. Here is where you will meet up briefly with the Astronomy Trail—an educational trail that seeks to illustrate the size of the solar system and the planets through a series of models placed on posts.

From here, the Blue Trail will soon cut off to the left (north), while you will begin a gentle downhill alongside an open field to the right. The trail will make a sharp turn to the left and head north along CR CC, still descending slightly. Soon you will turn west and meet up with the Blue Trail again, as well as meeting back up with the Ice Age Trail. From here you will pass the Powder Hill Road parking lot and cross the road. (Make sure to switch your mind from trail hiking back to road crossing mode briefly—the cars may be coming quickly.) Then duck back into the woods. The Black Forest Nature Trail will peel off to the right, but stay left and hike into a more open area before heading downhill and winding alongside a small pond before making a steep climb.

The trail will then merge with the Green Trail and head across Kettle Moraine Road before emerging from the woods and into an open prairie. This can get to be a pretty taxing area after a lot of hiking, so take water breaks where needed. You will then merge with the bike trail for the short stretch back to the parking area. Keep an eye out for bikers, and keep to one side of the trail.

The trail will meet up with the eastern shore of Pike Lake and go through a marshy area before ducking back into the woods, full of spruce and cedars, and emerging finally at the picnic area near the parking area and beach. A short, but fitting hill takes you out of the picnic area and up to the parking lot to finish the hike.

This great ramble up and down the hills and valleys of Washington County is a perfect look at southeastern Wisconsin's wooded landscape. Hikes like this one demonstrate how the last Ice Age dramatically shaped the land. And, with sore feet to attest to those hills, a great beach and glacial lake await at the end.

45

Nashotah Park

Total distance: 3.5 miles

Hiking time: 1 hour to 1 hour, 30 minutes

Difficulty: 2.5

Vertical rise: Minimal

Maps: USGS 7½' Oconomowoc East, Wisconsin; DeLorme Wisconsin Atlas & Gazetteer, p. 38 (D-2)

Sometimes you just need a park. You want a good spot to play volleyball, toss a ball, have a cookout, meet with friends or family, and simply relax. Throw in some great hiking trails that double as ski trails in the winter, a couple of lakes with some fishing, wetlands, waterfowl, wildflowers, and blazing fall colors, and you have Nashotah Park.

Admittedly, the county parks are sort of the little siblings to the other recreation areas in Wisconsin. By the time you get all the way down the ladder from the magnificent Apostle Islands National Lakeshore, the lush and wild Chequamegon-Nicolet National Forest, and the burly and breathtaking bluffs of Devil's Lake State Park, the county parks just don't seem that exciting sometimes. This couldn't be further from the truth at Nashotah.

A quiet park of good size, almost 450 acres, Nashotah is a very well-maintained and well-administered park. In fact, the park almost has to be this way as part of the agreement the Gallun family made with the county upon signing the deed. They wanted to ensure that this area would be a home for native plant preservation and recreation. That was in 1972, and while the Milwaukee area was growing back then, the Galluns' decision undoubtedly saved this area from the swarm of development that has engulfed every county surrounding the Brew City.

This hike takes you along the Green Trail, the longest loop in the park, and shows off everything that Nashotah has to offer. Starting off at the westernmost parking lot, the trail goes south along a ridge and

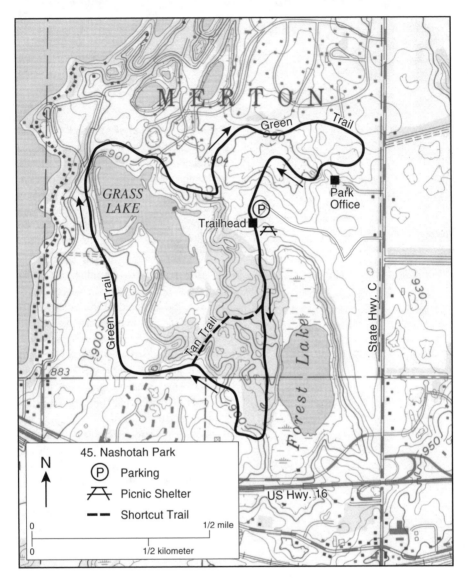

45. Nashotah Park

(P) Parking

🏕 Picnic Shelter

- - - Shortcut Trail

N

0 ——————————— 1/2 mile

0 ——————————— 1/2 kilometer

through a thick hardwood forest full of mature trees, offering great shade in the summer. The trail then turns west away from the lake and through a stand of pines, before heading out into the open and through a large prairie. From here the trail meanders along the western edge of the park toward Grass Lake, before turning east and up and down a series of small hills back toward the parking area. But, just before the lot, the trail turns north again and completes a mile-long loop through the largest prairie, alive with wildflowers in the warmer months, past the park office, and back up to the parking lot. This hike is actually somewhat taxing due to the rolling terrain and, in the heat of the summer, can make for a pretty strenuous trek.

How to Get There

From the south, take County Route C north from I-94 3.9 miles to the park entrance on the left. After passing through the park check-in, turn right and go 0.3 mile to the west parking lot.

From the east or west, take I-94 to the CR C exit and follow the directions above.

From the west, take WI 16 east out of Oconomowoc 3.8 miles to CR C. Turn left (north) on CR C and go 0.7 mile to the park entrance on the left. Follow the directions above to the lot.

There is a daily use fee, per automobile, payable upon entrance to Nashotah. In 2003, this was $4.50. Annual passes are also available. For more information, contact the Waukesha County Park System at 262-548-7801 or on the web at www.waukesha county.gov/parks.

The Trail

The trail begins at the bottom of the hill on the south side of the parking lot, below the picnic shelter. The Nashotah Park trail staff keep the trail pretty well padded with a thick bed of wood chips that welcome you to the trail and help you bounce up the first few hills. The trail is very wooded here on the bluff above the lake. As you head south you will pass the intersection with the Red Trail, but stay to the left and continue along the lakeshore.

The trail will eventually head uphill and through a stand of large white pines. One of them, which apparently died at some point, was used to make a small seat out of the stump. Turn west from here and uphill, through an open prairie area, to the Green Trail turnoff to the right (north). This section of trail takes you down through a deep valley prairie and up the other side, where the trail will head northwest and past the Tan Shortcut Trail intersection.

From here, you will head west and then curve north, past an old barn and down a long stretch of trail, until you come to the western shore of Grass Lake, a good spot for a rest and a water break. You are very close to the western edge of the park at this point, and the trail actually runs parallel to CR O over here. The trail will eventually turn back eastward at the northern tip of the lake and head down into a deep valley, before climbing back up into the rolling prairie on the north side of the park.

While you may even see your car from here, you will peel off to the north again and make a long, sweeping loop through this great prairie, which is alive with birds and butterflies and aflame with wildflowers. Once at the northeasternmost corner of the park, the trail will turn west again and up a steep hill, before passing the park office and dipping into the last valley. One final climb takes you up to the parking lot above, a picnic table, some water, and a much-deserved sandwich.

46

Kettle Moraine State Forest, Lapham Peak

Total distance: 5.8 miles

Hiking time: 2 hours, 15 minutes to 3 hours

Difficulty: 4.5

Vertical rise: 320 feet

Maps: USGS 7½' Oconomowoc East, Wisconsin; DeLorme Wisconsin Atlas & Gazetteer, p. 38 (D-2)

As the saying goes: "If you don't like the weather, wait ten minutes." Although this is somewhat true, we are now pretty well apprised of future weather, thanks to meteorological predictions and the work of the National Weather Service. This wasn't always the case, however. And, while not knowing about a pending storm is tough on anyone, it is especially life-threatening if you're a sailor on the Great Lakes. But for decades, ships set sail without knowing for certain what the winds would bring.

This all changed in the 1800s with the work of one man, Increase Lapham (1811–1875), atop a 1,253-foot hill—the tallest point in Waukesha County. It was here where Lapham received weather reports via telegraph from Colorado. It was this idea of forecasting that eventually led to the establishment of a National Weather Bureau (now the National Weather Service) and was commemorated by the renaming of this hill, originally Government Hill, to Lapham Peak.

Just off one of the two most-traveled interstate highways in Wisconsin, Kettle Moraine State Forest, Lapham Peak is as unique today as it was over a hundred years ago. But today's attraction is the exceptionally well-developed trail system traversing the hill and offering phenomenal hiking, mountain biking, skiing, snowshoeing, and horseback riding to visitors of all ability levels. There is even one remote campsite located here, accessible only off the Ice Age Trail, which also wanders through Lapham Peak. And in the winter months, there is a lighted ski trail for evening skiing, too.

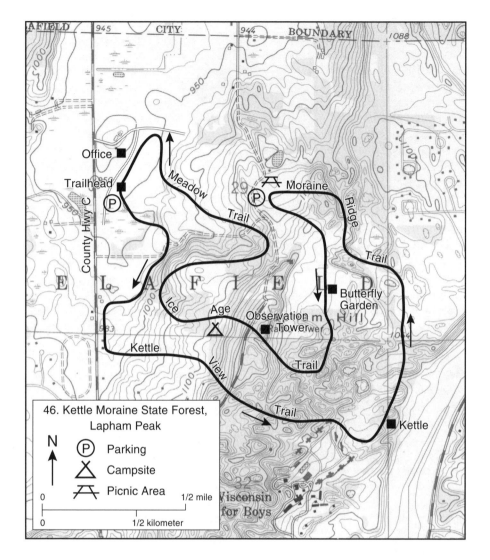

46. Kettle Moraine State Forest,
Lapham Peak

N

(P) Parking

△ Campsite

⛺ Picnic Area

0 ———————————— 1/2 mile

0 ———————————— 1/2 kilometer

The Kettle View (Blue) Trail is one of four loop trails comprising 16.8 miles of footpaths located here. This trail is the second longest at 5.8 miles and is a relatively strenuous hike, especially considering that two of the hills are nicknamed Gut Buster and Asthma. Gut Buster's long, sustained ascent is almost comically unimaginable on skis, but is quite a nice challenge on foot. The trail starts down in the more open prairie at the bottom of the hill before heading up Gut Buster and looping northward over a series of ups and downs. From here, the trail heads west over to the Homestead Hollow picnic area, which is great for a break and water before you head back south and up Asthma Hill.

To include the tower atop Lapham Peak itself, and to include a segment of the Ice Age Trail, we chose to leave the Blue Trail for almost a mile before joining up with it again and looping back to the trailhead via the meadow. This is probably one of the tougher hikes in this book, due to its length and the hills. Still, most of the climbing is in the first half the hike. You'll definitely get your day's worth of hiking in on this one.

How to Get There

From the south, take WI 83 north out of Wales 0.5 mile to US 18. Turn left (west) on US 18 and go 1.1 miles to County Route C. Turn right (north) on CR C and go 1.8 miles to the park entrance on the right. Turn right to get to the visitors center. Continue on the park road 0.2 mile, turn right, and follow this road to the Evergreen Grove parking area. The trailhead is on the left (east) side of the lot as you drive in.

From the north, take CR C south 1.0 mile from I-94 to the park entrance on the left. Follow the directions above from there.

From the west or east, take either US 18 or I-94 to CR C. Follow the directions above from there.

For more information, contact the Kettle Moraine State Forest, Lapham Peak at 262-646-3025.

The Trail

The trail starts just on the other side of the tree line on the east side of the parking lot. The trailhead, as with all of the trails at Lapham, is exceptionally well marked. Head off to the right (south) to start this counter-clockwise loop. You'll notice right away that this trail is meant for skiing. It is probably about fifteen feet wide and is mowed like a lawn, undoubtedly in anxious preparation for the first snowfall still months away. But for those of you who like more intimate trails, don't be too discouraged, because the trail will start to close in more as you leave the Green Loop and head up into the woods.

Because you are sharing with the Meadow Trail (Green Loop) for the first mile

or so, the trail is out in the open and fairly level, although the first 0.5 mile is a slight, gradual ascent, making it easy to get warmed up. You will turn to the southwest after this hill and cross the Ice Age Trail heading northwest toward the ponds, then continue south along a tree line before making a sharp turn, more into the woods, and beginning the almost mile-long uphill climb, known as the Gut Buster. While this probably applies to those poor souls attempting this ascent on skis, it's still a major hill for hikers—especially on a hot day.

When you cross an old paved access road, you know that you've reached the top, for now. There is a welcome bench off to the right, making for a great resting spot. Feel free to tap into up to half of your water, since you can always refill at the Homestead Hollow picnic area. After this the trail begins a substantial downhill that takes you deep into a valley. Since heading uphill, the trail is pretty shaded with large hardwoods and, since leaving the Meadow Trail, the trail looks more like a hiking trail than a wide ski track.

Soon you will come to a cutoff to the left for the Moraine Ridge (Black) Trail, the longest loop at Lapham. Stay right and head up a hill, a pretty good climb. Once on the top of this hill, you will find yourself right next to a kettle, which is a depression in the surface of the land, formed when sand and small stones settled where a block of ice melted. You will then rejoin with the Moraine Ridge Trail and cross the Ice Age Trail for the second time.

The trail will open up a bit again as you pass by a stand of white pines on the left side of the trail and aspens on the right. You will pass by the Kame Terrace (Purple) Trail twice on this eastern side of Lapham as you hike north. After another short climb, you will turn off to the left, leaving the Moraine

Ridge Trail, and the trail will really open up as you pass through a prairie area that can get really hot in the middle of a sunny summer day. This will make a welcome and long descent westward all the way to the Homestead Hollow picnic area. Once there, the trail will basically skirt the edge, buttonhook left, and leave. By heading straight toward the parking lot and to the right (north), you will find a water fountain. This makes for a great place to down the rest of your water, refill, and maybe have lunch or a snack—you're only about halfway through the hike.

From here, the trail will head uphill—up Asthma Hill that is—to the southwest. After you've conquered Gut Buster, Asthma won't seem too bad, but since it's halfway through this rather rigorous hike, you'll feel it. The trail will be more wooded now, and you will curve southward past the Butterfly Garden area, passing the Kame Terrace Trail twice more. After passing a dirt service road, you will come up on the Ice Age Trail. Take a right here and head up toward the observation tower. Soon after enjoying your first few steps along the Ice Age Trail, you will be met by a long series of riser steps taking you up to the tower. While we sometimes skip towers, this one certainly offers a great view. You can see all the way up toward Pike Lake, about 20 miles away.

After coming down from the tower, continue west along the trail toward the primitive campsite. You'll work your way downhill for a while before emerging in a prairie area, where an offshoot trail takes you to the site. The campsite is simply a fire ring and a grass pad below some cedars, so there's not much to see. But just imagine having the whole hill to yourself some night! From here, continue along the Ice Age Trail down to where it intersects again with the Kettle View, Moraine Ridge, and Meadow Trails, definitely a drastic change. Take this wide trail to the right (northeast) and follow it up your final, long ascent to the east before buttonhooking back west and back down into the prairie, where the trail will turn south and take you back to the trailhead.

This long hike along a Nordic trail and some of the Ice Age Trail is a pretty good day's workout. It's a great loop hike, offering varied terrain, trees, wildflowers, and great scenery.

47

Kettle Moraine State Forest, Scuppernong

Total distance: 5.0 (Green Loop 4.2 miles, plus Observation Loop)

Hiking time: 1 hour, 15 minutes to 1 hour, 45 minutes

Difficulty: 4.0

Vertical rise: 110 feet

Map: USGS 7½' Eagle, Wisconsin; DeLorme Wisconsin Atlas & Gazetteer, p. 30 (A-2)

Just yesterday, geologically speaking, woolly mammoths grazed Wisconsin's ground in the shadow of a mile-tall retreating glacier. Like a great plow of ice, this last glacier pushed forward and backward several times before eventually receding north. But it didn't leave without a trace. The remnants of the Ice Age—kames, eskers, and kettles, commonly known as hills, ridges, and depressions—all form what is Wisconsin today and mark, indelibly, its glacial past.

In an intrepid move by a group of Milwaukeeans in the 1930s, the Kettle Moraine State Forest was established to preserve this history. The grand plan, as conceived by lawyer and outdoorsman Raymond Zillmer, was for Kettle Moraine eventually to serve as the heart of a statewide, thousand-mile trail—as Baxter State Park in Maine serves as home to the Appalachian Trail. It was to be visited "by millions more people than use the more remote national parks," wrote Zillmer. While this dream wasn't entirely realized, and with the Ice Age Trail far from finished, Kettle Moraine South and this segment of the Ice Age Trail are exactly what Zillmer and his fellow conservationists were hoping for.

The Kettle Moraine State Forest includes more than 50,000 acres, making it the largest tract of public land in southern Wisconsin. The amazing part about Kettle Moraine is the fact that each one of those thousands of acres is within an hour's drive of the most populated area of the state. Equally amazing is that the entire area is set

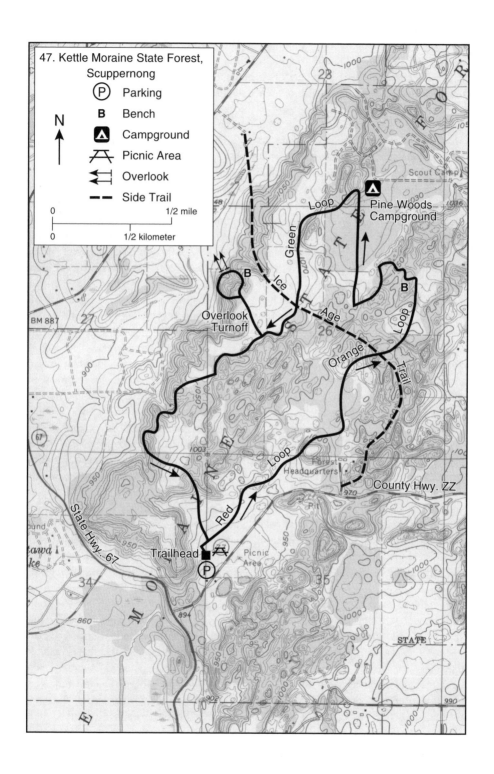

47. Kettle Moraine State Forest, Scuppernong

P Parking
B Bench
▲ Campground
🏕 Picnic Area
◀ Overlook
- - - Side Trail

N

0   1/2 mile
0   1/2 kilometer

Pine Woods Campground

B

Green Loop

Ice

Age

Overlook Turnoff

B

Loop

Orange

Trail

BM 887

Loop

Forest Headquarters

County Hwy. ZZ

Red

State Hwy. 67

Trailhead

Picnic Area

P

Scout Camp

STATE

aside for the silent sports of hiking, off-road bicycling, horseback riding, and skiing. On top of that, the scenery—as you stand atop an oak-covered bluff or meander through a pine-blanketed valley—is incredible.

This 5-mile hike follows one of the three loop trails available to hikers and skiers at the Scuppernong trail area. The trail weaves up and down and back and forth through a mixture of hardwoods and pines along a mostly shaded trail. While a ski trail, it isn't necessarily as wide and level as some, and the footing is a bit rocky and sandy at times. The hike takes you along a counterclockwise route past the Pine Woods Campground and crosses the Ice Age Trail twice before leading you out to a great overlook of the western edge of Waukesha County. The trail then turns southward and takes a bit of a roller-coaster ride (making you rethink whether you're ready for a trail rated as "advanced" for skiing) and back down to the trailhead.

How to Get There

From the south, take WI 67 north out of Eagle 4.1 miles to County Route ZZ. Turn right and go 0.3 mile on CR ZZ to the Scuppernong Hiking/Skiing Trail parking lot on the left side.

From the east, take WI 59 west from Waukesha 8.0 miles to CR ZZ. Turn right on CR ZZ and go 4.5 miles to the Scuppernong Hiking/Skiing Trail parking lot on the right.

From the north, take WI 67 south out of Oconomowoc 11.3 miles to CR ZZ. Turn left on CR ZZ and go 0.3 mile to the Scuppernong Hiking/Skiing Trail parking lot on the left.

For more information, contact the Kettle Moraine State Forest, Southern Unit at 262-594-6200.

The Trail

The trailhead is located in the north corner of the lot, and a large wooden map shows the three loop trails offered here. This trail, the Green Loop, basically follows the outer edge of all the loops and covers the most ground.

Upon starting, you will be greeted by a sandy path underfoot and pines overhead. The trail will take an immediate turn to the right, and you will head down a long, straight and flat stretch, giving you a good warm-up for the rest of the hike. The trail will turn more northward from here, and you will now encounter more hardwoods, mainly oak and some hickory. As you wind more eastward, you will climb your first hill before dipping down into a valley, a trend that will repeat itself several times on this hike.

Soon you will pass the turnoff for the Red Loop before heading down into a deep valley as part of an overall descent toward the Pine Woods campground. You will pass the Ice Age Trail in this area before curving east toward CR G. From here you will turn westward and zigzag down toward the grove of white and red pines next to the campground. You will actually skirt the edge of a few of the campsites on the eastern edge of the campground.

The trail will then come to the turnoff for the Green Loop, which takes you directly north along a long stretch of logging road flanked by pines, on the western edge of the campground. At the end of this stretch, you will come to an open area near the campground road, where you will turn left (west). Here you will begin a section of the hike that is a bit more exposed to the sun as you pass through a grassy prairie area that is home to many young white pines. In 30 or 40 years, this area will probably be shaded, too.

Again, you will cross the Ice Age Trail and meet back up with the Red and Orange

Scuppernong Ski and Hiking Area, Kettle Moraine State Forest

Loops. Just after doing so, you will come to the overlook loop turnoff. Take this to the right (north) and follow it to the overlook, which is on a high bluff covered in oaks, and offers a good view of the town of Ottowa and its environs. From here, head back to the main trail, turning right (west) and continuing along the Green Loop as it zigzags westward again. From here, it is mainly downhill toward the trailhead, especially a section just beyond where you will see a large sign with an exclamation point—a warning sign for skiers approaching a steep descent. This rocky and somewhat slippery downhill stretch must be an interesting undertaking on skis. Soon you will find yourself back in the familiar pine plantation and sandy soil of the trailhead parking lot.

48

Schlitz Audubon Nature Center

Total distance: 3.0 miles

Hiking time: 1 hour, to 1 hour 30 minutes

Difficulty: 2.0

Vertical rise: 100 feet

Maps: USGS 7½' Thiensville, Wisconsin; DeLorme Wisconsin Atlas & Gazetteer, p. 39 (C-6)

Anytime you try to stuff a million people into a sprawling coastal city, you'll run out of room along the shore. This has certainly been the trend in Milwaukee County, where shoreline property goes for millions of dollars and all the rest goes really fast. So it is exceptionally lucky that the single largest undeveloped tract of land in the entire county is protected within a nature conservancy.

Along the sandy shore of glistening Lake Michigan rests the 225-acre Schlitz Audubon Nature Center, a gift of nature to the county and its visitors from the residents of the town of Bayside. Like some of the other hikes in this book, the 6 miles of trails at Schlitz are found within the confines of a nonprofit, citizen-organized natural area. Originally called the Uihlein Nine Mile Farm for its distance 9 miles from the Schlitz Brewery in downtown Milwaukee, the land was given to the National Audubon Society. But, in a unique agreement, the community and the members of a friends group retained the right to operate the center independently.

Schlitz offers an incredible array of opportunities to the visitor, including birding classes, picnics, activities for children, nature exhibits, and of course, hiking. The trails meander around the grounds and pass through stands of evergreens and hardwoods, prairies, and wetlands, as well as taking you along the Lake Michigan shoreline. For an unbelievable view of the area, an observation tower takes you high above the lake, allowing you to perch in the treetops and see downtown Milwaukee to the south and up the shore to Sheboygan to the north.

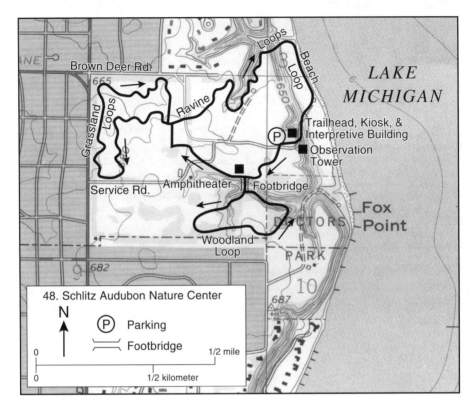

Hiking is generally defined as "a long walk." That being the case, this rather non-rigorous hike allows you to walk around the trails at Schlitz. We have essentially pasted together all the trails to offer one outer loop of about 3 miles. Offering varied scenery, it is mostly level, aside from one significant climb at the end. The trail starts by heading past Mystery Lake, a small wetland/pond before crossing a wooden footbridge and proceeding around the Woodland Loop. After crossing back over the footbridge, the trail takes a turn toward the more open Western Meadows area, where you will pass through a sea of wildflowers in the warmer months. Eventually, you will loop back eastward and along the very scenic Ravine Trail down to the lake and beach. From there, the trail climbs back up to the top of the shoreline and to the observation tower. In all, this definitely makes for a great day's hike to complement all the other educational offerings at the center.

How to Get There

From Milwaukee to the south, take I-43 north to WI 32 south/WI 100 (Brown Deer Road). Turn right (east) and follow Brown Deer Road to where WI 100 ends and WI 32 veers to the right. Go straight, being careful for oncoming traffic on WI 32, and stay on East Brown Deer Road. Follow this for 0.3 mile to the center entrance on the right.

From the west, take WI 74 east (Main Street) out of Menomonee Falls approximately 1.5 miles to WI 100 (Brown Deer Road). Continue straight on Brown Deer Road for approximately 9 miles, and follow the directions above from there.

From the north, take I-43 south to WI 32 south (Brown Deer Road) and turn left (east). Follow the directions above from there.

There is a daily use fee at Schlitz. In 2003, the fee was $4 for adults and $2 for children. Members of the friends group (which is open to anyone) have free access to the Center. For more information, contact the Schlitz Audubon Nature Center at 414-352-2880.

The Trail

Upon entering the center, follow the long drive to the check-in point outside the parking lot. The trailhead is close to that kiosk, so park nearby.

Begin by crossing the park road to the trailhead, following the sign for Mystery Pond and Woodland Loop. Soon thereafter, you can choose either route. We took the Mystery Pond option to get to the Woodland Loop. During fall and spring, you'll undoubtedly scare up some waterfowl by going this way. The trail follows along the shore of the pond, passing a couple of observation decks. When you get to the last deck on the western edge of the lake, turn left and take the trail toward the Woodland Loop. You will come to a fork in the trail; veer right toward the ravine.

The trail will head down a boardwalk and cross the ravine. The steps on the south side are somewhat rickety, but they seem stable enough. On the other side is a short loop through a mixture of hardwoods and conifers, and it marks your first sight of large white pines. This is a good spot to keep an eye out for deer. Take the trail in either direction, and loop back to the boardwalk over the ravine. Once on the other side, head left (west) along a trail that will take

Prairie blazing star, Schlitz Audubon Nature Center

you across a service road and over a long boardwalk, crossing a large pond.

Eventually you will come to the junction of three trails. Turn left (west) along the Grassland Loop and head straight past the old farm machinery. This trail marks the beginning of hiking in the open among blue vervain and coneflowers in the warmer months. As you pass any other offshoots of trails along this route, stay to the left and take the longest loop around. At the southwesternmost edge of the loop, the trail will pass back into the woods before emerging at a hidden pond, where there is a bird observation blind.

From here the trail heads north before curving east around the north side of North Pond along the Two Oak Trail, a mostly wooded section. You will then cut back south to the beginning of the loop, where you will turn left (east) and head across the park road. Once across the road, veer left, taking the Ravine Trail. This trail takes you through a mixture of oaks and birch trees before meandering along the ravine edge amidst towering pines and finally emerging in the open prairie north of the main building—an area covered in prairie blazing stars in the summer. Soon you will come to the intersection of three trails. Follow the Beach Loop, which will descend quickly along riser steps all the way to the beach level below. A trail just above the beach will take you past a deck for resting—a good idea before making the final push up a long, paved hill to the tower above. The view from the tower is pretty amazing and makes for a fun end to this hike. The parking lot is just down the paved access road that you took up from the beach.

This hike is a creative collection of trail loops at Schlitz, and does offer moderate length. It's a great spot for kids due to its level terrain and, in combination with the many other offerings here, could be part of an enjoyable day's visit to Schlitz Audubon Nature Center.

49

Wehr Nature Center

Total distance: 3.2 miles

Hiking time: 1 hour to 1 hour, 15 minutes

Difficulty: 2.0

Vertical rise: Minimal

Maps: USGS 7½' Hales Corners, Wisconsin; DeLorme Wisconsin Atlas & Gazetteer, p. 31 (A-5)

Like the seemingly innumerable, busy, big city streets, South 108th Street is abuzz with traffic lights, traffic congestion, and side-by-side storefronts. With very little green space and lots of cement, it's the epitome of urban. Add to that the occasional roar of a passenger jet powering downward toward General Mitchell Field Airport, and you really get the idea.

But just as you can't judge a book by its cover, don't judge the number and quality of southern Milwaukee County parks from the vantage point of a four-lane divided roadway. Just off South 108th Street lie Whitnall County Park, Wehr Nature Center, Boerner Botanical Gardens, a public golf course, and a segment of the 71-mile Oak Leaf Trail.

In a county where land is a hot commodity, there are over 140 parks and almost 100 miles of trails in Milwaukee County's park system, totaling 15,000 acres of open space to enjoy. Of these, Wehr Nature Center inside Whitnall County Park offers some of the best hiking in the system, with prairies, wetlands, and hardwood forests.

This hike takes you along the outer edge of all the loops available at the park, following primarily the Natural History and Lake Loop trails. Starting at the nature center, the hike begins by taking you between the prairie and the north shore of Mallard Lake before looping south toward the golf course. You will then head west, over boardwalks and across wetlands, before heading into the woodland section. You will meander northward in the woods before emerging in the Oak Savanna and looping back south to the parking lot and nature

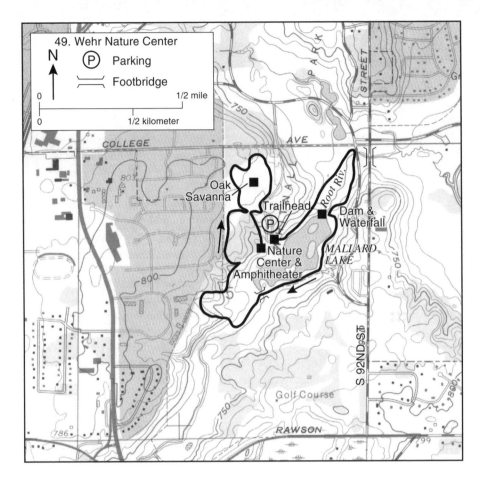

49. Wehr Nature Center

N

(P) Parking

⊐⊏ Footbridge

center. All told, the hike is about 3.2 miles and is easy to moderate in difficulty.

How to Get There

From the north, take I-43 south from I-94 for 5.2 miles to US 45 south. Follow US 45 for about a mile to the exit onto I-43/US 45 south. Follow I-43/US 45 1.9 miles to College Avenue. (Be careful, it sneaks up quickly.) Turn left on College and go 0.7 mile to the park entrance on the right. The park road will lead you to the Wehr Nature Center parking lot. Park down by the visitors center, if possible.

From the southwest, take I-43 north to US 45/WI 100 south. Follow US 45/WI 100 for about 1.9 miles to College Avenue. Turn left and follow the directions from College Avenue above.

Wehr Nature Center charges visitors a daily parking fee. In 2003, this was $2.50 plus tax.

For more information, contact Wehr Nature Center at 414-425-8550.

The Trail

To do the hike clockwise, start at the trailhead located in the southeast corner of the parking lot. Two trails will shoot off to the right almost immediately after you begin, but stay left and head between the prairie and the lake. The hillside is usually covered with wildflowers in the warmer months, and the lake will be alive with waterfowl in the spring and fall. The trail will eventually turn away from the lake a bit. You'll pass two trails, one that comes from the left out of the prairie and another that goes right to the dam. Stay straight and head toward the northern tip of the lake. (You will pass two other intersections with trails, but again stay straight.)

Soon you will come to the tip of the lake, which is actually at the junction of College Avenue and 92nd Street. Turn right and go over the 92nd Street bridge on a sidewalk, before resuming the trail on the other side. From here, you will follow the trail along the woods on the east side of the lake down to the dam and waterfall. In 2003, due to the extremely dry summer, there wasn't much of a waterfall at all. But the springtime undoubtedly finds water pouring over the dam.

From here, continue south through a small prairie below the overlook parking area. The trail will then meander through the woods before popping out below the golf course clubhouse. Take a right on the gravel service drive, past the southeast corner of the lake, and head west back into the woods along the drive. Soon you will come to a bridge taking you across the stream at the southwest corner of the lake. This area is pretty marshy, and you'll cross several boardwalks. Turn left at the first trail intersection and head southwest into the Woodland Loop.

Next you will head uphill amid a mixture of young and old hardwoods, and the trail will become pretty closed in. You will have a moderate climb along this stretch as you pass beneath the trees and past a mixture of woodland plants such as jack-in-the-pulpits, ferns, and wild geraniums. You will pass the first of many offshoot trails that allow access to area residents living in the homes and apartments nearby. Ignore these offshoots and stay on the main trail.

After the first offshoot trail, the main trail will turn directly east for a short distance before turning north again. (Make sure you turn left at the sewer lid.) You will pass over a bridge and head uphill slightly before making a sharp left turn, continuing on the Woodland Loop instead of heading toward the amphitheater. Continue on the trail north before cutting right (east) and past another offshoot trail to the left.

You will now be on the edge of the Oak Savanna. At the junction of four trails, turn left, (northwest) and into the savannah, veering left again at another intersection. The trail will then duck into the north woods where you will stay to the right (east) and cut just inside this mature woodlot before turning right (south) and back out into the eastern edge of the savannah, where you will find all sorts of wildflowers in the warmer months, including wild bergamot, goldenrod, and the curious-looking joe-pye weed. Stay on the easternmost option of the savannah trail and take it back along the road, turning west to the original intersection of the four trails. From here, turn south and take the short Glacial Trail back to the parking lot and nature center.

50

Richard Bong
State Recreation Area

Total distance: 4.2 miles

Hiking time: 1 hour, 15 minutes to 1 hour, 45 minutes

Difficulty: 3.0

Vertical rise: Minimal

Maps: USGS 7½' Silver Lake, Paddock Lake, Burlington, and Rochester, Wisconsin; DeLorme Wisconsin Atlas & Gazetteer, p. 31 (D-5)

Wide open vistas, full of wildflower-filled prairie, a lake and ponds, wetlands, and stands of hardwoods all in the same place is a scenario that is kind of hard to believe in southeast Wisconsin. With over 4,500 acres set aside for wildlife, prairie plants, trees, and trails, the Richard Bong State Recreation area is a welcome natural area in the most populated section of the state. The area is named for World War II ace fighter pilot and Congressional Medal of Honor winner Richard Ira Bong (1920–1945), a Wisconsin native.

But things weren't always supposed to be this way. In the wake of World War II, the land was slated to become a military airfield for fighter jets to use as a home base for defending the skies around Milwaukee and Chicago. Literally days before pretty much of all of this area was to be paved—and after topsoil was removed, land was leveled, and wetlands were filled in—construction came to a halt. Thus, like a charred battlefield, the would-be Richard Bong Airfield was left for dead.

A subsequent desire to turn the entire area into a modern, multi-use suburban development was thwarted, and the value of a large, contiguous tract of land in the southeast part of the state was realized. Now, instead of finding a 2-mile-long concrete runway, strip malls, or industrial parks, visitors are greeted with 16 miles of footpaths that wind throughout thousands of acres of prairie, wetland, and woods.

On this hike, you will follow the Blue Loop, one of six loop trails at Bong. The trail meanders through every environment the

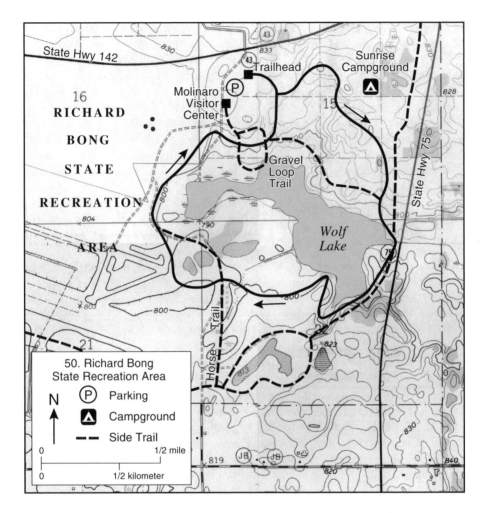

**50. Richard Bong
State Recreation Area**

N

Ⓟ Parking

🅰 Campground

--- Side Trail

0 ———————— 1/2 mile

0 ———————— 1/2 kilometer

park has to offer: prairies, wetlands, woods, and lakeshore. You will start near the visitors center at the trailhead parking lot and head immediately over a long boardwalk through a large wetland before crossing the park road and winding your way up to the hardwood stand on the northeastern bluff of Wolf Lake. From here you will wind down alongside WI 75, before turning west along the south shore of the lake. It is here where you will encounter some steep ups and downs in the woods before emerging again in prairie on the southwestern shore of the

lake. The trail then heads past the beach area and curves east back toward the trailhead parking lot. This 4.2-mile trail is a moderately difficult hike that would be tough for kids and, because it is sometimes exposed, can be a pretty strenuous hike for anyone.

How to Get There

From the north, take US 45 south out of Union Grove 3.1 miles to WI 142. Turn right (west) on WI 142 and go 3.9 miles to the park entrance. Turn left and, after passing through the entrance station, take another left and go to the trailhead parking lot about 0.25 mile down on the left.

From the west, take WI 142 out of Burlington 7.8 miles to the park entrance on your right. Follow the directions above to the trailhead lot.

From the east, take WI 142 east out of Kenosha approximately 17 miles to the park entrance on your left. Follow the directions to the trailhead lot above.

For more information, contact the Richard Bong State Recreation Area at 262-878-5600.

The Trail

The trail begins at the northeast corner of the trailhead parking lot. The trail immediately crosses a large wetland via a long wooden boardwalk, before crossing the park road coming to the intersection of the start and finish of the Blue Loop. Take a left, going clockwise, and head up a slight ascent alongside the road. The trail will soon leave the road, however, and head down toward the Sunrise Campground, alongside a large prairie filled with colorful wildflowers in the summer. You will duck into the woods for a bit as you skirt the edge of the campground. The trail will emerge again into an open prairie habitat as you climb your way up to the northeast corner of Wolf Lake, where you will find a bench and the intersection of several trails. All the trails are well marked, and it is easy to follow the Blue Trail out of this area.

After a short break, continue downhill and through the woods toward the eastern tip of the lake and alongside WI 75 very briefly, before turning off and into the woods at the southern shore of the lake. Along this part of the trail you will find the most hills, with several ups and downs, although nothing is too strenuous. Soon the trail will emerge from the woods and turn northward, directly toward the shore and another small woods. The trail will buttonhook through this area and head back out into the prairie, ascending slightly. It's in this open area that you are treated to an incredible view of the area. You are able to see in all directions, and the vastness of Bong is easy to capture. In the fall this area is alive with deep reds and oranges as the season changes, while in the summer it will be jumping with grasshoppers bouncing from one wildflower to the next. In the winter, you are treated to some of the best Nordic skiing in southern Wisconsin.

Soon the trail will cross the horse trail and turn northward toward the beach area, where it will cross the park road and head along a ridge above the beach. From here you will turn eastward and cross through yet another prairie area on the north side of the lake, crossing a gravel loop trail twice, and heading back up to the original intersection of the Blue Loop. Turn left and head back across the road, over the boardwalk, and back to the parking lot.

Index

---

map, 134
trail description, 134–136

Y

Z

Let Backcountry Guides Take You There

Our experienced backcountry authors will lead you to the finest trails, parks, and back roads in the following areas:

50 Hikes Series
50 Hikes in the Adirondacks
50 Hikes in Colorado
50 Hikes in Connecticut
50 Hikes in Central Florida
50 Hikes in North Florida
50 Hikes in South Florida
50 Hikes in the Lower Hudson Valley
50 Hikes in Kentucky
50 Hikes in the Maine Mountains
50 Hikes in Coastal and Southern Maine
50 Hikes in Louisiana
50 Hikes in Massachusetts
50 Hikes in Maryland
50 Hikes in Michigan
50 Hikes in the White Mountains
50 More Hikes in New Hampshire
50 Hikes in New Jersey
50 Hikes in Central New York
50 Hikes in Western New York
50 Hikes in the Mountains of North Carolina
50 Hikes in Ohio
50 More Hikes in Ohio
50 Hikes in Eastern Pennsylvania
50 Hikes in Central Pennsylvania
50 Hikes in Western Pennsylvania
50 Hikes in the Tennessee Mountains
50 Hikes in Vermont
50 Hikes in Northern Virginia
50 Hikes in Southern Virginia

Walking
Walks and Rambles on Cape Cod and the Islands
Walks and Rambles on the Delmarva Peninsula
Walks and Rambles in the Western Hudson Valley
Walks and Rambles on Long Island
Walks and Rambles in Ohio's Western Reserve
Walks and Rambles in Rhode Island
Walks and Rambles in and around St. Louis
Weekend Walks in St. Louis and Beyond
Weekend Walks Along the New England Coast
Weekend Walks in Historic New England
Weekend Walks in the Historic Washington, D.C. Region

Bicycling
25 Bicycle Tours in the Adirondacks
25 Bicycle Tours on Delmarva
25 Bicycle Tours in Savannah and the Carolina Low Country
25 Bicycle Tours in the Lake Champlain Region
25 Bicycle Tours in Maine
25 Bicycle Tours in Maryland
25 Bicycle Tours in the Twin Cities and Southeastern Minnesota
30 Bicycle Tours in New Jersey
25 Bicycle Tours in the Hudson Valley
25 Bicycle Tours in Maryland
25 Bicycle Tours in Ohio's Western Reserve
25 Bicycle Tours in the Texas Hill Country and West Texas
25 Bicycle Tours in Vermont
25 Bicycle Tours in and around Washington, D.C.
25 Mountain Bike Tours in the Adirondacks
25 Mountain Bike Tours in the Hudson Valley
25 Mountain Bike Tours in Massachusetts
25 Mountain Bike Tours in New Jersey
Backroad Bicycling in the Blue Ridge and Smoky Mountains
Backroad Bicycling in Connecticut
Backroad Bicycling on Cape Cod, Martha's Vineyard, and Nantucket
Backroad Bicycling in the Finger Lakes Region
Backroad Bicycling in Western Massachusetts
Backroad Bicycling in New Hampshire
Backroad Bicycling in Eastern Pennsylvania
Backroad Bicycling in Wisconsin
The Mountain Biker's Guide to Ski Resorts
Bicycling America's National Parks: Arizona & New Mexico
Bicycling America's National Parks: California
Bicycling America's National Parks: Oregon & Washington
Bicycling America's National Parks: Utah & Colorado
Bicycling Cuba

We offer many more books on hiking, fly-fishing, travel, nature, and other subjects. Our books are available at bookstores and outdoor stores everywhere. For more information or a free catalog, please call 1-800-245-4151 or write to us at The Countryman Press, P.O. Box 748, Woodstock, Vermont 05091. You can find us on the Internet at www.countrymanpress.com.